Other Books by Jane Ann McLachlan

Historical Fiction:

The Sorrow Stone
The Lode Stone
The Whetstone

The Girl Who Would Be Queen
The Girl Who Tempted Fortune
The Queen Who Sold Her Crown
The Girl Who Lost Her Kingdom

Science Fiction and Fantasy:

Walls of Wind
The Occasional Diamond Thief
The Salarian Desert Game
Midsummer Night Magicians

Memoir:

IMPACT: A Memoir of PTSD

Creative Writing:

Downriver Writing: The Five-Step Process for Outlining Your Novel

The Queen Who Sold Her Crown

The Kingdom of Naples, Book III

Jane Ann McLachlan

The Queen Who Sold Her Crown
Published in Canada by Kay Crisp Books
Copyright © 2021 by Jane Ann McLachlan

All rights reserved. No part of this book may be reproduced by any means, or stored in a retrieval system, or transmitted by any means, electronic, photocopying or recording, or translated into a machine language, without the written permission of the publisher. For permission contact: jamclachlan@golden.net

This book is sold subject to the condition that it shall not, by way of trade or otherwise, be lent, re-sold, hired out or otherwise circulated in any form of binding or cover other than that in which it is published and without a similar condition including this condition being imposed on the subsequent purchaser.

ISBN: 978-1-7774996-6-2

Cover Design by Heather Upchurch from Expert Subjects
Formatting by Chris Morgan from Dragon Realm Press
www.dragonrealmpress.com

http://www.janeannmclachlan.com

For my faithful readers,

Those who have participated in my launch teams, book after book, and those who have read every book in the series.

Thank you for taking this journey with me.

I write for you.

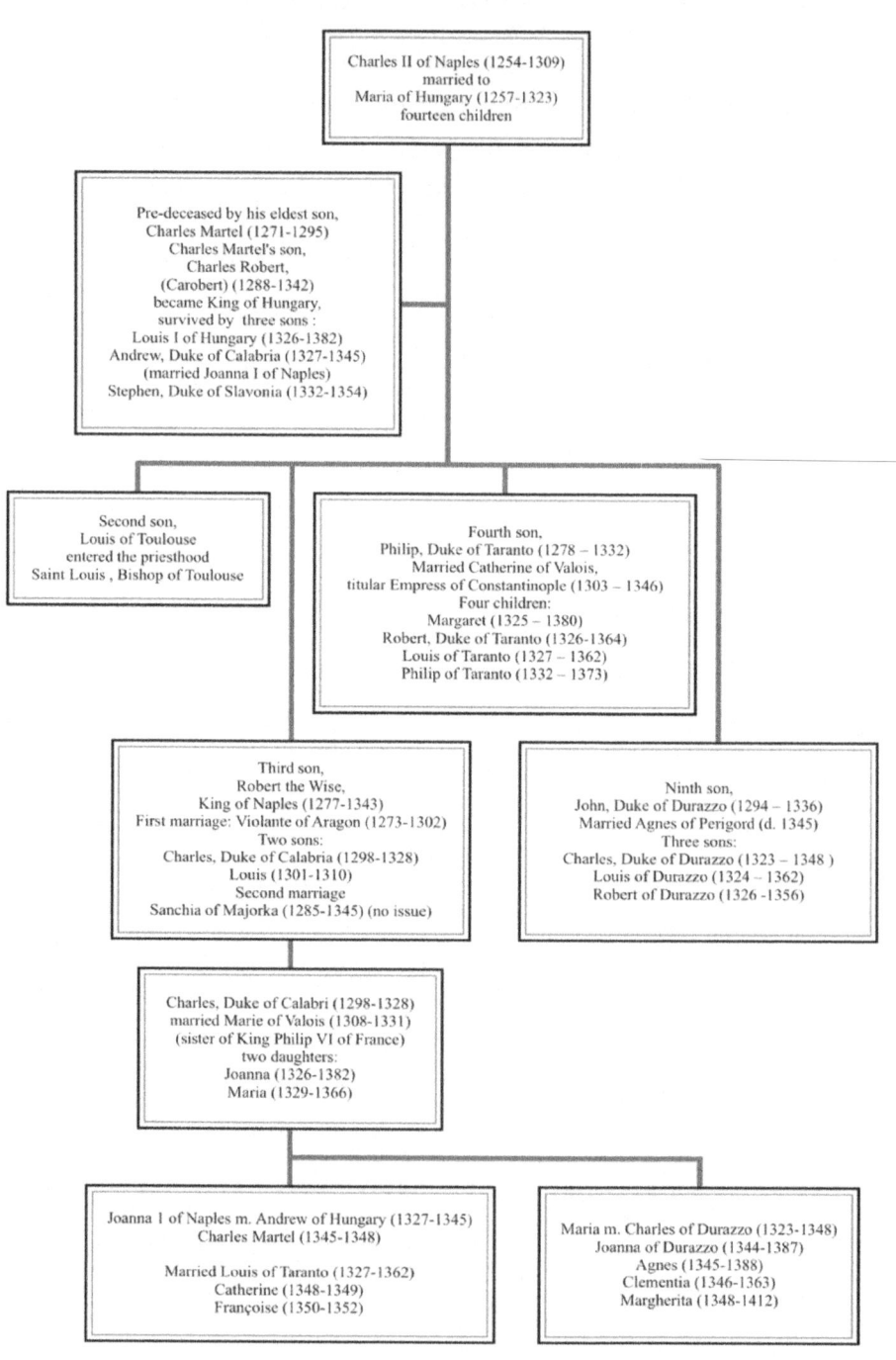

CONTENTS

Chapter 1: The Approaching Army 1
Chapter 2: The Defending Army 11
Chapter 3: Preparing for War 20
Chapter 4: Sisters and Allies 33
Chapter 5: Bloodless Battles 43
Chapter 6: A Ship at Night 54
Chapter 7: A Celebration 65
Chapter 8: Danger at Sea 74
Chapter 9: Midnight Flight 89
Chapter 10: Plague 99
Chapter 11: Orphans 112
Chapter 12: The Road to Avignon 122
Chapter 13: News from Naples 134
Chapter 14: Judgement 144
Chapter 15: A Terrible Sacrifice 154
Chapter 16: A Difficult Choice 162
Chapter 17: War 172
Chapter 18: A Rain of Blows 180
Chapter 19: A Royal Prison 189
Chapter 20: Allies and Adversaries 202
Chapter 21: Birth and Renewal 210
Chapter 22: Betrayal 217
Chapter 23: Rescue 226
Chapter 24: Marriage 235
Chapter 25: Captives 248
Chapter 26: Return to Naples 257
Chapter 27: Unfinished Business 264
Chapter 28: A Coronation 270

Chapter 1
The Approaching Army

Joanna 1 of Naples
April, 1347

I am standing alone on the northern outskirts of Naples. I hear the rhythmic stomp of marching boots, the hooves of horses, the creak of wagons pulling the machinery of war, all steadily approaching from beyond the hill in front of me. Behind me I hear the quiet bustle of my city as my people go about their business on this sunny day, unaware of the terror bearing down on them.

The darkened helmets of thousands of soldiers rise in an endless black line above the crest of the hill, then chests in chain mail, arms swinging with the relentless momentum of their approach.

"Stop!" I scream, my arms outstretched as if to ward off the oncoming menace. They give no sign of hearing or seeing me.

Now the cavalry appears behind them, the thunder of their approach deafening. No one will hear me, much less obey. I gape at them, terrified by their numbers. A mountain of men marching over the hills toward Naples as far as the eye can see.

A crowned man bearing the crest of Hungary on his tunic rides over the hill on his warhorse, both man and horse enormous. His armor gleams in the sun, black obsidian, blinding me. As I shield my eyes he raises his arm. His army stops, poised for the confrontation in a deadly tableau. The bowmen drop to their knees, arrows nocked, waiting for the fall of his arm. I will be mowed down, and my city behind me, by the silver rain of their arrows. I imagine my people falling in the streets, unaware of their peril until it is too late.

Suddenly a single figure appears between the massive army and where I stand. She is running toward me, her arms stretched sideways, skirts flapping in the wind, as though she can shield me against twenty thousand arrows.

"Philippa!" I scream...

I wake in my bed drenched in sweat, gasping for breath, still whispering her name. *Philippa.* My nurse, my surrogate mother, my most loyal friend, advisor, supporter, standing between me and disaster as she did all her life.

How can I hope to save my kingdom from the threat of war when I could not save her?

I close my eyes and indulge a single moment of despair, the moment I was told of her death. If I were an ordinary woman I would have taken to my bed to grieve, for the woman I called mother was dead, and her granddaughter, the most loyal friend I will ever have, along with her. If I were an ordinary woman I would have donned the white of mourning and washed their bodies with my tears and buried them with honor.

Instead I went to the Franciscan cathedral of San Lorenzo Maggiore and prayed. Not for their souls; their souls were innocent of the crime of which they were accused, and God knows this as surely as I do. I prayed for my country, for my people, enmeshed once more in shedding the blood of innocents, and for deliverance from the foes that surrounded me. For I am their queen, ordained by

God to wear the crown of Naples, to rule my country and my people. God will not fail me if I do not swerve from the purpose for which He made me.

And with that I open my eyes and sit up in my bed. I cannot undo the past, but the future—that is still within my power.

It is dark in my room and the night air is still cool—even if the heavy drapes keeping out the foul night vapors were pulled back, the sky would be black. But I have no desire to return to sleep. I ring the bell beside my bed for warm rosewater to wash my face, for my maids to dress me and comb my hair, for the four Clarissan nuns who are my companions to attend my morning ablutions. Another day has begun. I must arm myself with faith and duty to face what it will bring.

When I am dressed and coiffed I leave my rooms and go to my private chapel, accompanied by the four sisters from the Clarissan convent—Poor Clares, they call themselves—whom I brought to Castle Nuovo as my companions when I ousted Duke Robert of Taranto. As we walk through the lamp-lit halls we hear the bells of Naples' monasteries ringing Lauds, calling their monks and nuns to prayer in the hour when dawn breaks. How often have I come to this small, holy room, which I still think of as my Grandmother Sancia's chapel, to pray before my day begins. Every day of my childhood since I came to Castle Nuovo after my mother's death, and most of my adult years. My household priest and confessor is waiting when we enter and leads us in our Latin prayers.

When the time for silent reflection arrives I do not consider my sins, as I should, for I do not need forgiveness. What I need is succor.

I have lost all those who loved me and am surrounded by enemies, all because of my husband whose death I had no part in. I have had to sacrifice Philippa and her sons, who served me loyally, and her granddaughter, Sancia, whom I called friend. They had no part in the murder of my husband, Prince Andrew of Hungary, but they were guilty of another offense: the crime of rising above their station, for which they were hated and envied. I pray that they may find peace in eternity, and that they may forgive me for allowing their executions.

What choice did I have? With my Hungarian in-laws demanding justice for their prince and threatening war if they did not get it, Pope Clement VI insisting on executions to satisfy them, and my people, hungry from years of famine and stirred to revolt by my enemies, demanding blood also. I held it off as long as I could. I bend my head lower and let my sorrow spill over, feeling the hot moisture on my cheeks as I think of Philippa and her family.

I will have to give up Bertrand of Artois, now that his father Charles of Artois, bastard son of my grandfather King Robert, is dead. My Aunt Catherine, empress of Constantinople and Duchess of Taranto, was able to keep them under her protection while she lived but she, too, is gone now. Bertrand, I suspect, is not innocent, but one of the instigators of the plot against Andrew, for they were mortal enemies. His trial and brutal execution will be just, unlike that of so many of my other supporters. And yet I will miss him, a loyal ally and trusted friend to me. So many deaths, so many sacrifices, and yet King Louis of Hungary and his mother the Dowager Queen Elizabeth are still not satisfied.

This foul murder stains my reign and casts suspicion even on me, who had nothing to gain and much to lose by it! A violent, ugly death which allows that foolish, malevolent prince to reach from his grave to destroy me and my kingdom. How it would please Andrew to see his legacy!

Not only him. It pleases his brother, King Louis of Hungary, who has always wanted an excuse to break the treaty his father and my grandfather signed when Andrew and I were wed.

I cross myself. One should not be filled with anger and revulsion on one's knees before God. But how can I feel anything else when thinking of Prince Andrew and his brother, King Louis? Ruthless, cruel, and self-indulgent, both of them; Louis as determined to destroy my supporters to avenge Andrew's death as Andrew was determined to destroy them in his life. For those who most hated Andrew were those who most loved me.

And they are succeeding. Famine and conflict plagues my kingdom; it will require a miracle to prevent Louis of Hungary from swooping in and taking it from me. I bend my head lower, blinded by a blackness darker than the darkest night, which fills my heart with fury and despair.

As if he senses something behind my closed eyes and rigid posture, my priest and confessor touches my head in blessing. With great effort I pull myself out of the darkness. I am kneeling before the light. Darkness has no place here.

I turn my thoughts to my two-year-old son, living proof of God's blessing. Pope Clement VI wants him brought to Avignon where he will live in the papal palace under Clement's protection, but I will not allow it.

Clement's assurance that he will guard my son, whom I made his godson, may be sincere, but I am responsible for his care and upbringing as a future monarch. It is my task to teach him diplomacy and leadership as my grandfather King Robert taught me. I am responsible for his safety. Even a pope's resolve will not hold like a mother's love.

Since his birth Charles Martel has been the greatest source of joy in my life, a validation of all that I am and have done, a promise of peace at last for my kingdom and a secure succession. He belongs to Naples as much as to me, and Naples is where he must stay. I am a doting mother, perhaps inappropriate in a ruler, but I lost my own mother at a tender age and I will not have my son endure that. He is worth any sacrifice.

Though hardly more than a babe, he guards me as much as I guard him. He is a Hungarian prince through his deceased father, Prince Andrew, just as he is a Neapolitan prince through me. As such, while he is my heir and under my care, I may hope to prevent the Hungarians from attacking us. Whatever else Cardinal Bertrand de Deux and His Holiness the Pope take from me, I must not let them take my son. My life, at the moment, depends upon his presence at my side.

My son and my crown, I murmur under my breath, my head bowed in piety, in entreaty, in resolve. How often I have repeated this to myself, in my lowest moments when I feel I have lost everything, in my desperate moments when I fear what I must do, in my strongest moments when I remember who I am. In every moment when I reach toward God, my prayer a reminder to us both: *my son and my crown.*

My crown is who I am, who I was born to be. And my son, he is who we are, we Angevins, a river of royal right and obligation flowing from our imperial French Angevin ancestors down through us into future rulers. God's ordained sovereigns for his people in the kingdom of Naples.

I cross myself, murmur a final prayer for God to preserve my crown, my kingdom, and my heir, and rise from my knees. The four sisters from the Clarissan convent remain at their prayers. For a moment I watch them, envying the simplicity of their lives, then I straighten my shoulders. A queen must act as well as pray. With a swish of purple skirts I leave the chapel and returned to my presence chamber, where Cardinal Bertrand de Deux, the Pope's legate, is waiting to talk with me.

Louis of Hungary has sent His Holiness Clement VI a formal declaration of war against your kingdom, Cardinal Bertrand de Deux informed me when we met a week ago. He did not need to point out that my kingdom is in disarray, my royal cousins at war among themselves, spending against each other the forces that will be needed to repel the Hungarians.

And there are larger forces at work. That reminder was also there in the Cardinal's dark eyes. England's Black Prince, Edward III, is winning his war against France, and no doubt has been encouraging his ally, King Louis of Hungary, to attack France's ally, the Kingdom of Naples. The pope and his cardinals in Avignon, making no pretense of objectivity as they watch King Philip VI of France flounder in battle after battle against the English forces, are understandably distraught. Clement needs a unified Naples to stand with France and I have not provided it.

There it is. For generations my family has been loyal to the Avignon popes, supported their every cause and obeyed their injunctions; and yet I must acknowledge the Holy Father's willingness to sacrifice me now, if that will avoid war with Hungary, a country that has ever been a thorn in his side. I can only respond with dignity, prayer, and a most humble but resolute resistance, while protesting my innocence—and keeping my son by my side. King Louis of Hungary will be seen by all as the interloper he is if he attacks Naples while the Hungarian prince who is the rightful heir to the throne is here with me.

When has Louis of Hungary worried about how others see him? He will attack, I have no doubt of it. The only question is whether I will be able to unify my kingdom to defend itself before he descends on us.

Little wonder my dreams are troubled. And when I am not dreaming of disaster I lie staring into the darkness scheming how to bring my rebellious cousins into line.

My cousin Charles, Duke of Durazzo, married to my sister, hoping my defeat will pave the way for him and Maria to gain my throne.

My cousin Robert, Duke of Taranto, who would marry me

whether I will or not in order to make himself King of Naples—and likely murder me and my son as soon as he is crowned.

Between the two of them they could raise an army of knights and fiefs to defend Naples, were they not busy fighting each other and Robert's younger brother, Louis of Taranto, who has hired an army of mercenaries to defend me from them both. All of them wasting men needed to fight off the Hungarians! Oh, I have ground my teeth in the night at their colossal stupidity and arrogance as Louis of Hungary laughs behind his hand and lets them spend themselves on each other. Only he is not truly laughing; he is furious that one of them might beat him to my throne!

What can I offer each of these hot-headed, short-sighted cousins to bind them to me instead of against me? That is the substance of my nights, the sum of my days, and little by little answers have come to me. Certain things must be put in place, certain people convinced to support my plan, and all must be accomplished in rapid order if I am to succeed. Beginning now.

The sky showing through the windows is gray, growing lighter by the moment as dawn breaks over Naples. I take a deep breath. *My crown and my son*, I tell the breaking day as the cardinal follows me into my privy chamber and waits for me to seat myself. When I have done so, taking my time to remind him of the difference in our positions, I nod to let him know he might be seated at my counsel table.

We are both well aware he has been sent here as Pope Clement's legate to investigate myself and the princes of my realm with the aim of convicting those responsible for Prince Andrew's murder. The difference in our positions is fragile indeed, and yet he waits for my nod, and bows to me before sitting in my presence. I smile, for I have found in him an unexpected ally. Despite his instructions he has not taken Charles Martel from me, nor removed me from my throne, but instead sends reports back to Avignon protesting my innocence of Andrew's death, and the innocence of my royal cousins, the Dukes of Taranto and Durazzo, and assuring Clement of my maternal devotion to my son, whom I steadfastly refuse to release from my care.

Now I need even more from him, and I must use my strengths against his weaknesses to get it. He likes women, this cardinal, and possesses a natural deference to royal bloodlines. I raise my chin and take a deep breath, summoning all the skill, authority—and charm—I possess, to make him my ally today.

He waits for me to speak. This room, which was once filled with my councilors, today contains only him and me. My grandmother Queen Sancia, my most trusted advisors, my not-always-trusted aunts whose advice nonetheless was worth hearing, my beloved Philippa, are all dead. Her sons, my royal seneschal and the seneschal of my kingdom also dead, and I have not yet appointed new ones. My royal cousins are at war with me and each other. Niccolò Acciaiuoli, one of the few loyal councilors remaining to me, is away fighting with Louis of Taranto on my behalf. A queen with no trusted advisors in her council chambers save the pope's legate. Not an inspiring example of rulership. Nor a safe state for my kingdom should Louis of Hungary invade, I can imagine Cardinal de Deux thinking.

Well, I have had a legate sent to take my rule from me before. I know much more than I did then. He will see that I am a seasoned monarch now, who will not give up her crown so easily. I know what must be done to preserve my kingdom with or without this legate's counsel.

"It is time to bring my cousins back to this table," I tell the cardinal.

"Louis of Taranto?" he asks, knowing my preference.

I permit myself a cryptic smile. "Not yet. First his brother, the Duke of Taranto, and then my brother-in-law, the Duke of Durazzo.

Here is what we must do." I take a breath, exhaling with it a silent prayer as I begin to lay out my plan.

When I am finished he sits back and looks at me. He has often looked at me the way men look at a beautiful woman. He has looked on me tenderly when I am with Charles Martel, as good men will revere, for Holy Mary's sake, a woman caring for her child. He has smiled and blessed me at my prayers as a Church Father will smile on a pious daughter of God.

Today he looks at me as a man looks at his monarch, and bows low, and promises to do as I have bid him.

Chapter 2

The Defending Army

Joanna 1 of Naples
June, 1347

I have spoken to my sister Maria only a few times and never alone during the two and a half years since the birth of my son, Charles Martel, on January 25, 1345. The date my world changed. The date my succession was secured and I thought my problems were over.

Maria's second daughter, Agnes, was less than a month old when she came to share my confinement. We were close then, but the intervening years pulled us apart as my kingdom rose in revolt, my people made desperate by wide-spread crop failures and inflamed by rumors concerning the death of my husband. I could not save Philippa and her family, and I think Maria does not forgive me for that. But then, she could not prevent her husband from falsely accusing and torturing them, then working with Louis of Taranto and Hugo del Balzo to discredit me and those loyal to me. And I think *I* cannot forgive *her* for that.

I shake my head to clear it of such thoughts as I walk to my son's nursery. Personal feelings do not matter now. All that matters is that I bind my kingdom together before the Hungarian army arrives. Cardinal de Dieu has been as good as his word, getting the necessary permissions from Pope Clement for today's business.

First, he discreetly made it clear to Clement VI to delay sanctioning my union with Louis of Taranto. Nothing would be more certain to bring King Louis of Hungary roaring down on my kingdom with his massive army than to hear that I am betrothed. His mother, the Dowager Queen Elizabeth, has tried to have the pope declare that I may never marry again. Even Clement knows that a young woman of position and wealth cannot long remain unmarried, but he is also desperate to appease Hungary.

Nevertheless, soon I must have a husband to lead my army in defense of our kingdom, and I have chosen Louis of Taranto. He is stalwart and battle-hardened and bound to Naples by birth and upbringing. My people love him and will accept him. And incidentally, he is handsome and charming and fond of me as I have long been of him. He has defended me from the armies of his brother Robert and our cousin Charles of Durazzo and is eager to have his reward: my hand in marriage. But first I must appease my other cousins. And while I do so, it is best that he not know I am the one behind the delay of our nuptials.

Today I must secure the loyalty of my cousin Charles, the Duke of Durazzo, husband of my sister Maria. He is a treacherous one who will follow the course that best suits him regardless of previous promises, so I have had to offer him a future he cannot refuse that will keep him on my side until it unfolds.

Charles Martel runs to greet me as soon as he sees me at the nursery door. He is dressed in a cunning purple tunic and leggings like a little king. I take a seat and sit him on my knee and sing a rhyming song which ends with a bounce and a tickle, to his delight. He demands I do it over and over. I am happy to accommodate; I am as unlikely to tire of his deep belly chuckle as he is to tire of being tickled. Finally I settle him down for a short talk.

"Do you know why I am here today, darling?" I ask him.

He looks at me solemnly, waiting to hear.

"You are very little now, but when you are older you will rule this kingdom."

He nods enthusiastically. I have told him this already, before his homage ceremony six months ago. "Oui, Maman," he says. His voice is so thin and sweet I want to kiss him, but then he will giggle and I will have lost his attention.

"That is correct, Charles Martel," I say, keeping my face as serious as his. "And when you are king, you will need a queen."

He nods a little more doubtfully this time.

I resist the urge to hug him, and pat his head instead. He is so little. "Today you will meet her and we will hold a ceremony to bind you together until you are old enough to marry."

Behind me Cardinal Bertrand de Deux emits a snort of amusement. I almost blush, but manage to keep it from my face. He does not think Charles Martel understands a word I am saying, but even though my son is only two-and-a-half years old, he understands a great deal more than others might think. He nods or shakes his head with conviction, and appropriately, whether the speaker is addressing him in French, Italian, or Latin; and if asked to do something he does it, proving his complete understanding.

"Do you want to know who your queen wife will be?" I ask him.

"C'est toi, Maman!" he cries, his face shining as he looks up at me. I am struck with surprise and love, and barely manage not to laugh when the cardinal once again snorts with amusement behind us. But he can be very stubborn, my little prince, and I must have his best behavior today.

"I cannot be your queen, Charles Martel. I am too old. But I have chosen someone you will like just as much." I feel a twinge as I say it, looking down into his sweet face, and hope he does not ever like anyone *quite* as much as he loves me. Before he can object I continue quickly, "Do you remember your cousin with whom you played at Christmas? Cousin Joanna?"

He looks confused. He has heard me called Joanna and does not understand his cousin was named after me.

"Les deux filles?" I ask him, the name he used to refer to both of Maria's older girls.

"Les deux filles," he cries, clapping his hands. He ran after Joanna and Agnes all afternoon the day they visited, ignoring completely the baby Clementia.

"Les deux filles," I agree. "Your cousin is coming here today. She will be your queen wife when you are older. Her name is Joanna, the same as mine. What do you think of that?"

He nods happily and turns toward his nurse, Isabelle of Hungary, a fierce woman who was his father's nurse as well. I let him climb down from my lap, thinking he has been still long enough and wants to run, but instead he takes his nurse's hand, tugging her toward the door. When she does not move he says emphatically, "Le jardin! Nous allons-y!" I realize he means to go to the palace gardens where he played with his cousins when they visited, and this time I do laugh.

"We will greet your cousin in the great hall first, and then we will all have a special dinner together. Afterward, if there is time, your nurse may take you and Joanna to the garden to play." I hold out my hand. He drops his nurse's hand at once and walks with me out of the nursery and down the castle stairway.

I sit in my throne at the head of my great hall, with Cardinal de Deux standing on my left and Charles Martel leaning against my right leg as we wait for my sister and her husband to be admitted along with the guests I have invited: nobles of the realm who will bear witness to today's formality.

At my signal the guards open the great doors and announce the Duke and Duchess of Durazzo. They approach my chair and bow before me. Little Joanna, their oldest daughter and my namesake, gives me a very creditable curtsy for a four-year-old. I am charmed, and greet her with a genuine smile. They take their places at my left while the rest of our guests are announced and come forward to make their obeisance to me. It is a small company, only forty or fifty people, but we had neither the time to arrange a huge fête nor the desire to call too much attention to it. If I am lucky King Louis of Hungary will not learn of this subdued event for a while.

My sister and her husband do not look at me as the wine is poured into my cup and then into theirs. They are still angry about not being given Maria's full dowry. But I inherited heavy financial obligations from my grandfather along with his kingdom, which emptied my coffers. My people were starving after two years of crop failure due to heavy rains and flooding. I had no money for a sister who married without my permission a man who could bring neither new trade nor a strong political alliance to my kingdom. And then my own husband provoked my lords and filled my kingdom with strife and was murdered for his stupidity, bringing down on me a papal legate who further depleted what little resources remained. And now we are at war. And still in my sister's and her husband's eyes I see the bitter reminder of that unpaid dowry. Well, today's dealings should satisfy much of that resentment. I nod to Cardinal de Deux.

He steps forward. At my gentle nudge Charles Martel goes not toward the cardinal as I intended, but instead runs to his cousin, taking her hand without any prompting. Rather than take their hands as he intended, the cardinal leaves their little hands entwined and instead places his palms on each of their heads.

"Do you willingly and without any coercion affiance this boy, Charles Martel, prince and heir to the throne of the Kingdom of Naples, to this girl, Joanna, eldest daughter and heir to the Duchy of Durazzo?" the cardinal asks me solemnly.

I state my agreement clearly and sign my name on the parchment he hands me. My sister is beaming now. She catches my eye and I cannot help smiling back.

The cardinal repeats his question to my brother-in-law and cousin, Charles, who also gives his assent. He has what he wants: his daughter will be Queen of Naples. He is bound to me through this promised future for his family. I let out a breath I did not know I was holding as he signs the agreement.

Musicians appear and begin to play as tables and chairs are brought in and a feast laid for all my guests. Maria and Charles join me and the cardinal at the head table with the two affianced children, struck dumb with the wonder of eating with adults instead of in their nursery.

Neither Robert nor Louis of Taranto are here. I have assured Louis that his day will come as soon as Pope Clement approves our union, and he is out with his army scouting our borders. When he returns I will name him vicar-general of the realm for his faithful services, and Charles, as father of my son's future wife, will be given the position of captain-general of the army.

Which leaves only Louis' older brother Robert, Duke of Taranto. But I have found a solution for him, as well. At my suggestion the good Cardinal de Deux convinced Pope Clement to offer him a marriage to Maria of Bourbon, whose husband, the King of Cyprus, has recently died. She is from an influential family in France and has property in Achaia that will add to the Taranto family holdings he inherited from his mother, along with the title emperor of Constantinople. In return for this prize, Clement will have him swear loyalty to me and promise to join his cousins in defending Naples against the Hungarians. I have heard Robert is pleased with this arrangement, and although I shudder for Maria of Bourbon, I am relieved to have his cold ambition turned on someone other than me. I hope she is beautiful, pliant, and fertile, which is all he wants in a wife.

I sit at the feast of my son's engagement and feel a confidence I have not felt in a long time. Three months ago I dreamed I stood alone defending my kingdom; now I have three battle-tested warriors ready to lead their armies against our mutual foe. My country and my family, the royal Angevin line, are united once again.

I lean back in my chair, pleasantly filled with venison and orange-glazed chicken, mushrooms in an onion dressing, cheese-stuffed eggs and apple fritters. The dishes have been cleared and platters of honeyed walnuts and figs set out. Servers move among the tables refilling wine cups as the musicians, playing lutes, harp, drum and flute, fill the hall with lively dance music.

"Thank you…Your Majesty." My sister leans sideways to speak to me over the empty chair between us. Her husband has gone to dance with the pretty daughter of a count. I notice Maria's slight stumble over my formal title, as great a stretch as the empty space between us.

"It is a pleasing match for everyone," I lie smoothly. In fact my son could have done much better marrying a princess of France or of another country, bringing wealth and lands and a strong alliance to our kingdom. But these are desperate times and I need Charles' allegiance right now.

I look at the dancers. Little Joanna has enticed Charles Martel onto the floor and is leading him in something that roughly resembles a saltarello. The sides of little Joanna's skirts are tucked up into her waistband as she has seen the other women doing, to give them enough freedom for the sprightly footwork. Charles Martel is hopping forward and back and side-to-side beside her, laughing. She is patient and encouraging with him, accustomed to younger siblings, and he is eager to please her. Their heads bend together, plump, rosy cheeks and fair curls entwining as they regard their feet, trying to keep in time with the music and somewhat in line with the adult dancers.

"I remember my…engagement." I hope Maria did not notice my momentary hesitation. Andrew and I were married as children, not merely affianced. Is there nothing I can say to my sister that is not false? "They are pretty together. Joanna is a sweet child."

"She is very intelligent," Maria says—did I sound dismissive of her daughter?—"and loyal." The word is tarnished with past betrayals between us, but her tone is sincere. I do not know how to answer. We were that age once and very close, we believed nothing would ever come between us. Is it possible to love someone for a lifetime and never betray them? I am sure I will never betray Charles Martel, but perhaps I am doing so right now, marrying him to this cousin. My Grandfather did not know what Andrew would grow up to be. I do not blame him; he did what was necessary to preserve his kingdom—my kingdom, now—as I am doing today.

"I remember your marriage," Maria lets me know she caught my false wording. "I was only four, Joanna's age. I tried to get Andrew to dance with me after he had danced with you, but he was more interested in the marchpane."

"His father made him dance with me." I remember my embarrassment as my six-year-old husband stumbled over his feet and tread on mine. I was seven and very aware of my dignity. It was a relief when he broke free and went back to the feast table. I look at Charles Martel and Joanna and hope they are better-matched and will be happy, or at least content with one another.

"I hope this will be a new start…for us."

I glance at Maria and catch her blush as she looks down. She means it. She wants us to be friends again. She wants me to forget everything she has done and love her as she thinks she loves me.

"Keep your husband true."

She looks up at me. "This will do it." And in her eyes is a weary honesty. This will accomplish what she could not. He must be paid for his loyalty, that is the only influence he will allow.

The Queen Who Sold Her Crown

But then, what influence had I ever had over Andrew? I sigh. "We are sisters, Maria. We will always be sisters." There are no new starts, but blood is blood. "They will be married when Naples is safe and at peace and there is time for such things."

"I trust you," she says. The words, which we used to say so easily to each other as children, make me wince.

The music ends with a flourish and Charles of Durazzo returns to our table, flushed with the pleasure of dancing with the young countess. His wife, Maria, is not yet nineteen. I wonder if Louis will lose interest in me when we are married and I have given him children. I am twenty-one. Still beautiful, I have been told, with the figure of a girl despite having given birth, and the crown on my head casts its own allure. But when more children have stretched the firm skin of my stomach and Louis has his own crown…?

Maria smiles as her husband takes his seat between us. In contrast, I realize how weary she looks in repose. We have been through a great deal, her and I, and it has taken its toll. Do I look weary and older than my years when I am not roused to action or greeting someone? I let the troubling thought go. When am I ever not busy protecting my realm, my family, my crown, my son, my life?

Joanna returns, leading Charles Martel back to me. He is weeping—most likely with tiredness—and trying hard not to show it. I signal to a servant to fetch his nurse, wishing I could retire with him. But I must keep my smile in place and convince my nobles that all is well in the Kingdom of Naples, that the Angevins are united once more and there is no threat that can divide or conquer us.

Chapter 3

Preparing for War

Joanna 1 of Naples
July–August, 1347

The young soldier is pale and trembling, still gasping for breath. His legs shake so that he nearly falls and has to catch himself when he bows low before me. I wave him into a chair. He hesitates. It is a crime for a commoner to sit before a queen, but we are alone in my privy chamber and if he does not sit soon, he might faint before he can give me his message.

"Tell me your news," I say. My throat is so dry I have to force the words out. His presence before me can mean only one thing. I have been living in dread of it for three months, since Louis of Hungary first declared war on my kingdom.

"Your Majesty, the Hungarian army has been sighted in the northeast. They have not yet crossed our border but wait at its edge."

"Is King Louis with them?"

"No, Your Majesty. It appears to be an advance guard."

I nod. They will wait for their king before riding on to Naples, but they can do some damage while they wait. I ask a few more questions before I command him to keep this to himself and send him to the kitchens to be fed. As he leaves I order one of my house guards to have Charles of Durazzo attend me. It is time he repaid me for his daughter's glorious future.

I also send for Robert and Louis of Taranto, Niccolò Acciaiuoli, Cardinal de Dieux, and several others who must hear this news. When they arrive I lead them into my privy chamber and have the door closed and guarded.

I have recovered myself. It is a relief to have the uncertainty over, bracing to finally be able to act. I have had time to unify my country and plan my response and I am ready. I watch their faces as I give them the news. No one seems very surprised. The cardinal alone looks alarmed until he masters it. My three cousins look grim but determined, exactly as I had hoped, since they will lead my armies. We discuss strategy, the details of raising an army sufficient to repel the Hungarians when their full force arrives.

"What allies can we count on?" Robert asks. I would prefer not to answer this question, and even more that he had not been the one to ask it. He is the weakest link in Naples' defense, the commander with the least to gain in defending my kingdom. But as the Duke of Taranto he commands the largest number of knights and vassals sworn to his service.

"We need no outside allies," Louis says boldly in my silence. "We are Angevins."

Robert gives his brother a measuring look before turning back to me. "So the Florentine bankers will not spare us any men."

I nod curtly. Despite all my entreaties and our long-standing alliance with Florence, despite even the efforts of Niccolò Acciaiuolo who has influential family members in Florence, the Florentine elders have refused to send us the legion I requested, electing to remain neutral.

He does not ask about France. King Philip needs all the soldiers he can muster for his war with England.

"Cousin Charles, I need you to take as many men as are immediately available and ride northeast to Abruzzi. You are to keep the Hungarian soldiers at the border and limit any damage they might do while waiting for their king to arrive."

"I can do that," Louis objects.

"I need you here," I tell him curtly. Before he can press further I turn to his brother. "Cousin Robert, I want you to muster an army, as many men as you can order up among your vassals. Issue them arms and begin training them. Louis of Hungary's troops will be well-trained, experienced soldiers." I hope to distract him from the question I see in his eyes, the one I cannot answer yet.

But Robert will not be put off. "And what of our enemies?" he asks softly.

He means Sicily, on our southern border. We cannot be fighting on two fronts. "I have sent an emissary to the King of Sicily." My voice is steady, my expression more assured than I feel. "He has not yet returned but I am confident he will be successful in gaining a truce between us."

Robert opens his mouth, frowning, but Charles cuts off any comment he might have made. "I must marshal an army also. Louis can take a battalion to watch the border."

It is what Louis wanted, but now that his cousin finds it beneath him, he scowls. How will I turn these three into a fighting force when they cannot even plan the first steps together? And Louis must stay here with me. I raise my voice over their mutterings.

"Your brothers can muster your vassals in your name," I tell Charles sternly. "You are the captain-general of my army. It is your place to lead the first skirmishes against our enemy." I am relieved to see his chest puff out a little as I remind him of his new title. They are fine figures of masculinity, my royal cousins: arrogant, courageous, proud, and passionate. All they need is a wiser head to guide them and they will be invincible.

"I need you to find and hire more mercenaries," I tell Louis, the first reasonable excuse I can think of to keep him here. Charles and

Robert look ready to protest. They know the mercenaries are being paid by the royal treasury, while they must dip into their own coffers to feed and keep the vassals they call up to fight for them, and buy the weapons they supply them with.

"If Louis of Hungary takes Naples, he will claim for himself your castles and holdings, your forests and villages and fields of sheep and quarries…" I trail off letting them picture it, then finish sweetly, "But when we rout him and send him back to Hungary where he belongs, your queen will be greatly indebted to you for your service to her kingdom, and I have always been generous in my gratitude to those loyal to me."

I catch Cardinal de Dieux's gaze of admiration, gone before the others could notice it, and smile to myself. Has he forgotten I was raised by two of shrewdest monarchs in all Christendom? What Robert the Wise and Queen Sancia did not know about ruling a kingdom and controlling unruly nobles was not worth knowing. They began preparing me to reign the day I came to Castle Nuovo at five years of age.

As they leave I ask the cardinal to stay a moment and discreetly signal Louis to remain also. I wait until the others have gone and the guard has shut the door to my council chamber again. I have done what I could to secure the aid of Charles and Robert, but I know at their core they are loyal to themselves alone. Right now their best interests lie with me—until they do not. I must have at least one general leading my army whose loyalty cannot change.

"Cardinal de Dieux, Louis and I must be married."

After a moment's pause, the cardinal bows slightly. "I will write at once to Pope Clement for the necessary dispensations."

"There is no time for that now. We are at war."

My eyes are locked on the cardinal's, and his on mine. Louis, who still believes the delay has been the pope's doing, is judiciously silent. Good. Let him think I am finally putting my foot down.

I am. The cardinal knows as well as I that Clement, if asked, might refuse me permission to marry in order to mollify the Hungarians. But they have gone too far to back down now, bringing their army to my borders. Delaying my marriage any longer could cost me my kingdom if the fighting is hard and my cousins are tempted to retreat. Louis is no coward, but I must ensure that he will do all he can to keep them true.

He is also no fool. He will realize that marriage to me will seal his fate with King Louis of Hungary if he fails. I do not need to look at him to know this is in his mind. But he is too ambitious to refuse a kingdom. So it is not him that I keep my gaze fixed upon.

Cardinal de Dieux is silent. He admires me, he believes in my innocence and my virtue. I am the rightful queen of Naples, chosen by God and anointed by the pope, and in the last few months he has seen I am up to the task. But he is the pope's legate, acting on the pope's behalf.

"I did not start this war," I tell him quietly, "but I must win it."

He holds my gaze a moment longer, then nods once.

Louis and I dine alone together that night. Word has got round the castle; the servants, while not forgetting themselves so far as to smile at us, are unusually attentive, their voices warm with approval. Louis is dressed in his finest, gold and silver threads and jewels gleaming on his close-fitting tunic which follows the lines of his lean, muscular body. The tunic is a vivid blue, a color that stands for fidelity and virtue, and also happens to flatter his fair skin and deep blue eyes. His golden hair shines in the light of the oil lamps and a heady smell of spices and male confidence emanates from him, making me slightly dizzy.

He chooses the tenderest pieces of venison and feeds them to me from his knife. His eyes shine as I take each one into my mouth, licking my lips with a coy smile. I have flirted with him since we were children, and if I had not been of noble blood and married to another, I might have done more than flirted.

Tonight he gazes at me as a man in love. His eyes are warm pools of desire, travelling from my bosom over my body and back to my face with an intensity that makes me shiver. I have been bedded and I have borne a child, but I have never been loved. I dared not hope to be. A queen must marry for the advantage of her kingdom. It is only by some gift of God I will be married this time to someone I love, who says with every look, every touch, that he loves me back. I can barely eat for the tightness in my throat and chest, barely sit for the giddy feeling in my gut and the tingle between my legs. I want him to take me now and he wants it too, the air is thick with the tension of our desire.

"A month," I say, my voice catching. "We will be married in a month." *Can I wait that long?*

"Tonight," he says, his voice a low growl that sends shivers through me again.

I lift my wine cup and gulp the sweet liquid in a most unqueenly way. "We must first make an announcement, and invite those who will expect to be there, and arrange a feast—"

"We must be married before anyone can object," he cuts me off. "And then I shall bed you properly." He gives me a long look full of promise.

Properly, I think, tingling with anticipation. *Not like that rough, fumbling boy, Andrew.*

Louis smiles. "And then I will go raise an army of mercenaries to defeat your enemies."

I am jolted back to reality. He is right. He is thinking like a prince while I wallow in sensations. How could I have so forgot myself, even briefly? *A man who can do that to me is dangerous,* a small part of my mind whispers, but I quiet it at once. This is how it feels to be a queen with a strong king beside her, a man she can depend on. Louis has already insisted on being crowned King of Naples, he will not be satisfied living as my consort, and I have agreed. I knew a man like this would accept no less.

"Three days," I tell him, my voice firm now. "We cannot make the arrangements in fewer."

He leans across the table toward me. "We need not wait," he murmurs, so close his breath tickles my face.

But I am under control now, although my heart beats hard between my ribs. "Our marriage must be above question in every way," I answer, my voice as low as his even though the servants have withdrawn to a respectful distance. I gaze at him deeply, my eyes assuring him I am as eager as he is, that ours will not be a cold marriage bed. But I cannot afford any more rumors against my virtue than are already circulating because of Andrew's murder.

He sits back, a fleeting expression of coldness in his eyes, immediately hidden under a courtly smile. "I await the pleasure of my queen," he says, raising his cup in a salute before drinking.

Is he mocking me?

Before I can decide he lowers the cup and resumes his meal, his eyes warm and loving once more. He no longer chooses morsels for me to savor, so I help myself. I have lost my appetite but will not let him see that. He is a proud man and does not like to be denied, but he has got over it quickly. Already he is smiling and has turned the conversation to pleasanter subjects.

My emissary's eyes gleam as he stands before me in my privy council room, still smelling of sea and sweat from his journey home. "Sicily has agreed to a truce!" With a flourish he hands me the scroll signed by King Louis of Sicily.

I smile at his exuberance. "Tell me," I prompt, willing to sacrifice a little time to hear good news.

He bows once again. "I was taken to the great hall, where young King Louis sat, surrounded by the men who make up his regency."

I nod. Louis of Sicily has not reached the age of majority and must rule under a regency, which is in our favor. Old men do not like war. I signal the messenger to continue. His words have the smooth flow of practice, which makes me smile further as he proceeds.

"They were all old men, so I spoke as you directed me, of King Louis of Hungary's ruthless desire to claim all the land his father felt he was entitled to. They were already aware that King Carobert believed…" He clears his throat, glancing at me. I nod. "…Believed he had a claim on the Kingdom of Naples, and that he considered Sicily part of that kingdom. They showed no surprise when I mentioned this."

I listen without comment. Sicily is indeed a part of the Kingdom of Naples, and my grandfather never gave up trying to reclaim it, a fact I warned him not to bring up.

He continues quickly. "I emphasized that this was King Louis of Hungary's belief, and warned them that if they attacked us now it would only serve to deplete both their and our armies, weakening both our kingdoms and thereby assisting the Hungarians to overcome us both. But if they signed a truce with us, they need only stand aside and let us defeat the Hungarian army and send King Louis back to Hungary beaten."

Exactly what I had advised him to say. "Was there any argument?"

"Young Louis of Sicily asked what would keep us from turning on Sicily when we had vanquished the Hungarians?"

"And you said—"

"The truce!" He grins.

I smile back. "Well done." But I had sent him with a second directive: to learn as much as he can about Sicily's defenses.

Because of course, Sicily *is* a part of my kingdom and the young king holds it with no legitimate right. "Tell me what you saw while you were there."

He hangs his head, a slight flush creeping up his neck. "Very little of their armaments. I was escorted by an armed guard during my entire stay, with a guard at my door while I slept. I tried to walk out on the pretext of relieving myself, but I was escorted even there." He blushes crimson.

I sigh and raise my hand to dismiss him.

"I did see one thing, Your Majesty. It might be of import…"

"Speak," I prod, when he pauses.

"When the ship docked, a half-dozen guards were waiting to meet us. As we made our way from the port, I saw a man lying dead in the street. No one stopped to carry him to the church. Not only my guards, I mean, but no one. Indeed, those nearby averted their faces as though afraid to look at him. When we were passing, a terrible stench arose from the body, like nothing I have smelled before, although he could not have been lying there long. His clothes were expensive, he did not have the look of a man who would go unmissed."

He drew a breath. It had shaken him, this dead man.

"Every year people die of a summer fever. We have all seen them." *But usually in their beds,* I think, frowning, *attended to by their families.*

"No, Your Majesty, it was not that. I have seen and smelled dead men before. This was worse. I looked at him closely and saw black boils on his arms and neck, with pus seeping from them still… Before I could see more, the guards hurried us past. Strong fighting men they were, surely accustomed to the sight of corpses, but their faces were pale and they crossed themselves as we passed that stinking body, and moved to the far side of the road to avoid it."

"And no one remarked on it?"

"No, Your Majesty. Nor would they answer when I questioned them. I saw nothing amiss in the castle nor the grounds within its walls, but on the walk back to the port I saw three more bodies, two left on the street, another just outside her house, as though the poor woman had been shoved outside the minute she expired." He shuddered. "And a priest…" his voice shakes now. "I saw a priest cross the street to avoid the bodies and pass them by with his face averted."

I pause a moment as it sinks in. No last rites, no prayers for their souls, no washing the body and wrapping it in a white shroud, no burial in Church soil. No final dignity in death at all. It is unconceivable! "All of them with the same boils, the smell?"

"Yes, Your Majesty."

"A plague."

"I believe so. But one I have never seen before."

"You did not touch them?"

He pales and draws back. "No, nor any of my company. Indeed we were hurried past by the guards and barely given time to see them."

No wonder they were so eager to sign a truce. "Very well, you may leave me now."

I sit for a moment chilled by his words, and even more by the fear in his voice when he spoke of what he had seen. Priests ignoring the dead? Leaving them to face eternity with no absolution of their sins? What kind of priests live in Sicily? What kind of plague is this to cause such a reaction? Then I shake myself. Sicily is far away. What do I care if three Sicilians have died of an illness? I am facing a much more immediate threat to my own people.

The next day Louis arrives early at Castle Nuovo. He is wearing a silk brocade tunic which looks as though it has been spun of pure gold, so bright it challenges the sun. I catch sight of him as I descend the stairs and stop for a moment unable to breathe.

I had risen before dawn this morning, as nervous and excited as a maid of fourteen, unable to eat, barely able to sit still as I was washed and dressed in a pale green silk brocade kirtle, green for spring and new beginnings. It is laced with seed pearls in an intricate floral design and has tiny fleur-de-lis stitched in gold thread about the sleeves and neckline. My hair has been braided up under a green silk headdress glittering with emeralds and my neck is heavy with gold chains strung with pearls.

I have dreamed of Louis forever, never daring to hope this day would come. We walk out through the castle doors side-by-side, my hand on his arm lightly, lightly. I am afraid if I grasp too hard the entire scene will shimmer like a sunlit dream and disappear. I feel I am outside myself, watching this morning unfold like a vision in a still lake: the slightest false move and all my hopes and dreams could fall into it like a stone, sinking beyond my reach forever.

Louis hands me up into the royal carriage and sits beside me for the ride to the cathedral of San Domenico Maggiore where we will be married. We process through the streets, our two banners carried before us by guards wearing the royal livery, followed by six of my ladies-in-waiting in their most expensive kirtles and six of Louis' handsomest men-at-arms. Louis and I toss coins into the crowds cheering us on either side as we pass. Every coin I toss, every cheer I hear further convinces me this is truly happening. I am marrying Louis of Taranto. I am giddy with happiness and cannot stop laughing. How I have missed happiness!

Louis is tall and strong, sitting so close I can feel the heat of his thigh against mine. He smiles at my high spirits and waves to the Neapolitans lining our way shouting their approval. We are the stuff of minstrel songs to them, blond and blue-eyed and young, with royal blood in our veins and our family banners unfurling before us.

We are love and hope in a time of uncertainty and in our union lies the strength to carry them to safety with us.

I toss my coins far into the crowd, wanting as many as possible to share our joy. We have an entire city of witnesses to our wedding, as well as the nobles that could be summoned in haste to stand in the church while Cardinal de Dieux performs the ceremony, and to attend the feast that will follow.

No longer afraid of angering Louis of Hungary, I want this marriage public. This strong warrior beside me, who will lead my army, needs to know his fate is inexorably tied to mine. I do not doubt my Louis, no, he has proven his love already, he has fought for me against his brother and his cousin and now he will fight with them against our mutual foe. Today's vows will only give him what he has already earned.

Let Hungary see how we Neapolitans celebrate even as they ride to war against us! Let them see how we laugh and feast in the face of their threats. I toss another handful of coins out over my people's heads with a carefree smile. Tonight Louis will be my husband. Tonight he will move into Castle Nuovo and come to my bed and put his arms around me and love me. Tonight I will be his wife and need never be afraid again.

I lie impatiently in our bed, alone, having dismissed my ladies after they undressed me. At last I hear footsteps approaching the door and the rough voices of men who have had too much wine. As they get closer I hear the gibes men make escorting a groom to his wedding bed, but when they stop at the door the lewd laughter fades and Louis enters alone.

I watch him in the darkness pulling off his tunic and hose. He is not as drunk as he sounded, I note with relief. Then his shirt comes off, revealing his taut, muscular body fully naked and I am so struck by his beauty I catch my breath.

He turns, his eyes adjusted now to the darkness, and chuckles when he sees me watching him. He walks without haste toward the bed, every movement graceful and confident. I toss back the sheet so that I can enjoy the feeling of his eyes appraising me as he is enjoying my lusty appreciation of him. I smile as he hardens before he reaches the bed.

He climbs up beside me and twines his fingers in my hair lying like a spray of gold upon the pillow. He has not seen it unbound since we were children together. I lie still, forcing myself not to reach for him, determined to enjoy every moment of this night I have so long dreamed of. When he begins to stroke my breasts and down the little mound of my belly, I run my hands over his arms, his chest, marveling at the firm sculpture of his muscles. He kicks the sheet away and swings on top of me, smiling as he gently pinches my nipples and rubs himself against me, teasing me, entering just a little as I moan and part my legs, then drawing back, again and again, until I am in a fever of desire and move with him. Still he plays with me, drawing back as I arch up and slipping back in only enough to drive me to a frenzy.

When I can bear no more he enters me, his fingers continuing to tease me even as he satisfies me, until with a scream I feel myself explode.

I fall back, panting as after-ripples of delight pulse through me. Never, in all his fumbling, did Andrew make me feel like this. It is a revelation, an almost holy feeling, a sense of unity and fulfilment so deep it pierces my soul. I look at Louis, smiling beside me, and know he felt it too. I am filled with the absolute certainty that Louis loves me as I love him, that our love will last forever, that it is impossible to have experienced something as profound as this and not be bound forever by it.

Chapter 4

Sisters and Allies

Maria of Naples
September–November, 1347

Charles has come back from the north. A messenger came to tell me he is shut in with Joanna and her council discussing the war. No mention of how long he will be—I doubt he knows himself—but I am to have a good supper waiting.

"How many have returned with him?" I demand. The answer drains the color from my face. So many good men lost. I nod curtly and send the man away unhappy. I will not pay him from my housekeeping money, the little Charles gives me to run his household. Let Charles reward him for his services, he is Charles' man. Charles' mother, my Aunt Agnes of Perigord, had her own money when she ran the Durazzo castle, but I, a princess of Naples, second in line to the crown, have nothing but what my husband gives me.

I send a girl to fetch the cook. Charles will arrive home hungry; no doubt he is already feeling it after his long ride. Otherwise I would not have received a message at all.

I hear Charles' noisy entrance and come down to greet him in the great hall. It is late; my stomach has been grumbling with hunger for hours, but I ignore it and smile at him. The weariness and strain in his face makes me more anxious, but also more forgiving. I send for our dinner to be brought in: pigeon stuffed with minced eggs and roasted venison and a fish stew followed by fruit pastries.

"Tell me what happened," I urge when we have eaten our fill and Charles sits running his fingers around the edge of his wine cup, deep in thought. "I need to know."

Charles is not concerned with his wife's needs, but he is aware of what the second-in-line to the throne of Naples needs to know. He rouses himself with a sigh as though I have called on him to make another report. I sit straighter in my chair. Ever since I learned to love him less, he has learned to respect me more.

"Our fears were well-founded." His face is tight with the bitter memory. "Three of the northern barons had rebelled and joined forces with the Hungarian army. I made a stand at L'Aquila but their numbers were too great; I had to retreat." He takes a long drink of his wine. I frown over Charles' shoulder at the lad when he takes a step forward to refill Charles' cup. Charles has had half-a-dozen refills already. I want to hear the details of his trip as well as what he discussed with the queen and her council before he has to be carried to his bed. My life is at risk as well as my sister's if the Hungarians reach Naples.

"Fortunately, King Louis has not yet left Hungary, so I have time to raise a new, larger army." Charles is still staring into his empty wine cup. His voice has taken on a thick slur.

"What else was discussed at the council?" I ask sharply. But I am too late; his eyes have closed. I sigh and signal for two manservants to help him to his bed.

I should have a seat on Joanna's council. Both our aunts did, when they were only duchesses with no legitimate claim to the throne.

And Philippa, the daughter of a Sicilian fisherman, wife of an Ethiopian slave, even she had a place at Joanna's council table. I wince at the thought of Philippa and her family, all dead now, but my anger at Joanna is still ripe. She has always spurned me. If I were queen of Naples I would listen to her advice.

Or maybe not—let her see how that feels.

So I am left seeking news from my husband, when all he can talk about is the army he and our Taranto cousins are raising.

"1,500 knights," he tells me as we break out fast together the next morning. "And several thousand fighting vassals on foot, between our two Duchies. Plus all of Louis' German mercenaries besides." I note the satisfaction on his face and am greatly reassured. Surely that will be enough to defeat the Hungarians and drive them from our kingdom.

Charles is so busy arming and training his vassals for the war that I barely see him. Weary with sitting inside and seeing only servants, I swallow my pride and send Joanna a message asking to join her ladies-in-waiting. *Since you will not have me on your council,* I think but do not write. She responds at once suggesting I bring my eldest daughter with me.

It gives me pause when I read that. I still think of my Joanna as a baby, but she is four years old already. And she is affianced to the prince. My sister is right: they should be getting to know and trust each other. And my daughter needs to learn about life in a royal court. I remember Joanna and I as children at Castle Nuovo watching and coming to recognize the intrigues and alliances, both romantic and political, that bloomed in our presence chamber among card games and embroidery and music. Clever beyond our years we were, especially Joanna, as we discussed in bed at night which ladies and courtiers we liked and which ones we trusted, who was spying on us and on each other, and for whom. My daughter must understand such things.

I write back at once that we will come the end of the month. As soon as I have sealed the note and sent it off, I call for my daughter and our dressmaker. Joanna will need a wardrobe suitable for a lady-in-waiting! The thought makes me smile. I have had few reasons to smile for a long time.

Queen Joanna makes it clear among her court that I am in favor again. I am first in line behind her when we progress to dinner. I sit beside her when we sew in her presence room, little Joanna often on a stool between us, her head bent industriously over her embroidery. When she sends Joanna to play in the nursery or walk in the garden with Charles Martel and his nurse, I am the one chosen to play cards at the queen's table.

It is more than a balm to my ego; it is a balm to my heart to be close to her again. I know she will never trust me as she used to. Nor can I trust her as I did once, for she has not yet given me my dowry, and I with four children by my husband, three of them living. But I have been so lonely. For if my sister disparages me, my husband does so tenfold. If I cannot entirely trust my sister, I cannot trust my husband at all. My sister will put her crown and her kingdom ahead of me. I may not like that but I understand, even respect it, for she puts the crown and the kingdom of Naples before her own self. My husband puts nothing ahead of himself and as for me, he would put even his favorite hunting hound ahead of me.

I have come a long way from the girl who married her dashing older cousin for love, believing she was loved in return. I know now things I did not understand then. I know enough to laugh behind my hand when our cousin Louis of Taranto whispers in my sister's ear and she blushes with a little panting smile so unlike her usual regal bearing. But let her be happy. I will not disillusion her. Let her have a season of love if she can in these treacherous times, before she learns she is only a girl with a crown to Louis. As I am only a girl without a crown to Charles, who never lets me forget that he has not even received my dowry, let alone the crown to which I was second-in-line, in return for the gamble he made in marrying me.

Sitting in her presence chamber with her other ladies, I see when her councilors walk by, strutting with importance, and go into her privy council chamber with her, my husband among them, and shut the door. I remember Philippa and our powerful aunts getting up from their chairs and leaving their sewing to go in with the men. I was young then and did not want to join them, content to stay and gossip with the younger ladies-in-waiting and flirt with the handsome courtiers. But I am a woman now, the Duchess of Durazzo and a royal princess, and I burn with humiliation at being over-looked as her conceited councilors walk by. I keep my head down, as though my embroidery fascinates me, and pretend I do not see the other ladies glancing at me. My husband will tell me what little he thinks I must know when I take him aside and question him. And that, too, is an insult.

After many days, and with some trepidation, I muster my resolve during a game of cards. "Your Majesty—" I have got used to the formal title where once I simply called her Joanna, or sister—"I would speak to you privately if you will." I speak quietly, projecting humility though it burns my throat. And then I must wait until after dinner when she will walk with me in the garden, if she remembers.

Perhaps I do her injustice for she does remember and rises from the table while her husband is still drinking his wine and laughing at the antics of the court jester. She glances over at me and asks if I will join her for a stroll around the gardens. Charles gives me a suspicious look as I rise quickly from my seat beside him. I pretend not to notice, which is, of course, the worst thing I could do, but I cannot think quickly of something to say to allay his distrust. At least he will not dare launch into one of his tirades against me at the queen's table.

"What did you wish to say, Maria?" Joanna's voice is cool, neither friendly nor unfriendly. She looks around her garden as she walks, as though it is more interesting to her than I am. We used to run arm-in-arm through this garden, laughing with our cousins.

"I love this garden," I say, but it is the carefree days of childhood that I love, and the heady days when Charles courted me here. Days long behind us both. With a sigh I turn to look at my sister. In her brooding silence I know what she is thinking of.

"King Louis will never take this from us," I say, more fiercely than I intended.

She turns on me a look of anguish. "He will try, Maria. He will try his best, and even if he does not succeed, many will die in his attempt."

A chill goes through me. I have never seen my sister so close to despair. I think of our forces, led by her husband Louis of Taranto and my husband Charles and their brothers, the cousins we grew up playing with here in the palace gardens. "Even if he kills those we love," my voice catches for a moment. I do still love Charles despite how he has disappointed me. My eyes narrow at the thought of Louis of Hungary killing our husbands and cousins and I continue more passionately, "he will never take Naples from us! We are its rightful rulers and God will strengthen us." I toss my head. "And even if he does take Naples, he will never hold her. Our subjects love us and will only be ruled by you, their rightful monarch. Do not lose heart, Joanna. Naples is yours, and you are hers."

She smiles at me, tears glistening in her eyes, and grasps my hands. It is only a moment and then she remembers I asked her here. "What do you want, Maria?" she asks, letting go of my hands, but her expression is softer now and she looks at me, at least.

"I want to help you," I tell her simply.

"You are my lady-in-waiting. And my sister." She smiles. It does not entirely reach her eyes.

"I should have a seat on your council." I have rehearsed my arguments but nervousness makes me forget my speech. I hurry on, my points all out of order. "Our aunts sat on your council, and on our Grandfather's council, and even Philippa—"

"Our mother."

"Our nursemaid. Advised you. I do not mean to advise you, nor question your decisions, nor seek anything for myself—"

"You will be a rare councilor, then."

"I only need to be there. Should anything happen to you—may God forbid and the Virgin Mary watch over you! But if it does, I will need to know what is happening in our kingdom."

Her face is stony.

"Our Grandfather trusted me enough to make me your heir." I remind her. "Charles Martel is before me now, but he is a baby. Someone will have to be his regent and the most likely candidate is my husband. If I am not on your council I will be passed over and he will have sole regency." I let her think about that awhile and about Charles' ambition.

"You asked me to keep my husband faithful. How can I do so if I do not know your orders and decisions? If I do not even know how the war is going?"

"It is your husband who denies you a seat on my council."

I will myself to keep my face expressionless as I absorb this. I will not criticize Charles in front of his queen. When I can trust my voice I say coolly, "I did not know my Lord Husband chose your council for you."

"You have never been interested in politics, Maria."

"That is a failing I wish to rectify. Among others."

She studies me, wondering, no doubt, if there is something more to my request. There is, of course, but I meet her gaze steadily, once again showing nothing. I have Charles to thank for that skill, I was guileless as a child.

I hear a distant shriek of girlish laughter and the high-pitched voice of a small boy, and remember our children are playing here. Joanna turns her head toward the sound. I look away over the beds of flowers and shrubbery. The heat of summer has passed and the autumn colors are beautiful. Everywhere life is blooming and the scent of earth and sea and blossoms is heady. Another childish peal of laughter floats to us on the breeze.

"King Louis will murder me and my family as well as you and yours," I tell her quietly. "If he gets this far."

She turns and walks purposefully back the way we have come. "I will have a council chair set out for the Duchess of Durazzo," she says over her shoulder.

It takes me a moment to realize she means me.

My husband glares down the council table at me. I have not been seated beside him but near the foot of the table, where those who are not expected to speak are seated, ready to take orders when the decision-makers are in agreement.

That is fine with me. I have no interest in influencing Joanna's decisions. I only want to know them. And truth be told, I want what has already begun happening since the news spread that the queen has asked me to sit on her council: I am treated with respect. Courtiers flatter me, servants bow lower, musicians note the songs that make me smile. None of that matters as much as it once would have, but the fact that I am recognized as a princess, second-in-line to the throne after Charles Martel, and my daughters after me, that does matter. My people will protect me, will fight for me as their rightful ruler if anything happens to Joanna and her son. I was a child when I threw that away to marry my dashing older cousin, but I have learned its value since.

I tuck my slippered feet under my skirts and suppress a shiver. It is December and there is no fireplace in this room. The privy council room is small, enclosed within Joanna's suites with no external wall and only one door, easily guarded. I think there must be a secret exit somewhere, but I cannot see one.

"King Louis is riding toward Naples," Niccolò Acciaiuoli tells us. This time I cannot control my shiver, but I am not the only one shuddering at the news. The war is upon us at last.

"He left Visegrad with one thousand Hungarian knights," Niccolò continues. "Hand-picked, no doubt. His best." He is a useful man, Niccolò, with family and influential friends, not to mention spies, all across Italy. "By early December he was in Cittadella, and two days later, on December 8th, Verona opened its gates to him."

The speed of his movement shocks us. We sit motionless in our chairs staring at Niccolò, every face white and grim.

"They are not slowed down by foot soldiers or supplies," Louis says glumly from his seat beside Joanna.

They are not slowed down by resistance, I think as Niccolò recites city after city declaring neutrality and letting them pass.

"But only a thousand men..." Charles smiles.

"A thousand Hungarians. And some silver," Robert of Taranto drawls. "He is buying mercenaries as he comes." An easy task in northern Italy, as we all know, for he is allied with the Holy Roman Emperor, while we in the south are allied with Pope Clement, an ongoing conflict in which all Italy has taken sides.

No one speaks, as though there is nothing more to say.

Finally, Niccolò clears his throat. "He will come through Capua."

My husband nods. "He will have to come by the Via Appia. He will need a good road when he and his knights join up with his advanced army and the mercenaries he has picked up."

I feel faint. The Via Appia is the only road wide and firm enough for an army to travel on through the marshes and wetlands that cover much of our kingdom. Capua lies directly on the Via Appia. It is bordered on three sides by the Volturno River, giving it a natural moat. Because of its strategic location our ancestors have buttressed it into a nearly impregnable fortress. A good place to make a stand. But it is only twenty miles from Naples.

For the rest of the meeting the generals of Naples' army, Joanna's husband and mine, our cousin Robert and Niccolò, discuss strategy and timing. They agree to gather their army and leave for Capua this very week.

I can feel my knees trembling as I rise from my seat. I stand very straight and force my legs to move steadily, their betraying weakness hidden under my shirts. Joanna leads us out, her movements decisive and assured, her face calm. Her courage and resolution through this time fortifies us all. I school my features so I will look no less regal. We will surely prevail against these Hungarians, who are little more than barbarians. I remember the pleasure Prince Andrew took in his acts of cruelty to those beneath him, the mean satisfaction in the eyes of his Hungarian guards as they watched. I imagine an army of such men let loose on the citizens of Naples.

We *must* prevail against them.

Chapter 5

Bloodless Battles

Joanna 1 of Naples
December 1347–January, 1348

I strive to appear composed and confident, but inside I am trembling. I attribute it to my pregnancy, which makes a woman more prone to the sway of emotion, fearful of any threat to her unborn child. It is early; I do not show yet. Only Louis knows our secret. He clasps my hand under the table and squeezes reassuringly. I squeeze back before he lets go.

They will leave me here alone with only my city guard. If they lose the battle at Capua… An image of myself standing alone outside the gates of Naples, heavy with child, facing a massive army of brutal barbarians, comes into my mind. Try as I will, I cannot dispel it, or the terror it engenders. I hold my back rigidly straight, my head high, as I listen to talk of the impending war with every appearance of a firm courage I do not feel. It will come to me. God will fortify me to face whatever I must. But right now all I can think is that our enemy is rich and ruthless, and every city they pass, even those who have allied with us in the past, is swearing neutrality, afraid to oppose them. I feel like a sparrow shivering in the shadow of a hawk.

In bed that night I cling to Louis.

"Are you afraid for me?" he asks.

I cannot read his expression in the dark, but his voice is troubled. "No," I say firmly. "Our cause is just, God will protect you. And when you return in victory our Holy Father, Pope Clement, will recognize our marriage and crown you King Louis of Naples." I kiss him deeply, as though the prize is already his. "I will miss you when you are gone fighting for our Kingdom," I say, running my fingers down his broad chest and lower into the curly gold nest below until he groans. Then I show him how much I will miss him, and in which ways I will miss him, until we are breathless and neither of us is thinking of the other King Louis.

Niccolò's cousin informs us King Louis has gathered five thousand knights and four thousand foot soldiers, Louis writes to me from Capua. *Have no fear, we are resolute and righteous and well-prepared to defend this fortress.*

Edward Acciaiuoli would not misinform his cousin; he intends it as a warning. My husband and my cousins, the Dukes of Durazzo and Taranto, mustered up a little over half that many knights, and less than half as many foot soldiers. *Our men will fight harder because they are defending their homes,* Louis' letter continues. *Most of his soldiers are mercenaries.* But then, a portion of our force are the German mercenaries my husband hired, also.

I am pregnant and nauseous and cannot concentrate on anything as I watch for Louis' daily messages. Maria is pregnant also. She and her daughter have returned to her husband's castle where she is no doubt watching for messages from him as anxiously as I wait for word from Louis.

On Christmas eve I learn that Louis of Hungary has joined his advanced guard in L'Aquila. They will tarry at my border no longer.

I pace my rooms in Castle Nuovo until I fear I will go mad,

waiting in a fever of anxiety to hear that King Louis's army has engaged with my husband and cousins in Capua. They must know my army is there ready for them. Will it be enough? When I can pace no longer I have my horse saddled and ride through Naples, sitting straight and proud in my saddle to give my people courage. It is exhausting, riding out behind my banner with my chin up and my mouth smiling and my hands steady on the reins, but I force myself to do it once a day. My people are frightened, they need to see me. They line the streets and cheer as I pass, calling out their loyalty.

When I return to my castle I walk in the gardens alone. There, behind the thick shrubbery and shade trees, I let myself weep, remembering the trusting faces of my people turned up to me, applauding as I rode past them. I pray I will not let them down, that their faith in me will not be betrayed, that the crown on my anointed head and the rightful heir in my nursery will protect us all. *My son and my crown,* I remind God, fighting the unaccountable weakness that has me in its grip as I walk alone in a winter garden.

On the evening of January 11th a messenger dashes through my castle gates. Leaping from his horse he demands to be taken to me. I hear his urgent voice through the windows of my presence chamber as he talks to my guard, and hurry to meet him in the great hall.

My hands tremble so hard I can barely break the seal on the letter he hands me. He stands, white-faced and breathing heavily from his mad race to Naples. Is my army defeated? Is my husband dead? Is King Louis of Hungary at this very moment marching his bloodied army toward my city?

The letter is in my husband's handwriting. I let out the breath I did not know I was holding. He is alive. Whatever the news, my Louis has survived it. I feel my eyes well up and blink the tears away so I can read his note.

Your army is undefeated, he writes. I choke back a sob of relief and continue reading. *King Louis of Hungary, knowing how well-fortified we are at Capua, led his army north through the mountains and fell upon Benevento instead. Unprepared and with little ability to defend itself against so great a force, Benevento has fallen. Several men from the villages around Benevento, knowing we were camped in Capua, rushed to bring us the news and apprise us of the size of his army. We face a force much greater than we were told, one that has already taken a stronghold from which they can attack us more easily than they could out on the open road. Our brother and cousin, the Dukes of Durazzo and Taranto, have called me to a war council. I fear their resolve may falter with this news. I will do what I can to hold them to our purpose. Your loving husband, Louis.*

I read it three times over. All sense of relief has evaporated. "This is all?" I demand of the white-faced young messenger.

"Your Majesty!" he stammers, bowing so low his voice is muffled under his bent body. "My master said to go at once. He wanted you to receive his message…"

…So I will have time to prepare for the worst, my thoughts finish for him. *Prepare for what? How can I prepare when I do not know what has happened?*

"Get up and get out!" I order the prostrating boy. Then relenting, "They will feed you in the kitchen. Do not mention to anyone what you know."

"I know nothing, Your Majesty," he promises, backing out quickly.

I go at once to my private chambers, ordering a jug of wine and a supper brought up to me. Nothing can be done this evening and I need time to think. I bid the eldest of the Clarissan sisters attending me to sit with me in case I need something, and tell the other three to go to the chapel and pray. Then I send the few courtiers still at my court and my ladies-in-waiting down to dinner. Maria lingers behind the others. I am tempted to confide in her; a shared worry is always more bearable. But can I trust her? Even now her husband might be betraying mine. I ask her to lead my ladies into the dining hall, and touch my expanding belly by way of excuse for not leading them to dinner myself. Let them think me too nauseous to eat. Indeed I feel sick, but not from my pregnancy.

They will turn. Charles and Robert have proved false too many times before. Faced with an army they do not think they can defeat, they will capitulate, leaving my Louis with only a third of my army to fight the full Hungarian force. Why else sequester themselves in a war council as soon as they learn of the defeat of Benevento?

But I cannot be sure. It is only a sick dread in my gut, the weakness of a woman overwhelming me. What plans can I make when I cannot be sure what is happening? All I know for certain is that no one must know what I know. Louis has bought me a little time and I must not squander it.

The thought calms me. I have been given an advantage my enemy did not foresee. I eat my dinner slowly, considering all my options. I eat well, dipping my fingers in the bowl of rosewater when I am done, and send for the captain of my castle guard, a man devoutly loyal to me. When he arrives I take him into my privy chamber and set a guard at the door.

He does not grow pale or tremble when I tell him what Louis has written. Instead his expression, though grim, becomes firmer, more resolute, as though the steel he is made of is being drawn to the surface.

"I must prepare for the possibility of defeat."

His face darkens but he does not disagree. I left him in charge of Castle Nuovo during the uprising two years ago. I watch him remembering what happened to my friends and supporters under his guard.

I do not blame him. It was their decision to have him negotiate their surrender. I have no doubt he warned them that he could not guarantee their captors would keep the terms they agreed to. He knows I do not hold him responsible for he still has his trusted position as captain of my castle guard. This man did not prove false.

But he and I will never forget what happens to prisoners who surrender. And I would have to surrender eventually if King Louis took Naples and I stayed here. Castle Nuovo is nearly impregnable; Castle dell'Ovo *is* impregnable—but sooner or later the Hungarians would starve me out wherever I hid.

"King Louis will have me executed if he captures me."

"He will, Your Majesty."

I shiver at his confirmation. Did I hope he would disagree?

I realize I am thinking as though I have already lost to the Hungarians. Perhaps Louis has been able to hold my dukes firm. Charles must know his daughter's engagement to my son will be broken if King Louis takes Naples. Robert must realize Louis of Hungary will deal ruthlessly with anyone who raised an army against him.

"My army—my entire army—might even now be engaged in battle against the Hungarians. Might even now be driving them back."

"Yes, Your Majesty." His tone is respectful but his eyes are bitter, his lips thin with suppressed emotion. He will never forgive the Duke of Durazzo and the Duke of Taranto for breaking their bargain when he released my supporters into their hands.

"I must hope for the best," I say firmly. "But prepare for the worst."

"Yes, Your Majesty," he says, with more assurance this time.

"Go to the pier and charge three galleys to wait in the harbor. Tell them… the Lord who commissions them insists they be ready to set sail day or night. Give them this to keep them at the ready." I hand him three gold coins.

He bows and tells me he will go as soon as dusk has fallen. I appreciate his instant understanding and discretion. If my lords return victorious I would rather they not know I doubted them. If the Hungarians defeat my army, either by treachery or by greater force, King Louis must not suspect I have been warned or he will send an advance guard to prevent my escape.

"I will pray that our precautions are not necessary."

"And I also," he bows once more. "After I have secured the three galleys."

When he has gone I return to my presence chamber. I have my Clarisson companion pin a veil over my head and we go to the chapel to pray.

When I have prayed until my knees and back ache I rise and leave the chapel. The sisters refused my dismissal, staying at their prayers although they must be in great pain. But perhaps a life of prayer has strengthened the muscles necessary for it. I am grateful for their continued supplication. Surely God will reward their humility.

I hesitate at the door to my son's nursery. I am eager to see him as always, but what I must do now weighs heavily upon me. The guard looks at me, waiting to open the door, and I nod.

My son turns at once and runs to me, ignoring his nurse's reprimand. I catch his sturdy body in my arms and lift him in the air as if he were a little bird, a game that always delights him. He shrieks with delight and flaps his arms. Isabelle the Hungarian, who was his father's nurse before him, *tut-tuts* under her breath. She is a formidable, joyless woman made even more dour by the death of her first charge. Perhaps the only person who loved Andrew, she continues to wear mourning and despises me for setting mine aside. No matter, she hated me long before Andrew's death.

I set Charles Martel down and bid him fetch his cape for a walk in the garden.

"I am sending you and Charles Martel to Castle dell'Ovo in the morning." I had intended to send them tonight, but seeing my son I could not bear to part at once. Surely nothing will happen before morning, and I need some time with him before I send him away. Besides, any show of haste will only arouse his nurse's suspicions. "Pack up his nursery and alert his guards and other caretakers to be ready at first light."

"Will you be coming with us, Your Majesty?" She watches me closely.

"I must stay here until my army returns victorious."

Her eyes narrow. I watch her face working as she stifles the urge to question me further. She would be happy to learn what I know; she wants King Louis to ride in with his Hungarian army and claim my kingdom, would be delighted to see him put me to death. It will never happen, I would like to tell her, and slap that eager expression from her face. But I will not quarrel with a commoner.

She must not suspect I am planning my escape. The news of a messenger from Capua will have reached her by now. She knows something has happened and she will have spies watching everything I do. The moment she suspects the Hungarians are winning she will order Andrew's Hungarian guards, who are now Charles Martel's guards, to prevent me from leaving Castle Nuovo. I must get her and the entire Hungarian entourage away from me.

What can I say to allay her suspicions? If I seem to be explaining myself I will just make it worse. I settle for a confident smile as though my Louis had sent me only good news, and call Charles Martel in a cheerful voice to bring me the cape he is struggling to put on.

"King Louis will never harm Charles Martel," she calls as I take my son's hand to lead him out the door.

"No one will harm my son," I whirl on her. "Not ever! But when my army returns victorious after fighting Hungarians, they may not be best pleased to find you and my son's Hungarian guards lounging in my castle. There may be some confusion as to whether you are friend or foe. It is your safety that concerns me, so you will go to Castle dell'Ovo, every one of you, until my husband's and cousins' soldiers no longer want revenge for their comrades lost defending my kingdom from a usurper!"

She takes an involuntary step back and I usher my son out between the two wide-eyed Hungarian guards at his nursery door.

By the time we reach the garden my temper has subsided enough that I find myself chuckling at the memory of their expressions. Even if Isabelle still questions my motives, she will not convince any of my son's Hungarian entourage to stay behind and watch me now.

I set aside my worries, determined to enjoy this time with my son. We play hide and chase along the garden paths until he is tired. I lift him to sit on a bench beside me and we watch the clouds as I cuddle him close, wondering how long it may be before I can hold him again. He snuggles against me, his thumb in his mouth, and I have not the heart to reprimand him for it. Isabelle would take it out at once and slap his hand.

The thought reminds me of her final words before I left the nursery. She is right; no matter whom else he takes his vengeance on, King Louis would never allow Charles Martel, the son of his dead brother, to be harmed. He needs my son, the rightful heir of the Kingdom of Naples. I know this. It is the only thing that enables me to do what I must if my army is defeated: flee, leaving my precious son behind. Should I risk my son's life on a desperate sea voyage through winter storms rather than leave him to the care of his Hungarian relatives, to whom he is precious because of his father? Even if I could spirit him away without alerting his nurse and guards, it would be a selfish choice to do so.

Louis will surround Charles Martel with Hungarians and teach him to despise me and all Neapolitans, like a true Hungarian. Like his father, Andrew. I cannot bear the thought of my sweet, affectionate Charles Martel turning into a cruel and brutal man. My throat burns. I tighten my arms around my son's sturdy little body, warm against me, and pray I will never have to leave him, that my cousins will remain loyal and my army will triumph.

But what if I do have to leave without seeing him again, and what if it should take months or even years to win my kingdom back? Can I leave without a word?

"Charles Martel, there is something I must say to you." I sit him forward on my knee facing me and look searchingly into his face, memorizing it. He returns my gaze earnestly.

"Tomorrow morning you will go to Castle dell'Ovo and I will stay here. We will be apart for a while."

"Not long, Maman?" he asks hopefully.

"I hope not, darling. But it might seem very long, for we love each other very much, do we not?"

"Oui, Maman." He looks worried. "You could come with me?"

"I will come and get you as soon as I can, remember that. No matter how long it takes."

Now he looks truly alarmed. I force myself to smile. "Nurse will take good care of you."

"Nurse said…" he hesitates. I smile encouragingly. "A king is coming to visit me." His lower lip trembles.

She does, does she? "Well, you do not need to worry about a king. You will be a king yourself one day."

His face clears. He nods proudly. "A king is not afraid of anything."

"That is true. Can you be brave like a king while we are apart?"

"Yes! I will be very brave, Maman. As brave as a king," he promises.

I hug him tightly to me, kissing the top of his head. He lets me hold him a moment then struggles to straighten, leaning away from me. "Can we visit the tiger?" he says. "and the funny monkeys!"

I laugh and stand up, setting him on his feet, and we walk through the garden to the animal menagerie, staring through the bars of their cages at the exotic creatures my Grandfather received as gifts from emissaries to his court.

The next morning I watch from my window, hidden by the shutters, as my son is lifted into a carriage. There is an ache behind my eyes and a tightness in my throat as I watch Isabelle's arms reach out to receive him and settle him on the seat beside her. It is all I can do not to cry out at the agony that rips through me when he turns his little head up to look at the castle, as though he somehow knows I am watching. As the carriage starts up, a cloud passes over the sun and my sweet child disappears into shadow. I pull the window shutter open and lean out, careless of who might see me, staring after the carriage as though I will never see my son again.

Chapter 6

A Ship at Night

**Joanna 1 of Naples
January, 1348**

The next day, Charles of Durazzo and Robert of Taranto ride into Naples at the head of their men. I watch them from the window of my chamber which looks out over the walls of Castle Nuovo across my city. *I have lost my kingdom,* I think, as I watch their approach. It is a huge procession of able, unharmed soldiers who have obviously not seen battle. The messenger who comes to tell me, sent by my guard at the city gate, cannot look me in the eye but mutters his message with his head bowed, staring at the floor.

His shame rallies me. The dishonor of retreating from battle without drawing their swords is theirs, not mine. I have been anointed by God. As long as I live, I am the rightful monarch of the Kingdom of Naples. I will escape King Louis's vengeance and return with an army to exact my own!

But in order to do so, I must leave my son.

It is a worse blow than my cousins' betrayal. However I prepared for it, I never believed this would happen. It, too, may well be temporary, but I have never gone a day without seeing Charles Martel. He will ask his nurse, where is Maman, when am I coming to play with him? And I will not come. How long will it be before he stops asking? I stifle the sob that rises in my chest.

The messenger glances up and stammers, "I...I am sorry to bring you such terrible news, Your Majesty..."

I make a dismissive gesture with my hand, not trusting my voice as I blink back the moisture in my eyes and strive to master my features into a calmer expression.

"Go," I tell him. "Send the captain of my guard." It is all I can choke out. He bows himself out in as quick a retreat as he can respectfully make.

I linger in my privy chamber after the messenger has left, composing myself. My ladies-in-waiting will learn the news soon enough; what they must not learn is that I intend to flee. When I walk into my presence chamber I am composed.

"The battle is upon us," I tell my ladies-in-waiting, as though I believe my husband will engage Louis of Hungary with only a third of his army left him. I hope not; dear God, I hope he will see to his own safety! But I cannot help him now, and the longer I can keep the news from those close enough to watch my movements, the better. "Put on your cloaks and go to Santa Chiara to pray for our soldiers," I tell them. "Honoré, Jeanne, and Sybil, stay with me."

I have chosen my companions with thought. Jeanne is from Provence, the daughter of a noble family in Marseille. Honoré's uncle, the count of Altavilla, is second-in-command of my husband's forces, and Sybil is a relative of Niccolò Acciaiuoli. Both these men will have stayed to fight alongside my Louis, and their families will be punished. At least I can save the two girls. Charles of Durazzo's cousin, Margherita, and Robert of Taranto's sister, Marguerite, will have their traitorous relatives to protect them. They are also the most likely of my ladies charged to spy on me, so I send them with the others to Santa Chiara. I hope, kneeling at prayer in the cathedral, they will be the last to hear that I am defeated.

"Shall we return for dinner, Your Majesty?" Margherita asks before she leaves.

"Dinner?" I arch my brows. "Do you think our brave men will stop fighting to enjoy their dinner, Lady Margherita?" My voice rises with indignation. "Pray unceasingly, pray through the night, as I will be doing here in my private chapel with my Poor Clares. If you must have nourishment to continue, take your dinner with the good sisters, who pray while they eat. Let them be your example."

Maria does not leave with them. Nor did I expect she would, she knows me too well. I could never keep a secret from her, even as children. She knows I am keeping something from her now, I would not meet her eye when I spoke to my ladies. Her face is a masque of anxiety. She is afraid I am going to tell her her husband has died in the fighting. Would that he had, the coward! Sybil and Jeanne and Honoré discreetly draw away to give us privacy.

"Take your daughter and go home, Maria," I say, my voice tight. "Your husband is unharmed." I try to keep the bitterness from my tone, but her eyes widen in sudden understanding. I watch the color drain from her face with a sense of satisfaction. That, too, I cannot completely hide. She says nothing, but as she turns to go her eyes fill with tears—of shame, I hope.

And then I am sorry. "Maria—"

But what can I say? That we cannot help whom we marry? But she could. She married without my permission. I would never have given her to Charles of Durazzo. I wanted her to marry a French prince and seal our alliance with France. I could desperately use a strong ally now. So I let her take her daughter's hand and go home to the traitor she chose, without my forgiveness. If I never see her again it will burden my soul, but it is she, not I, who should ask forgiveness.

As soon as they have left I usher Sybil, Jeanne, and Honoré into my bedchamber and bid them pack up a trunk of my clothes and necessities. I tell them not to leave the room until I come again, and not to speak to anyone. They curtsy and do not ask questions, so that I need not lie to them.

I lead the captain of my guard into my privy chamber without a word, even though there is no one in my presence chamber when he arrives save him and me and the guards at my doors. Nevertheless I wait until the inner door is closed before I turn to him.

"I must leave tonight," I say in a voice hardly more than a whisper. He nods, for he, too, knows through the city guards that my cousins have returned.

"And I must take Charles Martel with me." The words burst out in a gasp of breath as though I have been holding something painful inside and can finally release it.

"Your Majesty, that is not possible," he says quietly, as though he has anticipated this.

"I cannot be separated from him." It is not the voice of a queen I hear but the anguished cry of a mother.

"You will be separated from him," my stalwart captain says, his face twisted with pity but his voice still firm. "They will take him from you whether you stay or leave."

"All the more reason I should take him with me."

"Everyone knows of your devotion to the prince, especially his guards. No one, not you, nor me, nor all your castle guards will get him away from Castle dell'Ovo without such a ruckus that all of Naples will be alerted to your intent."

I have thought of plan after plan since the messenger came to me, knowing none would work. Who takes a child for a walk in the garden at midnight? Isabelle the nurse is no fool. *Can you think of nothing?* I want to cry, but the look on his face is already my answer. If there were any feasible plan I would have thought of it, too.

"Your Majesty, you must flee or forfeit your life. You cannot help your son or your people if you are dead."

"I cannot help my son if I abandon him."

"Yes, you can, for then you can return to him."

I turn away, unable to look at him, hating him for being right. He does not try to tell me they will not hurt Charles Martel. There are many ways to hurt a child.

He is so little. He will weep when I do not come to him, and perhaps be punished for calling for me. Louis of Hungary will surround Charles Martel with Hungarians. They will see his gentle nature and call it weakness, and try to break him of it. I bite my fist against the pain that floods me.

My crown and my son. I did not know it would ever become my crown *or* my son.

I straighten my back and raise my head. I will be back. I am the Countess of Provence, my people there will raise an army for me, their sovereign ruler. I am the rightful monarch of the kingdom of Naples, Pope Clement will support me against this Hungarian usurper. My Neapolitan subjects will see what it is to be ruled by Hungarians and they will rise to greet me and join my army when they hear I am returning. I will come back and be victorious and heal whatever bruises my little boy's heart sustains, and never leave him again.

"I shall be ready at midnight. Come for me then." I tell the captain of my guard. "Choose six men you trust to go with me as my personal guards, and see that the galleys are armed in case we meet resistance."

He bows, assuring me he will be back at midnight. "Send Enrico to me," I add as he bows himself out.

Enrico Caracciolo, my chamberlain, arrives so quickly I wonder if he was waiting for my summons. As always, he is escorted by a guard, for he wears the keys to the two most important rooms in the castle: the royal wardrobe and the royal treasury. This day his guard is his nephew. He has no family of his own, thank God, for we would not be able to take them with us.

I tell him to have my most loyal noblemen join me for dinner, and bid him bring me my three best kirtles, the green one strung with seed pearls, the blue one sewn with silver thread and sapphires at the neck and sleeves, and the purple one embroidered with fleur-de-lis, which I wear for state occasions. "Bring me my royal jewels, also, that I might choose which I will wear to dinner tonight. And my royal blue surcote with fleur-de-lis of gold thread. And a large portion of gold to reward my nobles for their loyalty." I say this for the benefit of the guards at my door; it is always possible one of them will be a paid spy, though I trust the captain of my guard to have done his best to keep those at a distance.

When they return, I take Enrico and his nephew into my chamber where my three noble-born maids are waiting. I tell them all that we will be leaving on a galley for Provence at midnight. Despite the danger of a winter voyage, they know it will not be safe for any of them to stay and face the Hungarians, so they greet my news with a mixture of anxiety and relief. After I have chosen the blue kirtle with its lighter blue linen chemise, and a sapphire-studded necklet with a gold brooch to wear to dinner, I have the other two kirtles, the surcote, the sacks of gold and the rest of my royal jewels divided among my two trunks. Enrico and his nephew carry the trunks into my privy chamber and lock the door before they take the strongbox that held the royal jewels back to the treasury and lock it ostentatiously inside, so no one watching our movements will suspect it is empty now. I will need all the gold and jewels I can safely smuggle away with me to pay my expenses and raise an army in Provence.

By dinner time everyone in Naples knows that Benevento, just three days' ride from Naples, has been taken, that Louis of Hungary's army is undefeatable, that the Dukes of Durazzo and Taranto have surrendered and sent messages of homage to our enemy. There is little talk in my chamber as I am dressed for dinner. I have nothing to say either, and avoid looking at the stiff, pale faces around me. King Louis' wrath over the murder of his brother, Prince Andrew, has hung like a sword over our heads for two years, and now he will ride down on us with an army spoiling to fight and mercenaries eager for plunder. No one will be able to withstand his thirst for vengeance.

Terror wraps itself around my city like a shroud. The streets are nearly empty. People pass each other without greetings, avoiding each other's eyes. No one hangs from their window shouting down to passersby or calling children inside—the children are already inside, as well as all the young girls and pretty young wives. Even the market is subdued, although people still shop, buying what they can to store up enough food that they can hide inside their houses when the Hungarian army arrives. I leave the window and order the shutters closed against the depressing sight before I lead my ladies to dinner.

My nobles, arriving for dinner at my request, are pale and shaking. While the servants bring in our meat, I stand and address them. I thank them for their loyalty, their service to me over the years, and then I formally release them from their oath of allegiance to me, and through them, all my subjects. "Do not resist King Louis of Hungary when he enters Naples," I tell them. "If he asks it of you, swear allegiance to him while he controls my kingdom. Until such time as I come back into power you must look to your own safety."

My throat closes. I look over the great hall at them, my people whom I have loved and ruled to the best of my ability through such turbulent times, and I can say nothing more. Someone stamps his feet. Another pounds on the table. In moments every person in my hall is stamping and pounding and shouting "Huzzah!" proclaiming their love and loyalty to me now and always.

I bow my head and sit down, tears blinding me, and then I remove my crown and place it on the table in front of me, and the noise quietens as quickly as it began. I see grown men wiping tears from their eyes, unashamed, as I sit there before them accepting a tribute beyond any I could have asked for.

Before it becomes too much I signal for the servers to refill my wine cup. I take a long drink of wine as soon as it has been poured, releasing my guests to drink and eat as well. I nod to the musicians to begin playing. They look at each other, distressed and undecided, until I clap my hands together quickly, indicating a sprightly melody.

In the dead of night there comes a knock at my door. I am awake at once.

Honoré and Sybil, sleeping in my bed on either side of me, sit up wide-eyed. Jeanne rises from her pallet on the floor and I send her to the door in her night-dress, my heart in my mouth. It must be my guard, coming to help me escape. Unless my plan has been discovered by Robert or Charles, and they have sent their men to arrest me. What a prize I would be for them to hand over to Louis of Hungary. I dare not breathe as Jeanne opens the door.

And then I hear a quiet whispering, and she closes the door again and turns to me, her face solemn but calm, and I know it is my men. I climb out of bed and let Honoré and Sybil dress me in the rough travelling clothes I have borrowed from them. Jeanne, now dressed, braids up my hair under a dark headdress while the others dress themselves. We catch up our cloaks, preparing ourselves for the dangerous journey before us.

The captain of my guard is waiting with a dozen armed men whom he trusts when we emerge. Enrico and his nephew are there also, swords at their waists. I cross silently to my privy chamber and unlock the door. Four of the men hoist my two trunks between them, the others surround us, and we are away.

We steal through the night quietly, the captain and two guards in the lead, watching for anyone about who might give us away, the rest of us running from shadow to shadow after them. Fortunately, no one crosses our path on the short walk down to the harbor. My people are locked inside their houses, as frightened as I of the coming army.

We arrive at the port without incident. The night is very dark, the sky overcast with a brisk, cold wind from the north. The sea is choppy, the waves slapping angrily against the sides of the galleys and throwing spray onto the wooden pier, leaving treacherous rivulets we will have to navigate over. During the short walk to the pier the wind has increased; soon it will become a howling winter storm. Perhaps we can outrun it. Perhaps it will swallow our galleys and none of us will ever be seen again. Death lies in every direction. I will take my chances with the sea rather than with Louis of Hungary.

We stop at the edge of the pier. I hand the captain a sealed note and tell him it is for Niccolò Acciaiuoli. I have used his kinswoman, Sybil's ring to seal it. "See that this reaches Niccolò by morning," I say as he takes it. In it I tell Niccolò that I, writing as Sybil, have fled 'with the lady I serve' and bid him to seek his own safety and his lord's. It is all I can do for my poor husband, deserted on the battlefield. I pray he will recognize my handwriting and take my suggestion.

Jeanne pulls her cloak close and drapes its hood over her head, hiding her face. She walks onto the pier escorted by two of the guards carrying one of my trunks between them, and up the gangplank onto the first waiting galley. Honoré, similarly concealed, is escorted by two other guards onto the second ship. The last two guards hoist my second trunk and follow Enrico and his nephew, with Sybil between them, onto the third galley.

I clutch my cloak tightly around me, the hood falling forward, my face in deep shadow.

"Protect my religious companions from Louis' wrath," I tell the captain of my guard, referring to the four Poor Clares who have been with me over a year now. "If you can do so without arousing suspicion, send them back to their convent before he arrives."

"I will send them there tomorrow at dawn, and order them to remain in their cells." He hesitates, as though he wishes to add something.

It is a hard thing when an anointed monarch is forced to flee. It is as though God Himself were banished from that Kingdom. It burdens my soul to desert my people, and I have no doubt that Louis's wrath will fall upon them when he finds me gone, despite all I have done to mitigate it.

We stand in the cold wind, regarding each other soberly. I have known him since I was a child.

"Your Majesty," he begins awkwardly, but does not continue.

"I would take you with me," I whisper.

"You cannot, Your Majesty. I must be seen locking the castle gates as though to guard you. I must be there to keep my men in place as long as possible." He speaks firmly, proudly.

I want to weep. We both know it is a death sentence I am handing him and the men who stay at Castle Nuovo with him to guard my secret flight.

"God bless and keep you, thou good and loyal servant." My voice breaks as I bless him.

He cannot kneel or bow or make any sign that this fourth cloaked woman is more than the others, nor can I bless him with any sign that would give me away. We do not think anyone is watching, but one can never be certain. I turn and follow the guards carrying my second trunk up onto the third waiting galley, where I stand staring over the railing, my heart breaking, as the sailors row us away from the port. The sails catch the wind, pulling the ship forward, and Naples, my Naples, the most beautiful kingdom on earth, cradling my sweet son in its heart, fades behind me into the darkest night.

Chapter 7

A Celebration

Maria of Naples
January, 1348

"You have betrayed her."

I do not shout or scream as I wanted to when I first saw my husband riding toward our castle gates. I am beyond fury as I face him in the front hall. As though he has done nothing he ignores my accusation, demanding to know why I have not sent to the kitchens for a hot dinner after his long ride. All I feel is disgust as I look at this man who will grasp at any changing wind and wonders why his hands are always empty in the end.

"It would have made no difference to the outcome," he says when I stand my ground. "It would only have meant more bodies had Robert and I stayed with our men. We were hopelessly outnumbered. Would you rather a dead husband or a living one here to defend you when King Louis rides into Naples with his army, eager for spoils?"

"A dead one, rather than a traitor."

"Then you are a fool. If I had fought him, he would murder you and our children and all who rode with me. Now I will pay homage to him and he will spare us."

"You are the fool if you think that."

"I befriended Prince Andrew before he died! I sought out his murderers and tortured confessions out of them and had them executed! I encouraged King Louis to come here and promised him my support! He will remember all that."

"Yes, I am well aware of how often you have betrayed my sister. Betrayed your queen. All of Naples knows the value of your oaths."

His face is scarlet. He raises his arm to strike me but I have had my say, so I turn and leave him to order his own dinner from the kitchen and sit alone at the table to eat it.

When I reach the stairs to our private chambers I see little Joanna sitting on the top step, out of sight of the great hall.

"My Lord Father has betrayed the queen?" she asks in a small voice.

I hesitate, knowing how she adores her father, but then I reconsider; was I not trapped by his lies and falseness? "You will not marry your cousin now," I tell her.

"I do not care about that. Charles Martel is too little to marry, anyway."

"Do you not want to be queen of Naples?"

"My Lord Father will see that I make a good marriage. He wants what is best for me. For all of us," she adds, her bottom lip protruding defiantly as she stares at me. She is almost five and stubborn, like her father. I pray that is the only trait she has taken from him.

"Go to the nursery. You should not be here, listening to adult conversation."

"No one tells me anything. I am not a *baby*, Maman!"

I do not know whether to laugh or weep. Terrible times are coming, a ruthless enemy who hates us is only days away. My husband has turned traitor so many times no one will trust him and yet he believes he can convince King Louis to. I fear my Joanna will have to prove very soon that she is indeed not a baby.

"I will tell you what you need to know," I promise her. "And you will have to trust me and do as I say."

Her defiance turns to anxiety at my solemn tone, but she raises her chin bravely in a gesture so like her namesake that I once again feel tears behind my eyes. "I will, Maman," she promises, jumping up to run back to the nursery.

The next morning, on January 16th, wagons of flour and fish and meat and salt roll into the courtyard of Castle Nuovo to deposit their goods in the kitchen. After they leave, the castle gates are locked.

"She is preparing for a siege," my husband says when our spy in the castle stable brings us the news.

"She has left," I tell him, confident I am correct because it is what I would do.

"Her Majesty's horse is still in the stable, Madame," the spy contradicts me.

In mid-afternoon, at the height of a tempestuous winter storm, we learn that Joanna's husband, Louis of Taranto, has fled with Niccolò Acciaiuoli and a half-dozen others, leaving his army under the charge of the count of Altavilla. They are said to be out on the sea in a flimsy fishing boat, the only vessel immediately available. I wonder how Joanna is taking the news, if she is indeed locked in her castle. Betrayed by her own husband who will likely not survive his treachery. Perhaps she will be less judgmental of me in future, now that the husband *she* loves has shown his worth.

I sigh. Louis of Taranto could not defeat the Hungarians with his legion of mercenaries and loyal men. Perhaps our entire army could have prevailed, but not Louis with only his forces. It would be a slaughter to no avail. It is rumored his German mercenaries recognized their countrymen among King Louis' mercenaries and switched sides. Treachery and betrayal all around.

On the morning of January 19 my husband, dressed in his finest tunic and as exuberant as a man going to his wedding, bids me farewell. He is going with his brother Robert and our cousin Robert of Taranto to lead a large procession of Naples' highest-ranking aristocrats to Aversa, to make their formal obeisance to King Louis. Aversa, too, surrendered without a battle. The whole of the kingdom of Naples trembles before the size of the Hungarian army. King Louis has taken over the royal castle in Aversa where Joanna and I and many of our cousins passed the long, sweet summers of our childhood. The very castle where King Louis' brother, Prince Andrew, was murdered.

"Do not go," I beg Charles one last time. He gives me a disgusted look and stalks toward the mounting block where the groom is holding his tall black stallion. The horse stamps its hoof and shakes its head, as eager as its master to be off on this dangerous venture.

As he swings into the saddle Charles' head briefly blocks the sun, casting his face in shadow. I have loved this man all my life, whatever his sins. He is the father of my children, with another growing in my womb, and he is doing this to protect us as much as himself.

"My Lord Husband—" I want to send him off with a word of love, of support. Of warning.

Perhaps he hears only the last in my voice, for he turns his stallion toward our open gate and kicks it into a gallop without a backward glance.

The next day my husband's squire comes from Aversa with a message for my brother-in-law, Louis of Durazzo. He and Philip of Taranto, Duke Robert of Taranto's youngest brother, had been left behind to arrange a welcoming ceremony for King Louis of Hungary when he rides into Naples. I watch Louis' face as he reads the message, my heart stilled with fear.

He breaks into a broad grin. "King Louis of Hungary has accepted my brother's homage," he says with satisfaction. "He is throwing a banquet on January 22nd to celebrate this reunion of cousins. He wants me and Philip of Taranto to be there also. You have been wrong about him all along," he adds with a smug look in my direction.

My heart lightened at his news—until his final comment. For I am not wrong about Louis of Hungary, as I was not wrong about his brother, Andrew. I remember why I hated Andrew and shiver.

"And still you are suspicious!" Louis cries. "Read for yourself!" He tosses me the vellum marked with my husband's impatient script.

Indeed Charles' tone is jubilant as he tells his brother of King Louis' gracious welcome and orders him to attend the festive banquet and bring our cousin Philip. *All the male cousins,* I think. Everyone but Louis, Joanna's husband, who has escaped, or died in the attempt. I shiver again, but when I look up my brother-in-law has left to prepare for his trip to Aversa. And perhaps I am wrong. Perhaps Louis of Hungary is pleased with these cousins who betrayed their rightful monarch to support him, or at least refused in the end to bear arms against him. Perhaps it is only Joanna on whom he will take out his vengeance.

I hurry to my rooms, thinking to write a note, to warn my sister. But what should I say? That King Louis has welcomed her traitorous dukes and nobles, is holding a festive banquet for them? It will sound like I am pleased, that this somehow justifies their betrayal. Shall I tell her that I suspect Louis of Hungary of foul intent? That she is in danger and should not trust any of our male cousins? She already knows the danger she is in.

And why have I not been invited with Charles? I, too, am a cousin, and I am third in line for the throne. Am I in danger as well? No,

Charles would never let King Louis harm his wife, the heir to the throne he hopes I will acquire for him. Whatever the cousins are plotting, Charles will protect me.

I reach for the vellum and put it back and reach again three times as my thoughts whirl, but in the end I do not write. Joanna knows her danger and would not trust me anyway, the wife of a man who has once again betrayed her. And Charles does not trust me, that will be why I have not been invited to this feast. Charles will have someone watching me. Dare I expose my loyalty to the rightful Queen of Naples now that her enemy is coming? I have three daughters, the youngest still in her cradle, and a fourth child on the way. If Charles has found King Louis' forgiveness, I should thank God and be grateful my children are safe.

I do not thank God. Instead I pray, kneeling for hours in the cathedral, that this time Charles is right and I am wrong. I cannot focus on my sewing or give more than cursory thought to maintaining the household, but instead spend much of my time in the nursery with my daughters as I wait for the fateful banquet.

January 22nd passes slowly. I wonder anxiously how Charles is doing in Aversa, and alternately picture him drinking with our cousins or languishing in a dark cell. Ridiculous, I tell myself. If he or any of my royal cousins had been incarcerated the news would have reached us. My husband's squire would ride without rest to warn us. I am imagining the worst and only frightening myself by it.

To distract myself I walk in the garden with my daughters. Clementia, at 18 months, runs ahead on her fat little legs chasing butterflies and plucking at the flowers to her nurse's dismay.

"Let her," I tell the nurse when she catches Clementia's little fist and tries to extricate the scarlet rose petals peeking through her clenched fingers, while issuing a stern reprimand.

The nurse's tirade stops. She straightens and says stiffly, "There are thorns, my Lady."

"There always are. But she has learned to avoid them." I smile to ease the nurse's discomfort at not having stopped this behavior at the first offense, but my eyes are serious. I will not have my children rebuked today. "You may walk behind us," I tell her. "I will call if you are needed."

Agnes, nearly three years old, takes this as invitation to break from my side and scamper after Clementia.

"Not too far ahead, Agnes," I chide her.

"Look, Maman, a swallow." She stops and points into a tree. I look and indeed it is a swallow, with its long graceful tail and sweet song.

"What other birds do you know?"

"All of them." She puffs up her chest with pride, so like her father it breaks my happy mood. She looks at me, perplexed at not receiving the praise she expected, then shrugs and points out the bird to Clementia, explaining in detail how to tell the kind of bird it is. Clementia will have none of it, losing interest and running off half-way through.

We continue our walk. Once again I have been plunged into worry over what may be happening in Aversa. Immersed in my thoughts and in keeping an eye on my younger daughters, I barely notice Joanna walking quietly at my side, until Agnes turns and calls her to play.

"I am not a child, Agnes," she says, and returns to her silence.

Agnes points out a second bird, a swift this time. I remember to congratulate her, and she runs ahead with Clementia, satisfied.

"Is something bothering you, Joanna?"

"I am troubled, Maman," she says, as grave as only a four-year-old can be.

"Shall we sit and talk?" I match her solemnity as well as I can and point to a bench just ahead, set in a deep pool of shade under the wide green leaves of a palmetto tree. I nod to the nurse to continue walking with Agnes and Clementia as Joanna heads for the bench.

I wait while she gathers the courage to voice her fears, wondering what difficult question I am about to be asked now.

"Did Papa betray Her Majesty the Queen because I did not want to marry Charles Martel?"

I sit still a moment, taking care not to start or look at her until I can say calmly, "I did not know you did not want to marry Charles Martel."

"He is still a baby, Maman. Would you want to marry a baby? But I did not mean to make Papa betray Her Majesty. I do like my Lady Aunt, the Queen." Her voice, scornful a moment ago, trembles now.

"You did not make Papa betray our Queen. No one can make Papa do anything." I do not know whether that is consoling, but it is the truth. "All men are like that. They do as they will, regardless of what we want."

"But he knew I did not want to marry Charles Martel."

"How did he know?"

"Papa always understands me."

I manage to stifle my response. So I once believed of Charles. Are men born with the skill of deception, or do we women want to be deceived, conspire with them to believe their lies? And does it start so young? I look down at my small daughter sadly.

"You are not responsible for your Papa's actions. He would have married you to Charles Martel regardless of your feelings. As he betrayed Her Majesty my sister regardless of mine."

"Fathers know more than Mothers. That is why they make the decisions."

"So it is said." I wonder if she has heard this from her father.

"Thank you, Maman." I look down to see a tentative smile.

"But we are still responsible for our own decisions. As Papa is responsible for his."

"Is that why you are angry, Maman? Because he chose King Louis, when you would have chosen Queen Joanna?"

I am surprised at her perceptiveness and forget to hide the bitterness from my voice. "It does not matter what I would choose. Your Papa has chosen for us all. We must hope his choice was wise."

"Do not worry, Maman." She pats my hand. "Papa is very wise." She wriggles down from the bench. "I think I will play with Agnes and Clementia now."

I watch her run to her sisters, brooding a while longer on the bench before I rise and join them. What will be, will be, and I will not change it sitting downcast in my garden.

I have my dinner sent to my chambers and retire early to bed. Charles is probably sitting in the great hall at Aversa now, full of fine food and finer wine, laughing with the other false nobles and eyeing the serving girls to decide which one he will invite to his bed. I am worrying over nothing.

But why Aversa? Why would Louis of Hungary celebrate with the cousins he disdains on the site of his brother's murder?

Perhaps he has simply forgotten, now that he has what he has always wanted: the Kingdom of Naples.

What woman can ever understand what men will do?

Chapter 8

Danger at Sea

Joanna 1 of Naples
January, 1348

The ship rolls and pitches on the steep waves, and I heave with it. I have never been seasick but this rough passage in the dark of night has me vomiting until there is nothing but bile burning its way up my throat. I stand on the deck, knowing it will be even worse below, clutching the railing with white-knuckled hands as my feet slip and slide on the wet deck. Sybil, as indispensable as her kinsman Niccolò, stands beside me on the lurching galley, terrified but valiantly loyal. My chamberlain, Enrico Caracciolo, stands guard on my other side, his nephew beside him. They have lashed themselves and Sybil to the ship's rail and begged me let them do the same for me, but I will not face death bound like a slave.

The ship slides into a deep funnel causing me to heave again over the side even though there is nothing left in my stomach to dispel. Beside me Sybil gags in sympathy. Down, down we roll, the gathering wave on the other side of the trough rearing up to swallow us, but somehow the galley ploughs through it. Soaked through with salt spray we rise on the swell, only to crest and dive again. On and on it goes. Nobody says what we are all thinking: that King Louis' wrath could not be fiercer than this savage sea.

Dawn breaks and we are still alive but the storm, if anything, has intensified. Enrico insists on wrapping the rope around me and now I do not refuse. When I am not too miserable to think, I worry about the child I am carrying. Surely he will not survive this storm even if I do. I push the thought aside. I will survive, and my child also, for we have a consecrated and preordained life. Nothing, not Louis of Hungary nor all the tempests on earth can sway me from the path marked out from my birth.

The winter storm has one advantage: by the time it finally blows over we are far from Naples and well on our way to Provence, safe from capture. I am still throwing up, but now it is the baby, not the choppy sea that is the cause.

That night, exhausted, I fall into a deep sleep on the narrow bed that has been curtained off for me. I sleep past dawn and wake to the sound of rough voices cursing and shouting.

Sybil is already sitting up on her pallet on the floor. When she sees I am awake she jumps to her feet and curtsies.

"Get dressed quickly and go see what the commotion is about," I tell her, my heart pounding. What new danger has found us now?

The water is calm and the sun shines through our small window so it is not weather that has them furious with fear. Have King Louis's men taken faster boats and caught up with us after all? Have I left the stronghold of Castle Nuovo only to be captured at sea?

I stand quivering beside my bed, straining my ears to hear what is going on. How large a force has King Louis sent after us? My three galleys are armed with men as ready to fight for their vessel as to sail her; they would not be alarmed by a single ship.

Sybil slips into our private area with a discreet movement of the curtain that reveals nothing. "One of the sailors was sick," she says, her face pale. "They threw him overboard."

"One of the seamen died?" So much shouting, rough male voices filled with terror, over one dead crewman?

"He was not dead," she whispers, her eyes wide with shock. "They threw him into the sea alive, screaming…" she covers her face with her hands.

"Your Majesty," Enrico Caracciolo's voice calls from outside our enclosure.

"One moment." I gesture for Sybil to dress me.

As soon as I am clothed I wave impatiently for Sybil to pull back the curtain. I do not care if he sees my hair down. "What is it?" I demand.

"A plague. The captain says it started in the Tartar lands and spread to Constantinople, then Sicily. Now it is in Marseilles and spreading through Italy's port cities."

I remember the report from my messenger to Sicily. "Black boils in his armpits?"

"You have heard of it." He does not sound surprised. "If they think we have it on board we will not be allowed to dock. The captain swears he would not even approach the port with a sick man aboard. Two galleys were set on fire in the port of Venice, every man on board burned alive, when it was learned they carried infected passengers in their hold."

"Provence will always welcome me. I am their Duchess."

"Yes, Your Majesty, they will not turn you away, though they would burn the rest of us. But neither they nor any man possesses the means to cure this disease. You must stay here behind your curtains for the rest of the journey."

I am about to object but I recall my messenger claiming that even to glance at someone who has this plague is enough to bring the illness upon yourself. "Make sure none of our company goes near any of the ship's crew," I say instead. He bows and leaves, pulling the curtain back in place as he goes.

Fortunately it is winter or Sybil and I would be hot and breathless behind the heavy curtain in the airless hold. As it is, the four days we spend there seem interminable. I pace the little space, five steps one way and five back, when I am not praying. Three times we hear screaming on the deck until it is cut off abruptly with the splash of a body hitting the water. Once I hear Enrico's voice cry out. When he comes to bring our meal his eyes are red and his mouth a thin line of grief.

"Who?" I ask.

His face twists, confirming my fear. "I am sorry," I say. "He was a fine young man."

When Enrico leaves I kneel and pray that we will be delivered from this death galley, thankful now that I did not bring my darling Charles Martel with me.

At last I hear a cry go up on deck: land has been sighted. Sybil and I laugh and dance together as though we have been prisoners down here and are about to be released.

Within hours the ship slows and comes to a stop. I have arrived in Provence.

Thanks to the captain's ruthless behavior we do not have the plague on board and are permitted to disembark. Enrico pays him while I scan the other two galleys until Jeanne and Honoré appear at the railings of their ships.

"You are safe and well!" Sybil cries, running to Jeanne when she has descended the gangplank onto the pier.

Jeanne curtsies to me, flushing at the warmth of my smile—I am indeed relieved and pleased to see her. She returns Sybil's hug.

"It was a rough voyage the first night, we lost one of our guards—swept into the sea by the storm." She gives me a troubled look.

"I am sorry to hear it," I say. Two good men lost, this guard and Enrico's nephew. I hope there will not be more missing when the third galley disembarks.

"But you are all healthy?" Sybil persists.

"I was terribly seasick, but I am well now. How good and still the ground feels!" she stamps her foot lightly on the firm dirt. "But you are not talking of seasickness," she adds, catching the unease on Sybil's face.

"No matter," I break in before Sybil can say aloud that our ship carried the plague. "We are all safely arrived, and here comes Honoré to join us." I smile as Honoré dips low in a curtsy before the three women share a hug. Counting my men I am pleased to note that all aboard this third ship are here. They gather my two trunks and all our baggage ready to ride to Marseille. We are lucky to have lost only two of our group in this desperate crossing.

Marseille gives me a jubilant welcome. Word has spread ahead of us and its citizens line the streets, cheering and waving as we ride in. I dare not waste what money I have throwing coins to them but they cheer nonetheless, as though my presence is coin enough.

I am wearing my sapphire-studded kirtle over a pale blue silk chemise, with a cloak of purple velvet trimmed in ermine and sewn with gold thread in a pattern of fleur-de-lis symbolic of my French lineage. Two of my knights ride before me holding my banner and after them my three ladies-in-waiting, wearing their best headdresses and finest kirtles, and after them my last three knights. It is not a large procession, but it will do.

Every church bell is ringing, from the ancient bells of the Cathedral de la Major built on the sea coast just down from the port, all the way up to the majestic Notre Dame de la Guarde towering over Marseille alone on its hilltop. I wave to my subjects as I ride by, their love a welcome balm after the fear and bitter defeat of fleeing Naples. I am tired from my sea journey and the ride to

Marseille and I would be more pleased to take the shortest route to the Chateau d'Angevin where my family has always stayed when visiting Marseille. Instead our escort leads us down smaller roads, twisting off our route three times as though deliberately avoiding the piazzas and the cathedrals with their bells ringing so loudly for me.

I peer down the wide street leading to the Abbey de Saint-Victor, and draw back in horror at seeing a pile of bodies lying outside the Abbey doors. Some are wrapped in white shrouds, others are obscenely bare or still clothed in the garments they died in. The bells are not ringing for me, but tolling the deaths of the citizens of Marseille. Six rings for a single death, to speed the departed on his way to heaven. But this is not six tolls, nor twelve, nor eighteen, but a long, desperate, incessant tolling. How long would it take to acknowledge all those corpses? As we pass by the street leading to the Abbey I see a cart arrive, carrying more bodies, dead piled on dead.

I turn away, suppressing my horror, and look more closely at the people come to see me ride by, their mouths wide with cheering under hollow eyes. They wave at me frantically.

My own hand has fallen to my chest, my face frozen in a grim smile.

"Vive la Comtesse!" they cry, a note of urgency in their voices, in their frenzied waving. They are desperate for a celebration, for any distraction from the constant proximity of death.

I raise my arm slowly and wave back, forcing a fresh smile onto my face, seeking the calm benevolence that my people need to see. *All is well with the Countess of Provence who rules over you, and all will be well with you.* This is the message I project, while in my mind I can only think, *swallow*, as I hold my breath against the gorge rising in my throat. I dare not show any sign of illness now.

The gates to the Chateau d'Angevin open to admit our procession and close behind us with a resolute clang, shutting the horror out. Our host, a minor count, the head of the leading family in Marseille, hurries to greet us as though nothing is wrong in his city.

"Welcome, Countess! You grace us with your presence more than we deserve." His extravagant words and beaming smile contradict the worry lines on his brow. "We are planning a festive ceremony for you. We will do the best we can…"

"That is all any countess could ask of a loyal subject, and I thank you for it." I dismount wearily as he rises from his bow, but find a gracious smile for him. His anxious look disappears. "It has been a long journey," I add quietly.

"Of course, of course, Countess. We have had your chambers prepared."

As soon as I am in my room I dismiss everyone but Jeanne, Honoré and Sybil, who know of my delicate condition. Clutching the chamber pot in both hands I empty my stomach. I try not to think of what I have seen and finally I recover, weak and wrung-out. Honoré and Jeanne help me onto the bed while Sybil fetches rosewater to wipe my face and honey-mead to soothe my throat.

"Your Majesty." Enrico's voice is respectful, his bow deep. Only the clench of his jaw reveals his tension. "You are not thinking of going out?"

I have spent five days shut inside the Chateau d'Angevin at his insistence. If he had his way I would not have received the delegations and petitioners that came in a steady stream to seek my direction in their plans or my judgement in their affairs.

"It is time I rode through my city," I answer, with a single raised eyebrow to warn him against whatever he wants to say next.

"It is my duty to keep you safe," he answers stiffly.

"It is my duty to be seen. My subjects need the assurance of my presence during this terrible time." I had thought to attend a Mass but the memory of those blackened bodies piled in front of the cathedral waiting for burial was deterrent enough.

"Wear a veil over your face, I implore you, Your Majesty."

I hesitate. I am not as immune to fear as I pretend. But my people face death every day; I will not show less courage than they do. I walk past Enrico through the doors to where my carriage waits, with ten mounted guards around it to escort me.

Once again my people come out to greet me, but it is a thinner, quieter crowd this time. Perhaps they hoped my arrival would bring an end to the dying and I have disappointed them. I sit straight in my carriage willing on them and myself the strength and fortitude to face what lies before us.

Just as I think that, the sun pushes through the grey clouds above us and a beam of light illuminates me like a lance thrown by God. The shadows roll back and suddenly my people are smiling, cheering me as though they have been given a sign that I will bring them through this, that they will survive, if not individually then collectively, as a people. As *my* people. I feel their faith and a corresponding lightness, as though the sunlight has entered my body, infuses me with hope. Death cannot prevail, for we are children of the light and it will uphold us. I stand up in the carriage and raise my hands to the sun while my people cheer until they are hoarse and death slinks away searching for a shadow to hide in.

I return to my chateau invigorated and call for a scribe. The ceremony to celebrate my presence in Marseille has been set for January 29th, three days from now. The following morning I and my entourage will ride for Aix-en-Provence. Marseille, critically important as a port city and trade route, is not the seat of the government of Provence. That distinction goes to Aix-en-Provence. If I am to raise support to defeat the Hungarians and drive them from my kingdom, I will have to seek it there. I settle in to dictate letters, preparing the magistrates there for my arrival.

When the letters are written I send the scribe away and call for Enrico and my ladies-in-waiting to tell them we will be leaving for Aix-en-Provence after the ceremony.

"My reception there will not be so generous as it has been here," I warn them. Since the time of my grandfather, King Robert the Wise, there has been discontent in Aix-en-Provence. King Robert, as was his right, and I also, have given many choice administrative positions in the government of their city to Neapolitans whom we trusted and wished to reward. The local magnates have frequently complained that those positions should go to them, and I have heard rumors recently that their grievances have been inflamed by the dauphin of Vienne, my late husband's cousin, whose allegiance lies with Hungary.

Enrico signals to Jeanne behind me to close the window shutters. I have been leaning out to get some fresh air against the constant fires Enrico has burning in my rooms, which he has been told will ward off the vapors that carry the plague.

"Aix-en-Provence is not a port city," he answers. "The plague will not be as bad there."

"Then we will not argue so often over my riding out." I smile.

He looks about to say something but reconsiders. "Do you have letters for me to send, Your Majesty?" he asks instead, glancing at my table.

I sign and affix my seal to the six letters I have dictated, five of them announcing my imminent arrival to the noble families of Aix-en-Provence, and the last one going to Pope Clement in Avignon, entreating his support. I have sent him a letter every day I have been here, and received only evasions or no response at all. The thought disturbs me, but then I remember the sunlight piercing through me. Pope Clement, like the sun, is but an instrument of God.

When Enrico leaves I try to rest. My darkened, over-heated

chamber feels oppressive. Tonight I have been invited to dine with the local magistrates and their wives, no more than a dozen in all at a chateau nearby, but already my energy is waning. It is my pregnancy, I tell myself, rising to prepare for my dinner. But I know it is more than that.

Day and night I am consumed by worries. Is Charles Martel safe and well-cared for? What do they tell him when he asks why I do not come to him? Are my subjects bearing the brunt of Louis of Hungary's fury at finding I have escaped, or is he satisfied with his conquest of Naples? I gnash my teeth to think I have lost my son and my kingdom both. Only my driving determination to reclaim them prevents me from going mad. Unless I should die here first, of the plague.

I shake my head. I will not permit such thoughts. Did I not receive a sign from God this very day?

And yet as I sit at dinner I cannot dispel the sight of my son's face, his eyes solemn and brave but his forehead creased with a tiny frown as he assured me he would be very brave, as brave as a king, while we were parted. Nor can I dispel the image of King Louis making himself comfortable in Castle Nuovo, perhaps sitting in my dining hall this very moment, entertaining my lords and my noble cousins, calling himself King of Naples!

All the while these visions are taunting me, I must smile and thank my hosts for their unstinting efforts to make me welcome and comfortable and do me honor as their sovereign ruler. I play my part well, forcing aside thoughts of Naples and Charles Martel each time they intrude. Here I am not the Queen of Naples, but the Countess of Provence. These are my people also and they deserve my attention.

On the morning of the banquet I order my belongings packed up and instruct my ladies and guards to make ready; we will leave the following morning for Aix-en-Provence.

Jeanne and Honoré hold up my royal blue surcote, sewn with gold fleurs-de-lis, for me to step into. It is the outfit I keep for formal occasions of state, but I have already worn it here. I have so few clothes compared to my wardrobe in Naples. Will I look poor, wearing the same one again so soon, despite the costly jewels and thread of gold sewn into it? I bend my head and step under the folds of satin, careful not to disturb the simple lace head piece pinned over my braided hair. When I am ready to leave I will set atop the lace my jeweled crown, the symbol of my office and my right to rule. I am Queen of Naples still, no matter who sits on my throne.

The ceremony is being held in the large square in front of the Abbey de Saint-Victor. They will have removed the corpses, surely, but how many will have fallen along the way since the last cart cleared the streets? I suppress a shudder.

Sybil, always sensitive to my moods, asks, "Will you carry a posey, Your Majesty?" She holds up a small posey of flowers for me to dip my nose into when the stench becomes overwhelming. Many nobles do this now when they are out in the streets, but I shake my head. I will not let my people see any sign of fear or doubt in me. I bear my troubles in silence. Nor do I try to distance myself from theirs.

Every man, woman, and child of Marseille has come out to see the event, packed into the square, crammed into the streets and alleyways leading to it, the little ones on their parents' shoulders. Every balcony is teeming with people, all eager for a rare glimpse of royalty. My guards ride ahead and beside me, calling for people to move aside as my carriage rolls into the square. I have given instructions that no one may be hurt, however slowly we must go to give them time to crush together out of our way. I will not bring harm to those whom the plague has spared.

As I pass, people from the balconies overhead throw flowers down onto me, a blanket of perfume to drown the scent of death that lingers even though the streets have been cleaned. I smile up at them, and at those lining the route to stare at me with wide-eyed shining faces. The story of my sunlit omen has circulated. I have become their symbol of hope, as they are mine.

My carriage stops at the edge of the square. I descend and walk across it, followed by my ladies holding up my mantle and escorted by my guards. The piazza is quiet, my people watching with reverence as I climb onto the raised dais in front of the Abbey and turn to look at them.

My host, head of the city administrators and my representative in Marseille, says a few words of greeting to the assembled nobles and reiterates the honor I do them with my visit—as if they do not know I have run for my life from Louis of Hungary's army. But here for the first time, I feel no shame in that. I feel upheld, cherished. My enemies are their enemies.

"I thank you, my nobles, magistrates, merchants for your hospitality, for your loyalty and homage. I greet you all, my people of Marseille whom I love." The piazza fills with cheering, the streets around it take up the exuberant roar until it seems all of Marseille is shouting my name and swearing their devotion. The magistrates hold up their hands, but the voices of my people cannot be stilled, we must wait until they are hoarse and breathless before the purpose of this ceremony can begin: the exchange of oaths between ruler and vassals.

I pledge to defend the welfare of my people in Marseille, to rule them justly, maintain order in their city, and keep them safe with all the forces at my command. When I have finished the cheering begins again throughout the piazza and into the streets. It continues unabated as one by one my lords and magistrates of Marseille kneel before me. I have to lean forward to hear them under the roar of approval of the citizens of Marseille as they promise to obey, defend, and support me in my need. This last brings tears to my eyes, for this is indeed my time of need, and these good people are my defense and succor.

Never have I been given fealty with such a depth of sincerity, nor received it with such gratitude. The sun pours down on us again today as it did three days ago, so bright it seems to shimmer, the air itself shining around us. Loyalty unto death we swear to each other, with an earnestness that turns the oath between lord and vassals into a binding as strong as need, as deep as faith, as enduring as life, as full of grace as the holy, healing brightness that shimmers in a lance of light.

When the last oath has been given, I stand and wave to all, nobles, merchants, tradesmen, and peasants. The crowded square trembles with their cheering.

Again, tears come to my eyes. I could stay here, Countess of my beloved Provence, amid subjects who love me back, and live a long, peaceful life.

I push away the temptation as soon as it comes. I was born to rule Naples. I swore before God that I would do so, to the utmost of my ability, in times of peace and in turbulent times. I have a duty to my kingdom and a duty to my son, Charles Martel, to train him to be a good sovereign and to pass on to him in his turn a well-governed and prosperous kingdom. Nothing, not famine nor mounting debts passed on from my grandfather, not internal strife nor war nor pestilence nor any calamity thrown against me will deter me from that duty.

"As God is my witness," I whisper under my breath, "I will never rest until I have reclaimed my kingdom and made it once again peaceful, prosperous, and admired by all who speak of it." I touch my hand briefly to my golden, jewel-encrusted crown to seal my silent vow.

My host holds out his arm to escort me to the manor beside the Abbey where we will feast with all the highborn of Marseille. As soon as we are gone, tables of food will be set up in the square for the common citizens.

The next day I leave for Aix-en-Provence. The party that accompanied me from Naples has been bolstered by twelve knights and two more ladies-in-waiting who begged to serve me. Like someone who was starving and has been fed, I carry the gift of Marseille with me on the two-day journey.

We are met outside Aix-en-Provence by a delegation of hard-faced knights barring our way. My guards pull their horses into a circle surrounding me and my ladies, their hands on their swords. They are outnumbered two-to-one but I see in their faces that they will die before they give me up. I peer through the armored bodies of my men. Have I traveled so far over sea and land only to die on the road?

A large knight, the leader of the band before us, kicks his horse forward. "We are not here to harm the Countess," he tells my men in a rough voice. "She will be permitted to proceed on to Aix-en-Provence. Any of you who come from Marseille may go with her. But those who travelled with her from Naples must surrender yourselves to us."

The stomp of horses' hooves and the jingle as they chew their bits is loud in the silence that follows his words. Jeanne and Sybil stare at me wide-eyed, Honoré's head is bent, her shoulders shaking. Enrico removes his hand from his sword. That single act of intense loyalty breaks me.

"On whose command dare you speak to me this way?" I demand. I urge my horse forward, nodding my men to move aside. They do not move.

"We act on the command of the magistrates of Aix-en-Provence," the knight says. "Come forward, those who are from Naples, and name yourselves!"

"They will not!" I reply, hot with fury.

"Then all but you will die, Countess."

My hands shake on my gelding's reins. I urge him forward but still my men will not let me pass the safety of their arms.

Enrico kicks his horse. My men let him pass through their circle.

"Stop!" I command, but he rides straight toward the waiting knights.

"Enrico Caracciolo," he says.

One by one they ride forward as I watch helplessly, my five loyal Neapolitan guards, then Sybil, Jeanne, and Honoré, each stating their names. Honoré's voice breaks and Sybil has to give her name.

"Enrico Caracciolo…" The knight names each of them, "You stand accused of conspiring to murder Andrew of Hungary. By the authority of the magistrates of Aix-en-Provence I take you prisoner to await your trial and sentencing."

Louis of Hungary is behind this. I should have come directly to Aix-en-Provence. He has got to the governing body of Provence before me, with his money and his influence.

"They are guilty of nothing," I say, my voice cold and authoritative. "I demand you treat them well, as befits their station and the loyalty they have shown your Countess. If they are harmed in any way, I will hold you responsible. Where are you taking them?"

"They will be held in the dungeon of—" He names a castle I do not recognize and nods to his men. Ten of the knights break away to surround the prisoners, taking the men's swords. The rest escort me and my small remaining entourage from Marseille through the gates of Aix-en-Provence.

Chapter 9

Midnight Flight

Maria of Naples
January 22, 1348

A violent banging on the door of my bedchamber wakens me. As I struggle out of a terrifying nightmare of being set upon by outlaws, I realize the angry voices I heard in my dream are real. The night is alive with raucous shouts, screaming people and whinnying horses, ringing steel and objects breaking. The wild noises pour in through my bedchamber windows.

The banging at my door resumes. Beside me, my husband's cousin Margherita shrieks in terror.

"Enter!" I cry, sitting up hastily and clutching the covers around me.

Two of my husband's knights whom I had posted outside my bedchamber in a moment of fearful premonition before I retired fling open the door and rush in. The first one, Lorenzo, holds a lamp. Its flickering light casts demonic shadows across their faces and around the walls of my chamber.

"My Lady, you must flee," he cries. "The Hungarian army has entered Naples."

Outside my window the voices are getting louder. How long before they reach my husband's castle? A strange dancing light, like lightning, leaps up behind the wooden shutters at my window, belying the darkness of the night. The acrid smell of smoke and the crackle of flames confirms my fear. I leap from the bed in only my nightclothes and race for the nursery.

Joanna is already sitting up in her little cot. She turns to me, white-faced but silent, as I run into the room, followed by Lorenzo and Tomas who wakened me, and the guard posted at the nursery door. Clementia, my baby, bursts into howls. The night nurse stumbles up from her bed and picks her up, staring at me in alarm. The nursery is at the back of the castle; the outside noises are muffled here, she does not grasp what is happening.

"We are under attack," I tell her shortly. "Bring the children and follow me."

Agnes starts to cry. I pick her up and grab Joanna's hand. All undressed and unprepared we follow the men who lead us down the back stairs to the door behind the castle. Margherita meets us there and hands me my purse, taking Agnes from me. I wonder at her presence of mind, clasping the purse in one hand and holding Joanna's hand tightly in my other as three more of my husband's men surround us.

A cacophony of sounds breaks over us as we run outside: men shouting and running, swords clashing, horses screaming, mallets and axes breaking down wooden doors and shattering glass, and the shrieks of women and children fleeing for their lives. The night is alight with flames, hungry red tongues licking at the black sky, grey ash floating down over us as Naples burns.

"My Lady, I must see to my own family," the nurse cries, holding Clementia toward me. For a moment I consider asking her to take my baby, she will be safer in this woman's house. Whatever has happened, there is no peace between the cousins, which means I and my family are surely marked for death. But I do not trust anyone else to guard my children. Lorenzo sheathes his sword and plucks

Agnes from my arms, despite her terrified protest and I receive Clementia whose arms encircle my neck in a death grip as she buries her tear-stained little face against my shoulder. Margherita grabs Joanna's hand and we race through the back gate into the streets of Naples now seething with violence and murder.

"Go back," I tell all of the guards except Lorenzo and Tomas. "Guard my husband's castle as though we are still inside." We are too obvious a target surrounded by guards and there are too many Hungarian soldiers and mercenaries for a half-dozen guards to defeat. No one seeing two more women running through the streets in their nightgowns with babies in their arms will imagine one of them is the Princess Maria, heir to the throne. They will be occupied trying to break into my husband's castle to claim me.

We run in the shadows against the buildings, avoiding fighting soldiers and fleeing citizens, stumbling over bodies in a mad dash to reach sanctuary at the convent of Santa Croce. Tomas, sword at the ready, leads us, first me with eighteen-month-old Clementia balanced above my pregnant belly, behind me Margherita holding Joanna's hand, and last, guarding our rear, comes Lorenzo carrying three-year-old Agnes. My white nightdress flaps in the wind and clings to my body alternately, my bare feet are already bruised and cut by stones. As we dash across a road between two buildings I feel my feet sticking to the cobblestones and look down—the road is covered in blood, my feet red with it. A sob rises in my throat, threatening hysteria, but Clementia whimpers against me and I push my own fear aside. I must get my daughters to safety; nothing else matters until I have done that. I grit my teeth and run.

Out of the night three armed men appear before us. The middle one shouts something to Tomas in a foreign language—King Louis' mercenaries!

"Run!" Tomas commands me under his breath, raising his sword and blocking them from me with his body. I race around them, glancing back to make sure the others are following me. Lorenzo dumps Agnes into Margherita's arms and unsheathes his sword to aid Tomas. Margherita stumbles, dropping Joanna's hand to catch up Agnes.

"Joanna!" I scream, but my daughter has the presence of mind to grab the skirt of Margherita's night-dress and keep running.

The mercenaries' faces light up, now recognizing the men with us as guards, not brothers or husbands, and knowing that means wealth. The one nearest reaches out to grab Margherita but she dodges sideways. Lorenzo's sword slices into his shoulder. With a cry he turns back to the fight. One more block to the side street and then across the piazza to the gates of Santa Croce. If only Tomas and Lorenzo can keep these men occupied until we are safe inside the convent. Ignoring the pain in my side and my cut feet I put on a burst of speed. Each ragged breath burns my throat, my arms ache with the weight of Clementia and spasms of pain lance across my abdomen filling me with the fear of miscarriage. But we are almost there.

Lorenzo and Tomas catch up with us as we hesitate at the edge of the piazza. Two Hungarian soldiers are watching the gate of the convent. Tomas is limping, his left arm hanging useless at his side. He shrugs when he sees me looking at it and leads us in a circle back down another street which will bring us into the piazza closer to Santa Croce. Then there is no help for it, we will have to dash for the gates and pray the nuns will open them for us while Tomas and Lorenzo once again hold off King Louis' soldiers.

God hears our prayers; there are two holy sisters at the gate. One of them recognizes me and throws open the gate for us to race through. Lorenzo impales his man, pulling his sword clear in time to tumble through the closing gate after us, but Tomas is on his knees, fighting to his last breath that we may attain safety. The gate slams shut, leaving him on the other side. I hastily commend his soul to God while Lorenzo urges me to keep moving.

One of the sisters reaches to take Clementia but she clings to me screaming. I shake my head and carry her into the cloisters to a small dark room with a bed and a table. I sink onto the bed, my legs giving way, Clementia still in my arms. Joanna climbs up beside me and Agnes struggles in Margherita's arms until she sets the child on my lap also. I wrap my arms around the three of them as they cling to me and at last I let myself weep, my tears falling onto their golden heads. We have reached sanctuary unharmed. I whisper a fervent prayer of gratitude.

The nuns bring us a platter of cheese and olives and salted fish and the news that Maria of Bourbon, Duke Robert of Taranto's wife, has also made her way here with one of her ladies. Lorenzo is given a pallet in the courtyard, he insists on sleeping where he can watch our room. We lie down on the bed, Margherita and I and my daughters in a tangle of arms and legs under the blanket, and close our eyes. I think I cannot sleep, the night is yet alive with screams and fighting and I am still trembling from our narrow escape. But when I open my eyes again the room is alight with sunshine falling through the narrow window. I stare at it, wondering how the sun can shine so brightly after a night so wicked.

They must know we are here, or at least at one of the churches or convents of Naples. King Louis will arrive today or tomorrow. When he discovers we have abandoned the Durazzo castle, he will not rest until he finds us. What has happened to Charles? Where are Robert and his brother, and my brothers-in-law? My stomach is a knot of fear as Margherita helps me into a nun's habit, all that could be found for us to wear, and a good disguise should the convent be searched.

Breakfast is brought to us, the same fare as last night. After eating I go to the chapel to pray, then I pace the cloisters, unwilling to go outside where I may be seen through the iron gates. At mid-morning I am told a messenger has come for me. As he hurries across the courtyard I recognize my husband's squire. Lorenzo, standing beside the bench I am sitting on, makes a small gesture with his hand, restraining me from jumping up and running to hear what news my husband's man is bringing.

"My Lady!" The man bows, panting from his haste. He is nearly stuttering in his distress. "I have ridden straight from Aversa on your husband's fastest horse—"

"What was my husband riding?" I demand, full of a sudden dread and desperate to be wrong.

He blanches and stands speechless before me, his Adam's apple bobbing in his throat, his mouth hanging open.

"He has imprisoned them all!"

"Not all of them, my Lady."

"Tell me!" I cry, half-rising from my seat then falling back again, my knees suddenly weak. "Tell me everything, from the beginning."

He takes a breath, marshalling his thoughts. "My Lord Charles and his brothers, and the Duke of Taranto and his brothers, went together into the great hall of the palace at Aversa. The King of Hungary greeted them warmly and spoke with them pleasantly before he led them in to dinner. Water was brought for the king to wash his hands first, and then taken to my Lord, and the duke of Taranto and their brothers. The King of Hungary sat at the head table with his nobles and advisors. His royal cousins were seated at a separate table, each Neapolitan noble with a Hungarian knight or nobleman beside him."

I make an impatient sound in my throat, something between a

growl and a sob, and wave my hand. What do I care that they washed their hands or where they sat?

He continues more quickly. "I was standing behind my Lord Charles during the dinner in case he had need of anything, so when the Hungarian beside him, with whom he had been conversing pleasantly, leaned close—"

"Yes, yes! Get on with it!"

He swallows. "I heard the Hungarian nobleman whisper, *'Unfortunate duke, you have come to your misfortune! Believe me, and leave while you can.'*"

He pauses, waiting for me to exclaim, but I am too sick with dread to speak. The infant in my womb moves as if he feels my terror. I lay my hand over him protectively.

"The duke laughed, but his eyes flashed. He said he would report the man for maligning his cousin, if he did not know it was a cowardly jest made out of envy. They spoke no more. If only he had listened…" the squire wrings his hands.

"Where is your master?" I cry, at the end of my patience.

"My Lady, please, I am telling you!" His eyes bulge and he steps back as though I might harm him. I am tempted to order Lorenzo to beat him but then I will never hear his news.

"When dinner was over King Louis summoned Lord Charles and Lord Robert and their brothers to attend him. Lord Charles' smiled, expecting to hear his reward for…for…"

"Tell me what King Louis said!" I do not want to hear the name he gives my husband's betrayal of my sister, the Queen to whom he swore fealty.

"King Louis' pleasant expression disappeared. He stood, his face terrible to behold, and in a voice of thunder he said, *Duke of Durazzo, monster of iniquity, you are here to suffer the consequences of your crimes!*" The squire looks down, unable to meet my eyes as he recounts the rest of King Louis' words to my husband. "He accused Lord Charles of treason, of having his uncle, the Cardinal Talleyrand of Perigord, work to delay Prince Andrew's coronation, which delay made possible his terrible death. He accused Lord Charles of inviting him to invade Naples, and promising his aid in the invasion, only to turn traitor twice over and raise an army against him at L'Aquila." He takes a breath, his eyes sliding up to my face, trying to read my expression. I stare back at him stoically, knowing what is coming yet dreading to hear it.

"He finished by accusing Lord Charles of plotting to have King Louis' forces destroy Queen Joanna and all your royal cousins, my Lady, and then to murder King Louis and take the crown of Naples for himself."

"And what has he done with my husband and my cousins?" My voice is shrill. It is an effort to get the words out. Charles does not confide in me short of what he deems I must know to play my part in his schemes, but I know more than I let on. King Louis has it correct.

"Lords Robert and Philip of Taranto and your brothers-in-law, Lords Louis and Robert of Durazzo, were sent at once to the dungeon. My Lord the Duke of Durazzo…" He swallows, his Adam's apple bobbing with his distress, "…King Louis had him stand before a Hungarian tribunal, which condemned him for conspiring in the death of Prince Andrew. He then ordered Lord Charles to take him to the spot where Prince Andrew was assassinated. Upon the terrace from which the prince hanged to death before help arrived to cut him down, King Louis ordered Lord Charles beheaded, and his body thrown over the balcony to lie where Prince Andrew's body had lain.

"I left at once, my Lady, and rode all night to bring you the news, that you might be warned and escape." He looks around and lowers his voice. "I knew you would come here, Duchess, but King Louis will guess as I did when he arrives. This abbey will not afford you sanctuary for long after he learns you are here."

"I thank you for your loyalty," I say stiffly. "You will be rewarded." We both know how unlikely that is, that he had best run for his life, but all I can think of is to make him leave so I can sink into a chair and moan. Charles is dead. I can hardly take it in. Yesterday I was the Duchess of Durazzo, second in line for the throne of Naples, protected by my rank and my powerful husband who commanded thousands of vassals. Today I am the widow of a man executed for treason, left destitute with three children whose lives depend on me. What should I do? Where could I hide us from King Louis, who will surely blame me along with my husband for his brother's death?

The Abbess assures me Santa Croce will offer me sanctuary as long as I need it, but Louis of Hungary is no respecter of such things. I beg Lorenzo to arrange our escape from Naples as soon as possible.

That evening my husband's chamberlain arrives. I am warned that he is in a wild state by the nun who leads me to meet with him in the Abbess' meeting room.

"It is gone, my Lady, all gone!" he cries, tearing his hair and falling to his knees before me as soon as I enter. "All the Duke's castles and lands and money gone, divided among King Louis' nobles! They are already ensconced at your castle here in Naples. I barely escaped with my life!"

I sink into a chair, horrified.

"Calm yourself, sir," the Abbess says sternly. "Tell the Duchess of Durazzo what you know."

He rakes his hand through his hair, breathing deeply. In a slightly calmer voice he says, "King Louis entered Naples just before dusk and went straight to Castle Nuovo. Finding the Queen already gone he flew into a rage and ordered the citizens of Naples to pay him an enormous sum, in the form of a tax, if they did not want their city sacked. Next he divided the palaces, lands and property of the Queen and the Dukes of Durazzo and Taranto among himself and his generals. Our Queen has been declared a murderer, and all those who rode to Aversa against him, whether they fought or not, are named traitors and conspirators, their lands and wealth forfeit. All this I learned when three of his generals burst into Castle Durazzo. They questioned me, demanding the keys to your wardrobe and jewels and all the documents for your holdings." He pauses for breath, his eyes watering.

"I told them you were dead, my Lady, dragged from the castle and slain by the mercenaries last night. While they were gloating over the deeds to your lands and castles, I made my escape, penniless as you see me now."

Penniless. The word echoes in my mind. I have lost everything. I am nineteen years of age, with three children and a fourth on the way, wearing a borrowed nun's habit, and I, too, am penniless.

He waits on his knees before me. I know what he waits for. He has said I am dead, yet he has seen me here. I remove my husband's ring, the only thing of value I own save for the coins in my purse that must buy my escape.

"I will remember your loyalty when I come into my own again. Meanwhile, tell no one you have seen me, but spread the tale of my death." I hand him my ring. "This ring is a token of the wealth that will be yours when I return. Bring it to me then for a fitting reward for your service this day."

Chapter 10

Plague

Joanna 1 of Naples
February, 1348

Settled in the Angevin ancestral castle in Aix-en-Provence, I pace my presence room, pausing at the window alcoves to look out at the capital of Provence. I stand back, unwilling to be seen at my windows by the people who have come hoping to catch sight of me. My ride into this city was a troubling and frightening experience. There were many who cheered me, lining the streets to welcome my arrival. It has been many years since a royal has visited Aix-en-Provence. My father came once, I have been told, but I have never come till now.

But there were also many who shouted curses at me and called for my death, without fear of punishment for their treason! The plague, only a week ago limited to port cities, has by now made its way inland, arriving in Aix-en-Provence just days before me, as though it is a poison leaking across the land to signal my arrival. I still hear the echo of his voice, that nameless man shouting above the cheers of my faithful subjects: "Your crime has poisoned us!" blaming me for the death that preceded me.

More voices joined in, claiming my sin has brought down this judgement on them, that I must be punished for the murder of my husband before God smites them all for my crime. They are not the majority, but they are a vocal number, and their voices will increase as the plague increases. I was glad of the very knights who stripped me of my Neapolitan attendants and sent them to the dungeon, for they became my protectors, shielding me and delivering me safely to my castle gates.

I glance down at the people walking on the other side of my castle walls. Would they cheer or denounce me if I stepped up to the open window? Not knowing, I stand back, not out of fear but prudence. Their accusations do not frighten me for I have not sinned. Andrew's murder was none of my doing. If anything he brought it on himself, threatening my powerful lords with his vengeance once he was crowned, swearing he would destroy them for belittling him. I made it known among my lords and royal cousins that I would not condone violence against him, hoping to restrain their hot tempers, but they are not mealy-mouthed men without spirit or pride, not the kind of men who would tamely wait for their own ruin.

The dauphin of Vienne has been more successful than I would ever have imagined, whispering rumors of my guilt here on behalf of his Hungarian cousins. It annoys me to hide from my people, as if there was any truth to his vile claims. But I must negotiate with the governing lords of Aix-en-Provence and regain their loyalty, and it will not help my cause if they hear even a small faction of their citizens calling for my execution in order to stay God's wrath.

It is time to dress for my meeting. I choose my blue kirtle—blue for faith, virtue, and loyalty—with silver threads woven through it and sapphires at the neck. I have not come to them a beggar but a queen, and I shall look the part. The two ladies-in-waiting who accompanied me from Marseille help me dress and braid up my hair. When I am ready I raise my crown and place it on my head over my veil.

I walk calmly into the great hall where the governing council of

Provence awaits me. They are not fools; they know the plague is everywhere, and they know as well that only the Pope can judge me, if judgement is required. Nor do they care about Andrew's death or the dauphin of Vienne's rumors. They care about royal appointments—everything else is only a negotiation tactic.

I walk into their presence confident and regal, yet projecting the assurance that I am willing to hear their grievances, prepared to be sympathetic and accommodating in order to reconcile our past differences. There can be nothing about my appearance or demeaner that says I need their support. No, the message must be that I am a just and mindful sovereign, worthy of their fealty, here to resolve the rift that distance and misunderstandings have caused between us.

It is not entirely an act. These are my people, as willing to love me as the citizens of Marseille, and their complaints are not without basis. It is my right, as it was my grandfather's, to appoint whom I wish to administrative positions in the seat of government in my duchy. But I have worthy subjects here, willing to prove their loyalty, who know the needs of Provence better than the Neapolitan noblemen I rewarded with those appointments. It was short-sighted; I did not foresee needing to seek haven in Provence. The time has come to correct this mistake.

They stand and bow as I enter the room and take my seat at the head of the table. When they rise from their bows I leave them standing as I look directly into the eyes of the man to my left, the Neapolitan lord I appointed to represent me here. He returns my look uneasily, unable to meet my gaze yet afraid to look away. In allowing these men to imprison my retinue he has failed me miserably.

I turn to the man on my right, obviously the head of their council. He looks back at me with a mixture of apprehension and resolution. I am the Countess of Provence and my wrath over the way I have been treated, should I care to exercise it, will fall on him. I am tempted, when I think of my loyal subjects lying in a dungeon, and I hold him in a cold and merciless gaze long enough to let him see that. "You have something to say to me?" I ask at last.

He rallies, aware of his fellow councilors also watching him. "My Lady Countess of Provence…" he bows again and hesitates, hoping perhaps that I will allow him and his fellow councilors to sit. It is permitted to sit in the presence of a Countess, but not in the presence of a Queen. I leave them standing.

He launches into a lengthy speech, praising me, expressing their appreciation that I have honored them with my presence, but also going into their many grievances, as far back as my Grandfather's reign.

When he has finished I look around the room. "So say you all?"

There is some shifting of feet, sideways glances, but all murmur their agreement.

"Be seated, then," I say graciously. "Not you," I glance left briefly at my appointed lord.

"I find there is merit in your concerns, if not in your recent behavior. This man is relieved of his post," I tell the councilors of Aix-en-Provence. "Choose the most worthy man among you, one who is loyal to my family and steadfast in the interests of Provence as well. Give me his name and he will have this appointment."

I am gratified by the expressions on their faces—amazement, relief, delight—and equally gratified to note at the corner of my eye that my Neapolitan lord slumps in disgrace. His family surrendered to the Hungarians with Charles of Durazzo and Robert of Taranto. In one sentence he pays for his own failure here and their betrayal in Naples.

"Your chairman, naturally, will not be considered for this appointment." I will not reward the man who ordered loyal Neapolitan subjects thrown into prison, no matter how just their grievances. I cannot ask for their release. Having trumped up grounds for their imprisonment these men must stand by their action. It is up to me to prove myself and my supporters innocent of any crime, and I will be called to do so in Avignon. For now I can see in their uneasy expressions that they have received my warning to treat my subjects well.

"As for the rest of your concerns…"

By the end of the meeting I have the full and enthusiastic support of the governors of Provence. On February 19th, at a public ceremony, I give my solemn oath to henceforth appoint only noblemen native to Provence as its governors. In return I receive the oaths of fealty from every aristocrat and administrator in Aix-en-Provence. At the end of the ceremony I ride with a magnificent entourage through the streets of the city, my banner carried proudly before me, to the cheers of my people. If there are any who yet maintain I am the cause of the plague that swept in ahead of me and stalks them in their streets, they are silenced by the wall of my supporters.

Provence is mine. Here I will build an army and return to reclaim my kingdom. But none of this can happen until I clear my name, once and for all, of any suspicion of complicity in my husband's murder. As well, I must legitimize my marriage, performed and consummated in haste on the threshold of battle, without the necessary papal dispensation. And soon, for I am now four months pregnant with Louis' child. Only Pope Clement can pronounce me innocent and free those who followed me from Naples, and only he can validate my marriage. But will he?

He has postponed taking a stand against Hungary for too long! Between the promise of his wealth and the threat of his army King Louis has Pope Clement bent like a sapling in the wind, swaying with indecision. Unlike the other princes of Christendom who at least hesitate at the threat of excommunication, knowing their citizens will not stand for it, King Louis of Hungary and his mother, the Dowager Queen Elizabeth, practically dare Clement to defy them. They want me dead and Louis of Hungary declared the King of Naples. But I am an Angevin, descended from the Kings of France, my own mother the sister of King Philip of France. And King Philip will not countenance having his line disgraced. Thus have France and Hungary kept the pope swaying between them. I cannot go to Avignon until I know which way Clement will bend.

I ply him with letters from my castle in Aix-en-Provence, entreating his support and requesting a public audience, only to meet with excuses and delays. My arrival in Provence is awkward for him. He is the Holy Father of all Christendom, and all Christendom, it seems, is at war. Edward III of England is at war with Philip of France and each has recruited allies who have their own reasons for arming. King Edward supports Hungary's invasion of Naples because it distracts Naples from arming with France, and Hungary supports England's invasion of France as it prevents King Philip from sending forces to help me. Spain watches eagerly to see where an advantage lies for her, and German mercenaries fight with whoever will pay them. The northern cities of Italy—Verona, Venice, Rome—want a Roman pope, while the southern principalities—Florence and Naples—support Clement in the papal palace in Avignon. In his pursuit of peace and prosperity—mostly the latter and that for the Church—Pope Clement would rather not visibly choose sides, but sue for reconciliation.

I need support not reconciliation, and I need it now. I pace the halls of my castle beset with fears. Where is my husband? Did he escape Louis' army? What of my son? Is he being well-cared for? And my people, my beloved Neapolitan subjects, are they suffering Louis' wrath in my place? Surely he will not plunder my treasury and burn my city. He wants to be King of Naples, not to leave it in ruins. But he is a violent man, a man who enjoys watching others suffer, who seeks vengeance for imagined slights let alone real ones. I wake in the night from nightmares of what he may be doing to my city, to my people, and lie in the dark trying to convince myself it was only a dream, not real, when I know that the reality is very likely worse even than my dreams.

Another nightmare is unfolding around me in Aix-en-Provence. The plague continues to spread throughout the city, killing more wantonly than any invading army. The crowd that stood at my walls to catch a glimpse of royalty has gone, scurried into houses and churches and other places that offer only the illusion of safety. My guards advise me to lock my gates and stay inside my castle, but after a week of confinement, tormented by frustration at Pope Clement's delays and my own inactivity, I ride out for fresh air against their advice.

The roads and piazzas are nearly empty, silent except for the church bells constantly ringing the death knoll for the dead. Those who venture out to buy food or conduct business creep through the streets, handkerchiefs pressed to their noses, avoiding each other. The friends and neighbors they would have stopped to greet a month ago might today be carrying the deadly disease, might have a bubo already blossoming in their groin or armpit, hidden by their clothes. Corpses lie on the streets, men, women, and children, their faces puckered with the agony of their last moments, their bodies blackened by the buboes and stinking with the foul stench of this death. They have been thrown onto the streets by relatives, piled atop one another to wait for the death carts that will carry them to mass graves.

"Mercy! Have mercy, I beg of you!" a woman's voice cries from the building we are passing. I slow my horse and look for her. She is leaning out of an upper window of her home, a burgher's wife. I see no sickness in her face, only terror. Below a dozen men are boarding up the doors and lower windows of her house. They ignore her screams, refuse even to look at her.

"What are they doing?" I ask the guard riding nearest me. He mumbles something too low for me to hear clearly. "What did you say?" I demand, certain I have misunderstood.

"Entombment," he repeats.

I stare at him in horror. "They are boarding her up in her house?" A small head appears in the window beside the woman. She bends quickly and lifts a child, no more than a baby, to show me, all the while screaming, "Help us, Countess! Please help us!"

"Her and all her family," the guard replies to my question.

"But she does not look sick. Surely they are not all sick?"

"Her husband, perhaps, and she and their children have looked at him, fed him, touched him. They cannot be allowed out to spread it to others. My Lady Countess, we must keep riding, you should not even look at her." He looks around quickly as though to see if anyone has noticed.

"But how will they send in food?" The men boarding up the house have left no openings that I can see.

"No one will bring them food. They were dead the minute they sheltered and nursed one struck by the plague. The rest of the families on the street must look to their own lives. Please, my Lady Countess, you are not safe here."

I look at him, mute with horror at the fate of the woman and her children. "For tending her husband in his illness? What do other families do?"

"They call the street cleaners."

"I mean before their husband or parent or child has died. When they still need care."

"They call the street cleaners."

My stomach heaves. I am nearly five months pregnant now and

easily made ill. My guard's face blanches.

Suddenly I think, what if I throw up here in the street? What will they do to me if they believe I am ill?

"We must go back," I say.

"Yes." His face crumples with relief. "Yes, Countess, at once."

I throw my reins to the stable boy and hurry through the double wooden doors into my castle, telling my maid to fetch me some wine and water to wash my hands and face. Eleonore, one of the ladies-in-waiting who accompanied me from Marseille, follows me up to my presence chamber. She reaches to remove my riding cape, still dressed in her own from our ride. As she unclasps it I glance at her face.

"Eleonore, you are weeping!"

"I am sorry, my Lady Countess," she whimpers, swinging my cape off my shoulders with her head bowed and dipping into a curtsy, all in one motion.

"Is it the woman?"

She nods. "I am sorry," she repeats.

"I could not help her." My voice is heavy with regret.

"Of course not, my Lady Countess. It is the plague." She makes a helpless little gesture, trying to hide the tears that accompany her words.

"You know someone who has sickened with it." I cannot say 'died of it', but there is rarely another outcome.

She nods, her shoulders shaking. "My L...lady Aunt." The words come out in a sob. She throws her hands over her face, weeping unreservedly as she chokes out the story. "My cousin Henri sang as he left their house in the morning. He was back before the monastery bells tolled terce. My uncle fled as soon as he saw his son stumble to their door; we have not heard from him since. My aunt helped

Henri onto his bed and sent her younger children to us. By midday Henri could not sit up, nor eat nor drink. By nightfall he was dead and my aunt lay screaming for help in the throes of her own death. I crept past her house but dared not go inside the gates. I will remember the sound of her screams as long as I live."

I pour two cups of wine and hand her one, speechless with pity. When her sobs subside and she has taken several gulps of wine, I ask, "Are your little cousins well?"

She shakes her head, fresh tears leaking from beneath her closed eyes. "My father would not let them in. He ordered a servant to leave food and small ale at the gate and send them away when they had eaten, refusing to listen to my mother's pleading. We saw them twice more at our gate, but after a few days they did not come back. Cecile was eight years old, little Charles was only six."

"Your father did what he had to, to protect you," I say, more to comfort her than because I believe it. Would I send my niece Joanna and her sisters into the streets to die? Of course not, but they are royal children. I could have them cared for by servants and keep them away from me and my darling Charles Martel.

But Eleonore's family must have had servants. If a man will desert his own family, if an uncle will turn his niece and nephew away, how could one expect servants to stay? Perhaps Eleonore's father knew they would desert his household if he took in children who had lived in a house with the plague. I feel a rush of gratitude that this gruesome illness is not in Naples, remembering a moment later that Naples is at the mercy of a conquering army as cruel and merciless as any disease.

"These are very hard times we are living through. Between wars and famine and plague we are every one of us beset with grief and fear, country against country, neighbor turned against neighbor, husband against wife, parents abandoning their own children," I tell Eleonore. "After we have drunk our wine we will go to the chapel and pray."

Later that day a message from Pope Clement arrives. He cannot grant me an audience now, Clement writes, but he bids me travel to Chateaurenard, not far from Avignon, and wait there for him to contact me.

I am safer here in Aix-en-Provence, surrounded by my subjects and their newly-secured oaths of fealty. In Chateaurenard I will be easily accessible if King Louis's ambassadors convince Pope Clement to take his side and arrest me. But Chateaurenard is still in Provence and a show of obedience might dispose Clement more favorably to granting me a public audience.

Avignon is my city. I own it and I am its rightful ruler. I may go there at any time. Indeed, Clement himself is a guest in my city. But he is also the Holy Father of Christendom. I must have his support. I cannot risk going to Avignon until I know he will receive me publicly with all the ceremony due the Queen of Naples. I will not go and be spurned, nor meet him in private where he can promise me anything and I must pretend to believe him without the benefit of witnesses to hold him to his promises.

The last line of his missive assures me his cardinals will send eighteen knights to escort me, in recognition of my rank and position. That is good. He knows I will not come to him as anything other than the rightful monarch of Naples. Not a supplicant but an equal, ordained by God as much as he is. I toss the letter on a table. Why will he not grant me an audience? He did not refuse to hear King Louis' ambassadors.

I put my hand to my forehead, trying to think. The bells in every church, cathedral, abbey, and monastery throughout Aix-en-Provence and every nearby town ring day and night, a constant, pitiless clamoring marking the dead. And still they cannot keep up.

Death on death on death they toll, alerting heaven to the passage of souls. Who would ever have imagined such a relentless rush of souls fleeing this life, such a weight of grief and terror falling upon us? But there is no time to grieve, no silence for reflection and mourning. There are no last rites to cleanse the dying of their sins, no funerals, no prayers beside the graves, no grave markers. Only the constant hammering of the bells and the dull thud of bodies falling into mass graves like slops tossed into a pig sty.

It is the end of the world, I have heard people whisper, and in the dark as I wait for sleep, wondering whether I will wake in the morning, I fear they are right. Yesterday two of my cooks died, this morning one of my maids. My voice shook as I ordered the fires stoked up and locked myself alone in my chamber as though the wooden doors could keep death out. And through it all the bells tolled: *doom…doom…doom…* I am going mad with the sound of the bells!

I cover my ears and lay my head on the table…

…Brave as a king, my little boy's voice comes to me.

I raise my head and square my shoulders. How pleased King Louis and his mother would be to hear of my death. But I will *not* die until I have reclaimed my kingdom and passed it on to my son. I reach for Clement's letter. Chateaurenard is neither a trade port nor a seat of government, but a community of wealthy estates. The size and opulence of the castles and vineyards will create a necessary distance from each other. The plague might not have taken hold there as it has elsewhere in Provence.

I walk to my door and send for a scribe to attend me in my chambers. When he arrives I dictate a reply to Clement. I will be ready by February 27th to proceed to the castle in Chateaurenard that has been offered for my temporary accommodation.

I must wait on the Pope's bidding, but at least it will be somewhere a little farther away from the eternal sound and sight and smell of death.

Chapter 11

Orphans

Maria of Naples
February, 1348

"It scratches, Maman!" Agnes complains, wriggling in the rough peasant's shift they have dressed her in.

"Agnes, be still," Joanna scolds, shifting her shoulders a little as she herself resists the urge to scratch where the badly-carded wool fabric touches her skin. "And do not call our Lady Mother 'Maman'!" She turns to me. "Is that not right, Maman?" She claps her hand over her mouth.

"You are right, Joanna. You must call me Brother Giovanni, all of you, until we are far from Naples and safe."

"But you are our Maman still?" Agnes asks anxiously. Beside her, baby Clementia sucks hard on her thumb watching me fearfully. Her doubt is perhaps warranted. Even without the benefit of a mirror I can well imagine how odd I must look swathed in the brown robe of a friar from my head to the ground, with my hair braided tightly out of sight and my head buried in the cowl of my habit. The rope at my waist is tied loosely, letting the too-large robe bury my woman's figure in folds of heavy cloth. Even though it has been washed it still carries the scent of male sweat, which hides my identity as effectively as the cloth. And itches—how it itches! I have to grit my teeth to endure the rough, ill-smelling cloth against my skin. I push the hood back and smile at my children with as close to an air of gay mischief as I can summon.

"I am most certainly your Maman. I will always be your Maman. But we are going to play a little game. Like a …masque or a mummers show! You are to pretend I am a man, a friar, and you must call me Brother Giovanni. And I will pretend you are orphaned peasant children that I am escorting to an abbey in France where you will be cared for. What fun we will have playing this game!"

"But you are not really going to leave us in an abbey." Joanna says this stoutly, trying to look confident for Agnes and Clementia. Her eyes slide sideways to make sure I will agree.

"Never," I swear. "I will not leave you ever, my darlings. Not…for any reason." I was about to say, *not as long as I live,* but I do not want to add another element of uncertainty. "You are more precious to me than all my titles and all my jewels and fine gowns! *You* are my jewels!"

Agnes giggles. I have told them this before but never while I was standing in front of them with neither a fine gown nor a jewel in sight.

"But we will come back to Papa when the game is over, and put on our nice clothes that are not itchy," she says.

"We will come back when it is safe," I promise her. I cannot tell them yet about their father, any more than I can warn them of the dangers we are about to brave. It is my job to keep them safe now.

"You must call me Sister Margherita," my husband's cousin says. Dark-haired, brown-eyed Margherita will never be mistaken for an Angevin and so has been allowed to keep her sex, dressed as a nun. "And if you have a question you must ask me, not Brother Giovanni." She winks at my children, making Agnes giggle again, though Joanna only nods solemnly.

Lorenzo arrives dressed like a priest with a silver cross hanging from a chain around his neck and a book of hours in his hand. He will accompany us to the imagined abbey near Tuscany, where he will claim he is to become their spiritual leader and priest, taking the place of the old one who has gone to his reward.

"You must call Sir Lorenzo 'Father Lorenzo'" I tell my children, "if you speak to him at all." I pull the hood back over my head. "And now, *mes petites cheres,* it is time for us to begin our little game." I straighten my shoulders and raise my chin with a smile at Lorenzo.

"Now?" For the first time Joanna's voice betrays her tender years. "But it is supper-time, Mam—"

I look at her sternly.

"—Brother Giovanni. It will soon be dark. I do not want to be out in the night. Will there be soldiers?"

I bend down, my face even with hers and Agnes'. "It was very frightening the last time we went out in the night. And there may be soldiers on the streets again tonight. But we will try to avoid them, and even if they see us they will not bother with monks and a nun and children. You must be very brave and very quiet and do what we say at once, and we will be alright."

Joanna nods, her eyes huge. Three-year-old Agnes, taking her cue from her older sister, nods as well. I pick up little Clementia, not trusting her to be quiet in anyone else's arms, and take Joanna's hand while Margherita lifts up Agnes. We walk briskly to the abbey gate. The Mother Superior whispers a brief prayer over us as one of the sisters opens the gate quietly, looks out both ways, and opens it wider. Lorenzo leads us out of sanctuary into a damaged and dangerous city I barely recognize.

The mercenaries who fought for King Louis have been plundering the homes and businesses of Naples since they arrived. Bodies lie in the bloodied streets and the doors of shops and households rich and poor stand open as Louis' forces seek their fortunes. It is the way mercenaries are paid for taking a castle or city, but it is horrible to see the devastation. Yesterday the citizens rebelled, setting up blockades, killing a number of King Louis' soldiers and taking many of them prisoner. King Louis was forced to rein in his men and pay them with his own silver in order to stop the looting. Tonight the streets are quieter, and we can wait no longer.

We walk in the shadows of the buildings as we did before, wrapped in our guise of poverty, heading north. We are nearly out of the city when a rough German voice shouts "Halt!"

We keep walking, hoping he does not mean us, or that a second look at our modest attire will convince him it is not worth the effort to stop us.

"Halt!" the command comes again, this time two voices shouting.

Lorenzo stops, the rest of us huddling behind him. I hold Clementia close to me, whispering to her to stay quiet, and motion Joanna back behind my habit as three soldiers approach us.

"Where are you going?" the first one shouts in the harsh syllables of Germany.

Lorenzo spreads his hands as though he does not understands and answers them in Latin.

"Who are you?" one of the other mercenaries demands in strongly-accented Italian, his hand on the hilt of his sword as he peers into our faces.

I hold my breath. I want to pull the cowl further over my face but dare not draw attention to myself.

"Father Lorenzo," Lorenzo replies in Italian, clasping his hands piously and bending in a humble bow. He points to me. "Friar Giovanni."

"Where are you off to, then?"

"To the Abbey Santa Maria." Lorenzo points vaguely north. Clementia, feeling the tension in my body, begins to wail, setting off Agnes. Joanna peeks from behind my robe. "To take these orphans to be cared for," he adds, looking challengingly into the soldiers' faces.

"Give us your money and you may be on your way," the man who speaks Italian says, glaring uncomfortably at the crying children. "Do not tell me you have none, you will have some for your journey."

"We have already given it up." Lorenzo shows them two strings hanging from his belt, previously attached to a missing purse." It is all I can do not to gasp. What has become of my purse, which I gave him to pay for our journey?

"What about you?" The soldier turns to me. I shake my head, holding out empty hands.

"He is under a vow of poverty and silence," Lorenzo says. "Here, this is all we have." He reaches for the chain around his neck and pulls the silver cross from under his robe.

The man who ordered us to stop reaches out to grab it and waves us away in disgust.

"Go," Lorenzo murmurs, motioning us ahead of him as he bows once more to the soldiers. A woman's scream reaches us from a few streets away. The soldiers turn like hounds scenting a hart and run off seeking wealthier victims.

I cannot stop myself shaking as we hurry away. The children's wailing continues. "Shh-shh," I whisper to Clementia and Agnes in a voice that quivers. I need a moment to catch my breath and calm myself but Lorenzo keeps us moving. I pray ceaselessly under my breath, imploring Mother Mary to keep us safe. Perhaps she takes pity on me for we are not stopped again as we leave the city.

When Clementia, exhausted from crying, falls asleep Lorenzo plucks her from my arms without missing a step. The relief of no longer having her pressing against my swelling womb revives me temporarily, but is soon swallowed by the ache in my legs and the pain in my feet from shoes not designed for hours of walking.

The hills surrounding Naples make for slow and tiring walking uphill and down. It is so dark I cannot see my own hands by the time we reach the Via Appia, which will take us north to Tuscany where we will catch a galley to Provence. There are many days of travel ahead of us before that, however. An army can walk it in ten days, Lorenzo tells me, eight if they are pushed. I am exhausted already and we are barely out of Naples. It may take us a month, I think.

Margherita and I are stumbling with weariness before Lorenzo finally leads us off the road to a little copse of trees and lets us rest hidden among them.

"When we are far enough from Naples I will purchase a donkey and perhaps a cart. You will have to walk when we pass towns or villages, my Lady, to maintain your appearance as a poor friar, but we will travel faster with the children riding. And you can ride when we are on the empty road." He grins at my surprised expression. "I have your purse safely tied under my habit."

"If they had found it and exposed your lie—"

"They would have found the blade of my sword first, Duchess, and been sorry they had not let us go. But it was better to give them a silver cross and leave quietly, in case they had comrades nearby."

It seems I have barely fallen asleep when Lorenzo wakes us. The sky is already lightening and I hear in the distance the bells of a monastery ringing Lauds, calling its monks to their dawn prayers. He gives us each a hunk of bread and a piece of cheese. It is early for breaking our fast, but he tells me he does not want to stop again until midday. I brush off his apology; I know as well as he that we must put as much distance as possible between ourselves and Naples. I dip Clementia's bread in the goat's milk Lorenzo has also brought and let her suck on the sop and swallow pieces of the soggy bread. She cries for the breast but her wet nurse is far away in Naples. She is so small for such a difficult journey that it breaks my heart, but she would not fare well locked in a clammy dungeon, either, and I doubt King Louis would take pity on Charles' daughter. I pray for her and Agnes and Joanna and for Margherita and Lorenzo, so loyal in my time of need. My conscience compels me to pray as well for Charles' stewards, knights, vassals and servants, whose lives are surely in danger now for their association with us. When I raise my head Lorenzo is waiting with ill-disguised impatience, anxious for us to resume our journey.

The walk is more difficult today. Before the sun is half-way up the sky I am limping, and I notice Margherita is also. She is carrying Clementia who whines with fatigue and hunger. I ache to soothe my baby but there is nothing I can do. I have no milk in my breasts, nor can I put her to nap in her cradle, and though she might take some comfort in my arms, my abdomen still aches from her weight upon it yesterday. I cannot risk one child to soothe another.

Lorenzo is carrying Agnes. She peers over his shoulder to keep an eye on me as though afraid I might abandon her in his strange company. She is not accustomed to being carried by a man—Charles was not one to play with daughters—but neither Margherita nor I responded to her pleas of "up, up" and lifted arms. After running after us for a while she was willing to accept his offer to carry her. So would I, I think ruefully, trying to walk on the heels of my feet to ease the pain in my toes. Joanna, clutching my hand, drags behind me. She does not utter a word of complaint, which hurts me more than if she whined and wept. I look down at her pinched, pale little face and whisper encouragement and praise. She has barely the energy to smile back at me.

At midday we stop for water and another meal of bread and cheese. Clementia sucks eagerly at her milky bread and swallows every morsel. I give King Louis an ironic nod for holding off his invasion until Clementia is old enough to eat whole food.

A horse whinnies behind us. It is hidden from sight by a bend in the road, giving us time to scramble to our feet and pack away our bread and cheese. I scoop up Clementia and turn to the woods at the side of the road but Lorenzo touches my arm, staying me.

"We must look like people with nothing to hide," he murmurs, leading us onto the road in full view of whomever is coming.

I pull my cowl over my head, hiding my braids and casting my face in shadow, and follow behind him, forcing myself not to limp. My heart is pounding loudly enough to frighten birds away and the sweat that covers my skin under my robe is not from the heat of the sun. What if they are King Louis' soldiers, scouring the roads to find me? I hear them coming up behind us and dare not turn to look.

"A horse and wagon," Lorenzo murmurs.

Not soldiers, then. I let my breath out unevenly.

When the wagon is no more than a few feet behind us, Lorenzo turns and raises his right hand in the sign of the cross, conferring a blessing on the man as any priest might do.

"I thank you, Father," the driver says as he reins in his horse. He is dressed in a woolen tunic and hose, but they are clean and not too worn. A freedman or a merchant, perhaps. His face is young, no more than a decade older than I am, with an open expression and cheerful brown eyes.

"You are alone on the road," Lorenzo observes before the man can make the same comment about us. "Where are you going, my son?" I see his eyes glance over the wagon. It is carrying a dozen large wadmal bags and two barrels but there is room among them for Margherita and I and the children, and the seat is big enough for Lorenzo to sit beside the driver.

"Minturno, Father, across the Liris River."

"Your name, my good man?"

"Thomas, Father."

Lorenzo looks taken aback. He appears to recover quickly. "God will provide to those who place their trust in Him." He crosses himself reverently. "It is no accident we have met. We," he gestures around at us, "are going to the Abbey Santa Maria where I will take the place of the abbey priest, Father Thomas. Yes," he nods when the young man starts at hearing his name. "It is a sign. Father Thomas was a good man who reached a good age and has gone to his reward. God will reward you also, his namesake, for aiding us in our journey."

The poor man swallows, looking a little stunned to be a sign from God. Belatedly he realizes he has been asked to do something. "I...I am honored, Father, to give you a ride?" His voice rises, turning it into a question. Lorenzo waits. "I have a dinner packed..." He looks at us all, his eyes bulging a little. "It is yours, of course. I hope it will be enough."

"What God provides is always enough, friend Thomas," Lorenzo replies with a hint of reproach in his voice that makes Thomas flush.

"Of course, Father!" he says as Lorenzo places Agnes in the wagon.

He jumps down to lower the back plank and lift Joanna in while Lorenzo helps Margherita in. I climb in last and Thomas replaces the back plank while Lorenzo hoists himself up on the wagon seat, leaving room for Thomas beside him.

We leave Thomas at the market in Minturno where he intends to sell the sheep's wool in his wadmal sacks and the vegetables in his barrels. At an inn near the edge of the town Lorenzo buys a donkey and a cart and a hot dinner for us all at the inn's long table. He arranges for us to sleep in the stable.

The next morning before dawn we continue our journey. Margherita and I take turns riding in the cart with the children. It is eight more days of walking before we reach Tuscany.

The long trek gives me time to reflect on the delights and bitter disappointments of my five-year marriage to Charles. I mourn the older cousin I adored as a fourteen-year-old bride more than the coolly ambitious husband whose betrayals and counter-betrayals have led to our ruin. And yet, what person can be summed up so simply? We all gamble with the wheel of Fortune. What other choice have we? Those she smiles on are considered the brave and those she drags down are villains. My husband was murdered by a treacherous, black-hearted man more ambitious and cruel than Charles has ever been, and that man Fortune has rewarded with the crown of Naples. I know better than to imagine life will be fair, and it is in that knowledge that I mourn for Charles. And a little of my sorrow is for me. Will I ever again love a man as completely as I loved Charles of Durazzo when I was an innocent girl of fourteen?

In Tuscany we stay at an Abbey while Lorenzo arranges our passage on a galley going to Provence. He sells the donkey and cart to pay our fares, and buys Margherita and I linen kirtles and leather shoes and snoods for our hair. He himself stays in his priest's garb, inventing a new story of escorting two merchant's wives and their children to visit relatives in Provence.

Indeed I intend to do just that. My husband's uncle, Cardinal Talleyrand of Perigord, will surely want vengeance for his nephew's life, let alone the full return of our family holdings.

When the galley casts off, carrying me beyond Louis of Hungary's reach, I heave a sigh of relief. The boat rocks on the waves like a cradle, lulling me into the first good night's sleep I have had since I raced through the night from my husband's castle to the convent of Santa Croce.

Tomorrow I will tell my children their father is dead. They have been brave long enough; it is time for us to grieve together.

And it will not hurt our case if we all arrive weeping and distraught at the Cardinal's door.

Chapter 12

The Road to Avignon

Joanna 1 of Naples
March, 1348

He is alive!

His child kicks in jubilation. I stroke my hand across my womb, grinning, and open Louis' letter again. How often I have imagined him dead on the battlefield in Capua, or sinking on a storm-tossed boat into the sea, or lying black and bloated in an unmarked grave. But he is alive and he is here in Provence!

Louis writes that he received the note I sent before I fled Naples, that he and Niccolò Acciaiuoli escaped in a flimsy fishing boat, the only vessel they could procure, into a violent winter storm. Beaten by savage winds, drenched to the bones and barely alive they landed at Sienna and journeyed inland to Niccolò's family estate outside the locked gates of Florence. Their petitions to enter the city were denied, the Florentine elders too frightened of King Louis' army to admit his enemy, but Niccolò's cousin, the Bishop of Florence, came out to confer with them and together they all took a ship to Marseille.

I blush as Louis describes his joy at learning in Marseille that I am alive, and shake my head as he recounts his anger on hearing of the imprisonment of my Neapolitan entourage by the elders of Aix-en-Provence.

They have all settled for now with Cardinal Guy de Boulogne at his estate in Villeneuve-d'Avignon, who has promised us his support. I thrill at the thought of how close Louis is, just across the Rhone from Avignon. From there he promises he and Niccolò and the Bishop of Florence will add their voices to my suit for Pope Clement to grant me an audience.

I smile and call for wine, feeling my hope renewed. Niccolò Acciaiuoli, our Neapolitan banker, will serve as a reminder to Pope Clement of his financial affairs and holdings in Naples, which Louis of Hungary now has his greedy hands on. The Bishop of Florence will have weight with the Cardinals as well as with Clement, and I have been told the King of France, my uncle, having recently lost Calais and Crecy to the invading English army, has sent his ambassadors to sue the Pope to sanction my marriage to Louis of Taranto and support our efforts against Hungary, England's ally. King Philip's castle in Villeneuve-d'Avignon, across the Rhone from Avignon, is easily visible from the Papal Palace and currently occupied by my cousin the King's nephew, a constant reminder to the Pope of his ties with France.

Surely it is only a matter of time until all is restored to me. But I cannot feel that time is my friend. Every day I am here in exile my kingdom, my subjects, and my precious son, Charles Martel, are in Hungarian hands.

In the midst of this a second messenger arrives from Villeneuve-d'Avignon, this one from the powerful Cardinal Talleyrand of Perigord.

As he enters and bows before me I feel myself trembling. What terrible news might he tell me of the house of Durazzo? Have Charles and Maria taken my throne? Or has Louis of Hungary murdered them both to claim it? Could something have happened to my son? I wait in dread to hear what news this messenger brings.

"Your Majesty," he rises from his deep bow, "I am come to inform you your sister has arrived at the house of Cardinal Talleyrand. With her children," he adds as I stare at him speechless.

I feel a rush of relief. Maria, alive and well and here in Provence. I dared not tell her of my plan to escape nor offer to take her with me, but I would have blamed myself if she had died. "What of her husband, the Duke of Durazzo?"

He bows his head once more. "He is dead, Your Majesty. King Louis had him tried and executed for the murder of Prince Andrew."

I draw in my breath. How dared he? Only the Pope has the right to judge a member of the royal family. "And my other cousins?" I force myself to ask.

"He has imprisoned them, Your Majesty, and divided their holdings among his generals."

My cousin dead. For all the grief he gave me, I am saddened. Images of him come to me from my childhood. He was the oldest of my Neapolitan cousins, three years my senior, the leader in our youthful games. I remember my Grandfather sending him to war with Sicily, trying once more to regain our family's rightful title there, and my relief when Charles returned defeated but alive, as my father and grandfather had before him. He has betrayed me many times over and drawn my sister into his web of betrayal, but he was my royal cousin, my sister's husband, and Louis of Hungary's action was not a legal execution but an outrageous act of murder.

An act that will cost him, a part of me thinks. Pope Clement will not be able to overlook this for all Louis of Hungary's bribes and threats.

"The Duchess of Durazzo and her children are unharmed?"

"Yes, Your Majesty, and safe at the Cardinal's castle in Villeneuve-d'Avignon. As safe as anyone," he finishes glumly.

I have heard that the plague is now running wild in Avignon.

"Does Pope Clement know of the murder of my cousin, the Duke of Durazzo?"

"Cardinal Perigord has gone to speak to the Holy Father and the other cardinals in person, at the same time as I was dispatched with this message for you." He holds out a letter.

"I will have a response for you before you leave." I accept the letter and send him to the kitchen for wine and food, tearing open the seal as soon as he has left the room.

It is from Maria, recounting her narrow escape and terrible journey, as well as the pillage of Naples and death of so many of my citizens, including her husband. I am sick at heart upon reading it.

The next day I receive a missive from Pope Clement inviting me, with all due ceremony, to come to Avignon.

The plague has been raging in Avignon since January. I have been told that nearly a quarter of the citizens have died already and each day more people die than died the day before. The church graveyards were filled weeks ago; Clement purchased and consecrated a field near the city and now it, too, has been filled. The bodies must be disposed of quickly for the very sight of them infects others with illness, terror, and spiritual doubt. Thus does this vile plague destroy not only people's bodies, but their minds and souls as well. In desperation the Holy Father has sanctified the Rhone itself as a funeral grounds.

Nor is the plague all that I have to fear in Avignon. It has been visited on us as retribution for the sinfulness of the world. Pope Clement himself has said so in his sermons, and now a plague of blame-finding has settled over the land. I will attract that blame as a flower attracts wasps, all the more so when I submit myself to trial for complicity in the murder of my husband.

My maid, Eleonore, has become staunchly loyal to me since we prayed together for her family and everyone afflicted by this terrible plague.

"Nowhere is safe, Countess," she responds sadly when I ask if she would rather stay behind when I go to Avignon.

"I may not be able to…continue affording you my protection there," I say.

She looks at me quietly, waiting. I am not accustomed to explaining myself, but there is such trust in her large dark eyes and I have had no one to talk to for so long. "I will have to stand trial for the death of my husband," I say, bitter and humiliated to admit it.

"No one can imagine you would be involved in such a crime. In any crime at all," she says loyally, then adds a more worldly observation: "The Angevins have supported the Avignon popes for generations."

"King Louis' advocates are very persuasive." I cannot ignore the fact that Clement, stung by King Louis' accusations that he would not punish guilty royals, charged his legate, Cardinal Bertrand de Deux, to convict me if he found any evidence of my guilt. Fortunately the good Cardinal recognized my innocence and defended me, but he is not here to speak for me now. "By finding me guilty Clement will appease the anger of Hungary and deflect the blame for this plague from himself," I tell Eleonore.

"Do not go, Countess." She seizes my hand impulsively.

Her love warms me. Nevertheless I raise an eyebrow causing her to drop my hand quickly. "I have no choice," I tell her gently. "There is only one path forward for me, and it lies through Avignon." Only the Pope can proclaim my innocence, legitimize my marriage, and lend my cause the moral support I need to raise an army to reclaim my kingdom. But will he?

"Then I will go with you, Countess."

She accompanies me once more to the chapel and kneels beside me, praying no doubt for our safe deliverance from the plague and the pope equally.

I bow my head and pray for strength, courage, and protection when I ride into Avignon. I pray as well for humility. Louis of Hungary would never submit himself to the judgement of the Pope and the Sacred College of cardinals. Few monarchs would. The authority of a legitimate monarch is as great as that of the pope in all but spiritual matters. But I am without power or authority now; I need guidance. It comes to me in the words of the Psalmist: *Yea though I walk through the valley of the shadow of death I will fear no evil for thou art with me.*

I have been legitimately anointed by birth and by God to rule the Kingdom of Naples. Doubt and fear are beneath me. I rise from my knees and go at once to authorize the arrangements for my procession to Avignon.

If it is God's will that I fail, then I will fail. But it will not be *my* will that fails.

On March 15th I prepare to set out for Avignon. *The Ides of March,* I think wryly, remembering Caesar who went to his death this day. But I am not going to my death; I am going to my resurrection, for I am determined that it will begin this day.

My ladies dress me in my royal purple kirtle of silk brocade adorned with gold thread and jewels. They braid up my hair under my veil and place my crown upon it, before covering my dress with a purple velvet cloak, trimmed in ermine and embroidered in gold thread with a recurring design of fleur-de-lis. Even my shoes are purple, their elongated pointed toes peeking out below my robe.

I ride upon a pure white mare with golden bridle and stirrups and under her saddle a cloth of purple silk also embroidered with gold fleur-se-lis. Two men walk on either side of me holding over my head a canopy of purple silk with a fringe of gold.

After me ride my ladies-in-waiting, some who followed me from Marseille and others who joined my court in Aix-en-Provence. They are dressed in their finest silks and velvet cloaks, wearing stylish headdresses embellished with braided coils of false hair made from yellow silk.

And behind them ride our escort of thirty armed knights on horseback, their chain mail polished until the sun glinting off it hurts the eyes. They hold their lances in one hand and in the other carry bright pennants emblazoned with their ancestral coats-of-arms.

As we draw near to Avignon, the wind brings us first a whiff and then the increasing stench of death and decay. It vies with the warm sunlight and the life-affirming colors of my entourage. The church bells ring the endless lament I have become accustomed to. Catching a glimpse of the Rhone I notice large white blobs floating in its water.

Ahead I see the guards leading my procession glancing at the river, their faces transformed by fear. When I am close enough to see more clearly I realize with horror the white objects I saw are corpses, sewn into their tightly-wound shrouds, floating on the river's current. They drift alongside the road forming a macabre parade, a second procession running parallel to mine. It is a fearsome and ominous greeting.

As the road winds closer to the river the stench becomes overpowering. Eleonore's eyes stream. Beside her, two of my other ladies are gagging. One of the younger guards leans sideways over his horse and vomits onto the road. His horse skitters, spooking the other horses, their wide eyes rolling with fear behind their blinkers. I shiver, suddenly cold despite the hot sun. Is this a portent? Has Death himself come to greet me on the road to Avignon, attended by these white shrouded ghosts? If we continue, will any of us ever ride out again from Avignon?

Surely we are riding through the valley of the shadow of death. I grit my teeth so hard they hurt to keep my face expressionless, clench my throat and stomach against the urge to be ill. Any sign of fear, any hesitancy at all from me and my entire retinue will turn and flee.

I ignore it all: the death tolls, the foul smell, the river of corpses, and hold my crowned head high, eyes straight ahead, under my purple canopy. We ride forward silently, white-faced ghosts on our nervous mounts, barely breathing, until ahead we see a living delegation come to greet us.

A group of church and government officials, including the eighteen cardinals of the Sacred College dressed in their scarlet hats and robes, waits to welcome us at the gates of Avignon. They join our retinue, together forming a flamboyant parade of color as they escort us through the narrow streets. Townspeople line our route, come out to gape at the glorious spectacle of the Queen of Naples and her entourage. Some glower at me as at a notorious murderess, some shake their fists at the sinner they hold responsible for their misfortune, but most are caught up in the grandeur of royalty and cheer until their throats are raw, waving their kerchiefs and even weeping with joy, as though our vibrant pageantry might ward off the grayness of death. Children run along beside us, calling out, until they are pulled back into the crowd by anxious relatives. The balconies above us are decorated with garlands of flowers, their railings draped with rich tapestries, as the nobility of Avignon, dressed in their most elaborate attire, cram out of their upper stories to watch me pass.

I am no longer competing with the plague. I have beaten it back with my royal presence. I raise my face to the sun as though I am even now receiving God's blessing and the people of Avignon call out their love and make the sign of the cross as I pass. Let them remember this moment when I stand on trial for a crime I did not commit. Let the cardinals remember their people blessing me when they presume to judge the anointed of God. Let them consider King Louis' mercenaries sacking my city and murdering my citizens and compare his foul invasion of Naples to my joyous and blessed procession through Avignon. Let them consider who brought death with him and who brought life with her when they hold my life or death in their hands.

We stop at the grand courtyard in front of the Papal Palace. I sit still and silent staring at it before I catch myself and replace my expression of awe with a more regal bearing. I have never seen anything so huge, in height as well as circumference. Its stone walls dwarf other castles, its vaulted ceilings arch upwards like a soul straining toward heaven, its towers and spires soar into the sky.

When I dismount I am offered the traditional refreshment of wine and a pastry. Then the cardinals lead me into the enormous hall of the consistory where kings and ambassadors are received by the pope and monumental decisions are made: the canonization of saints, the proclamations of new cardinals into the Sacred College. I am accustomed to cathedrals and royal palaces, yet the beauty and significance of this room gives me pause. Heavy wooden beams traverse the ceiling as though to remind us of the cross Christ died upon, and along the full length of one wall are life-sized frescoes showing in stages the life of John the Baptist, he who prepared the way for Christ. This is a room in which lives change.

As mine, too, will change soon enough. Today, however, I am here to be received with all the pomp and ceremony of a visiting monarch. Visiting, yet not a visitor. This is my city, as I have just dramatically demonstrated; the Pope and all his cardinals are my guests here.

At the far end of the great hall is a double dais. On the top tier are two thrones draped with velvet and gold. On one sits Pope Clement, magnificent in his tiara and white robes, waiting to receive me. On the lower tier of the dais the eighteen cardinals seat themselves in an open semicircle around the sides of the two thrones.

The hall is filled with regents, princes, and ambassadors from every known kingdom—every nobleman who could wrangle an invitation has come to see the notorious Queen Joanna of Naples. They will be even more eager to attend my trial.

I offer an aloof, imperial smile to them all. Without a breath's pause I walk down the hall toward the Pope, my mantle held by two pages, as regal as though this hall as well as this city belonged to me. An appreciative smile plays upon Clement's face at my composure and my beauty—it is well-known that he is an admirer of beautiful women. I give him time to enjoy my face and figure, the gracefulness of my movements; time to note the royal purple of my robes and the crown of Naples sitting where it belongs upon the head of its rightful queen. I step up onto the tier the cardinals are seated upon and kneel on a white silk cushion to kiss the gold cross embroidered on the Pope's slipper. He raises me up and kisses me formally on the mouth, and then I take one more step up onto the highest tier to sit on the throne beside his.

We talk of nothing important during this most important meeting, exchanging the exaggerated compliments and surface conversation of diplomacy, in which I am well-versed having been raised to it. I watch his face and the faces of the cardinals as I am sure they watch mine. We are all well-practiced in the art of saying and showing little while speaking at length. Even so I learn a great deal from the glance of an eye, the effusiveness in a compliment, the tap of a foot, the occasional smile that is too wide or not quite wide enough. The way they react to each other tells me more than the way they respond to me, and I note, too, the way some look to Clement, and the way some do not.

I am aware of every word I utter, every smile I give, every modest lowering of my eyes and confident raising of my chin, every graceful movement of my hand. These nineteen men will be the judges at my inquest. No word I utter, no glance or movement I make is insignificant. In this hour they will decide whether they hope to find me innocent or guilty, and I am determined to fashion that hope to my advantage.

The reception is short, but I am satisfied with what I have learned and what I have conveyed to them. I am content to have it over so I may lead my ladies and knights to the chateau where I will stay until my own palace in Avignon can be completed and made ready for me.

At the chateau my ladies-in-waiting remove my velvet and ermine cloak, my crown and jewels and my silk brocade gown sown with gold thread. I have Eleonore of Marseille take them to be locked up while the others help me into my night clothes and let down my braids and comb out my hair. I allow myself to relax at last as my maids chatter quietly of the exciting procession through the city and the magnificence of the Pope's palace. None of them mention the river of corpses.

Eleonore returns with the light dinner I have ordered, cheese and olives and figs with mulled wine. She stays to serve me when the others leave, murmuring only, "Did it go well, Countess?"

I smile wearily at her, the only one who realizes today's importance. "I believe so, Eleonore," I answer. She nods and says nothing more, her presence enough, until I have eaten and she helps me into bed.

Finally I am alone in my bed, a single lamp burning, the scented oil sweet in the dark room. I go over the day, remembering the stink of the corpses, the celestial beauty of the Papal Palace, and the cold vast cavern of the hall in which I must submit myself to judgement under the zealous eyes of John the Baptist. I consider all I have learned today about the eighteen cardinals who will be my judges and what I must do to convince them of my righteousness. My husband and my advisor, Niccolò Acciaiuoli, and perhaps his cousin the Bishop of Florence, will join me soon. I close my eyes and allow myself to sleep.

Chapter 13

News From Naples

Joanna 1 of Naples
March, 1348

"Good!" Louis leaps up from his chair, his face dark with rage. "He deserved to die! He was a traitor. He betrayed me!"

"He betrayed *me*," I remind him sharply. Charles swore his allegiance to me, his queen, not to Louis of Taranto.

My husband paces the small room off my chambers that I have made into a privy council chamber. His eyes are wild, distraught. I imagine that moment as he waited on the battle field when he learned his cousin Charles of Durazzo and brother Robert of Taranto would not be coming. That they had departed with all their vassals, over two thirds of his army, leaving him to face the massive Hungarian force with his remaining supporters and a band of hired mercenaries. And half of those had friends among the mercenaries hired by Louis of Hungary. One look at the size of the enemy and his mercenaries would go over to the other side as well. He had stared death in the face at that moment, with no choice but to run. A terrible choice for a proud man. He would never forgive them for making him run from a fight.

"Charles might be alive today had he not retreated before the battle was even engaged," I tell him. "And your brother Robert would not be imprisoned." *And my kingdom would not lie at the mercy of a conqueror,* I finish under my breath. Oh, I am easily as furious as he, if that were of any use to us now. "They have paid for their cowardice and treachery." I take a calming breath. "Yet despite his deceit, Charles was our cousin. The blood of kings flowed in his veins as it does in ours. Louis of Hungary had no right to judge and execute him, nor to imprison your brothers and Charles' brothers."

"They betrayed me, all of them." His voice is low, tight.

"And we will not trust any of them again. But our real enemy is Louis of Hungary. It is his actions we must put in doubt if I am to regain my kingdom."

Niccolò Acciaiuoli gives me a sympathetic glance. No doubt he has heard my husband rant on this topic already, and he understands how much is at stake. My reputation, my kingdom, and my head will all be forfeit if the Sacred College finds me guilty of Andrew's murder in two days' time. King Louis has already sent a small army of ambassadors and lawyers armed with false proof and clever arguments and more gold than I could ever hope to raise. He will stop at nothing to convince Clement to find me guilty and execute me, and name him King of Naples.

Louis sits down again, leaning his elbows heavily on my council table. "Niccolò is right," he says. "We will deal with our devious kin later."

"That is wise, my Lord," Niccolò says smoothly with a second quick glance at me.

I let it go. Louis loves me, as I love him, but he is too proud a man to accept counsel from a woman. I lean back in my chair at the head of the table and let Niccolò talk for me.

"I will accompany the queen to the inquest and speak on her behalf. We must not only convince the Sacred College of her innocence in Andrew's murder, but also cast doubt and suspicion upon her accuser, Louis of Hungary. We must make sure no one wants to see him become King of Naples."

Louis snorts. "He is a usurper. If Clement supports his claim no monarch in all of Christendom will trust the judgement of the Holy See. Any man with an army may take their crown and have his claim validated as easily."

"That is true, Prince Louis," Niccolò agrees. "But first Queen Joanna must be acquitted of any wrongdoing and have her right to the throne of Naples upheld."

I blink. When did Niccolò begin calling Louis 'prince'? I have promised that he will be crowned king beside me when all this has been settled and our marriage legitimized, but he is not a prince for all his royal blood. He is not in direct line to the throne.

Niccolò smiles at me. I return his gaze coolly. I do not mind when he manages my husband—hot-headed Louis needs managing at times—but I do not care to have my financier attempt to manage me.

He turns to Louis giving no sign of my reproof although I know he has registered it and will take more care in future. "You should not speak ill of your relatives in captivity, my Lord. Rather be aggrieved on their behalf. What right has King Louis to throw them in a dungeon and steal your and their ancestral titles and holdings? Even the Duke of Durazzo, your brother-in-law, you must defend. His death was murder, not justice. I will have my cousin the Bishop of Florence speak in this vein to the cardinals."

Louis looks at his empty hands lying on the table in front of him. He clenches them into fists so tight his knuckles whiten, then opens them again stiffly and clasps his hands together. He gives a curt, angry nod.

"And speaking of cardinals," Niccolò continues, "we have a powerful one on our side: Cardinal Talleyrand of Perigord, the Duke of Durazzo's uncle. Already he has all the French cardinals sympathetic to us after the terrible ordeal his nephew's wife and children have been through." He leaves Louis to chew on that like a man struggling to swallow a piece of gristle.

Louis' jaw clenches, but he finally acknowledges the value of Niccolò's advice with another reluctant nod.

"I have sent word to my sister, inviting her to dine with us tonight," I say, my tone conciliatory. "I—we—need to hear what she witnessed of King Louis' actions in Naples." I am desperate to hear what has happened to my kingdom. Maria's news will be nearly two weeks old, but I pray it will not be as bad as what I have been imagining ever since I made my own escape.

"Your Majesty." Maria curtsies low before me. I expected contrition, shame on behalf of her husband's actions, but I am unprepared for the gaunt, lined face before me. She is thin as a pauper and trembles in her curtsy as though her legs can barely support her. I step forward impulsively, take hold of her hands and raise her into my embrace.

"Maria," I whisper, kissing her. "Thank God you are alive." I hold her away from me and look at her, and she at me. Our eyes are moist.

Behind her, her man bows. "Your Majesty," he says formally, then turns to my husband, bowing again, "Lord Louis."

Maria lets go of me. "My husband's knight, Sir Lorenzo," she says. "He brought us out of Naples."

"I am indebted to you," I say, motioning to a servant to set another place.

Louis extends his arm to take me in to dinner. There is only the smallest hesitation, then Niccolò steps up and holds out his arm for Maria, and we go in, six of us to sit at a table that holds twenty in a room meant for two hundred.

Maria, despite her exhausted appearance, is dressed in a stylish new mi-parti gown, the left side and sleeve a white silk with a pattern of pale blue threads running through it, the right side and sleeve a deep blue. It is generously cut over her expanding belly—once again we are pregnant together. While we eat, Maria tells us of her flight north disguised as a friar charged with taking three orphaned children to an abbey. She tells it as though it were a gay adventure, and only the occasional strain in her eyes and the mirthless face of Sir Lorenzo beside her bears witness to the hardship and terror she must have endured.

I tell her of my midnight flight onto the waiting galleys, of lashing ourselves to the ship in the storm while the sailors prayed and cursed as they worked the sails to keep us from drowning. Louis and Niccolò tell us of riding out the same storm alone in a flimsy fishing boat. We all speak lightly, as if our desperate escapes were a summer's outing, the way we might reminisce about lounging on barges in our youth, singing as we boated along the shoreline looking for a pretty spot to make our picnic.

Not one of us mentions the plague. My windows are all shuttered, as they have been since I came here, to keep out the foul air which might carry the disease to us. The room is lit with oil lamps which I burn day and night for light. I have had to cut back, for good olive oil is expensive and I will not have the smell of cheaper oil permeate my rooms, so the few I have lit cast shadows everywhere. I have used all the coins I brought and sold nearly half of my jewels to pay my household expenses and I do not know how much longer I will be here. Pray God, not long. I am so tired of being shut in, of not seeing the sun or the sky or riding out into the city. No one goes out except when they must. I am sure everyone at my table feels the same but none of us talks of it.

The plague is too horrible to bear thinking of, let alone to insert into table conversation. The sheer numbers of the dead are beyond imagining, the speed with which it kills terrifying. Any one of us might rise from this table healthy and sated, only to fall into agony and die before the sun rises tomorrow. Death sits beside each one of us, a gruesome companion that we push aside with every gay word or story we recount, with every forced trill of laughter or unconcerned expression we summon up to cover our fear.

When the servants have cleared away our meat and brought us cheese and fruit and nuts to end our meal, I turn to Maria. "Tell me about Naples," I say. The smile leaves her face.

Silent moments pass while she sits pale and quiet, trapped in her memories. I think she will not answer but then in a low and husky voice, she begins. "King Louis' soldiers roamed the streets, slaughtering anyone they found associated with the houses of Taranto and Durazzo, even the servants. Thank God I had been warned in time to flee to Santa Croce. They treated the citizens just as brutally, raping the women and stealing everything they saw and wanted." She closes her eyes as though to dispel the memories these words recall. Then she breathes in deeply and opens her eyes again. Making no apology for her temporary faintness she continues, a half-smile now easing her face.

"After five days the citizens elected eight leaders who organized them into a militia. They dug up the streets and made blockades forcing the mercenaries back and pelting them with rocks through windows and doorways and from balconies, killing many and taking those who surrendered prisoner. The rest retreated. And thus they forced King Louis to agree to end the looting and pay his soldiers out of his own silver.

"I was in hiding all this while at Santa Croce. My husband's chamberlain told the nobles who came to our castle that I and my children had been dragged into the streets and killed. There were so many bodies that night it was impossible to tell if he was lying, and he escaped before they could torture the truth out of him."

Her smile fades. "Others were not so lucky. Louis sent his soldiers scouring the city to find anyone he could implicate in the death of his brother. Many people were taken for interrogation and few returned without at least the loss of their nose or a hand. Noblemen even of the highest order were tortured and threatened with death unless they put forward the name of someone from their own family as a collaborator. Fathers handed over their sons and sons their brothers, uncles named nephews, cousins betrayed—" she stops and flushes. I overlook her deserved shame over her husband's behavior and signal a server to refill her wine cup, then wait impatiently as she drinks.

"It was only a matter of time before they searched the abbeys. The monasteries had already been raided and those in sanctuary dragged out and thrown into dungeons. On the sixth day, after the citizens fought back and King Louis stopped the general looting, Sir Lorenzo and the Abbess arranged my escape."

"On the day I was to leave, my husband's chamberlain came to me a second time, to warn me to leave. He told me all that I have told you. Some of it I had already heard, and worse. King Louis has had a wheel devised, with sharpened blades affixed to it. The condemned man is tied upon it so that as it turns the blades tear him to pieces. His torment can last from third mass until well past vespers, and all the while his screams are heard throughout Naples." She shivers and takes a gulp of wine.

"I am so glad you escaped, sister." My voice shakes. What if I had lost her? I reach down the table and grasp her hand. She clasps mine tightly back, as she did when we were children, orphaned so young and sent to our grandfather's castle to be raised as his heirs. What would I do without her, this sister who causes me so much grief and yet whom I love so unfailingly? As she does me.

After a moment I loosen my hold, but before I can withdraw my hand she clasps it in both of hers. "Sister," she says in an odd, uncertain voice. I wait uneasily for her next words.

"I escaped with nothing." She looks down at the table, not

meeting my eyes.

I suppress a shiver. No moment is too tender for Maria to use to her advantage. It is an unkind thought and I dismiss it as unworthy. I try to ease my hand from hers but she grasps it tighter.

"You are fortunate in the kindness of your uncle," I tell her. The Cardinal Talleyrand of Perigord is a very wealthy man with much family feeling. I have no doubt she wants for nothing.

"I must have my own money. I am a royal princess of Naples. How can I hold up my head, living on the charity of my husband's uncle? While you live here extravagantly on the wealth of our kingdom?"

I frown. She does not know how desperate my situation is. Misreading my frown she hurries on, her voice nervous and quick. She has practiced this speech. Did she only come tonight to ask me for money?

"You have never given me my dowry. I must have at least a portion of it now to live on. It is mine by rights."

"Maria—"

"Princess Maria," Niccolò interrupts me before I can tell my sister of my own present deprivation. "You do your uncle a disservice. Only yesterday my cousin, the Bishop of Florence, was speaking to Cardinal Talleyrand. He told my cousin how pleased he is to have you staying with him, how fortunate he feels to be able to honor his deceased nephew by helping you and your children at this difficult time."

Maria looks from him to me. But I have been reminded of the importance of keeping up appearances. I cannot afford to look defeated. If Pope Clement thinks I am beaten, with no chance of regaining my kingdom, he will surely side with Louis of Hungary and find me guilty. I cannot trust Maria not to tell Cardinal Talleyrand anything she learns tonight, and Cardinal Talleyrand has the ear of the Pope.

"Do you dare come to me for money, Maria?" I ask coolly, withdrawing my hand from hers. "You demand your dowry after your husband betrayed his Queen and opened my kingdom to our enemy? You should be glad I am not the kind of monarch who destroys traitors."

She looks as though I have slapped her. I feel a brief regret until her expression hardens. It is only a moment, and then the smooth mien of a courtier, which we have both learned from childhood, hides her feelings once more. "There is something more I have to tell you, Your Majesty," she says.

Down the table from her, Lorenzo clears his throat. Maria starts as though recalling herself, and looks away.

What has she to tell me that she cannot bear to see my face when she says it? I straighten, leaning away from her again. What new betrayal does she have to confess?

She licks her lips and pinches the white linen table cloth. We are all waiting, silent, except Sir Lorenzo who looks aside when I glance his way, and has put down the piece of fruit and cheese he was nibbling at.

"Tell me, Maria." My throat is tight around the words.

"I do not wish to cause you pain, sister." Despite the anger still etched in her tense posture, she bites her lower lip as though genuinely distressed.

"Charles Martel!" I gasp. *No,* I think, *it cannot be. He is Andrew's son, King Louis would never harm him!*

Her eyes flick up to my face and away again. "He is alive," she says quickly. "Unharmed." And then in a lower voice, "as far as I know."

"What is it? Tell me! What have they done to him?" I cry in a panic. *I should never have left him! I should have stayed and let them murder me, if that would have kept him safe. Oh, Charles Martel! Oh, my son!*

"Tell us your news!" my husband orders roughly. "And tell us how you know of it!"

"They have sent him to Hungary. Along with our cousins, prisoners of King Louis. Not that Charles Martel is a prisoner. I am sure they are taking great care of his safety," Maria adds quickly. She looks at my husband. "I only know by messenger, the day before we left, but I have no doubt of its truth."

"It is true," Lorenzo says, his deep voice regretful. "I heard it also from a palace servant at the market. She was complaining of having been busy all the morning packing up Charles Martel's clothes and supervising the smoking of meat and preparing other foods for the journey to Hungary."

He is unharmed, I think, momentarily weak with relief. And then, *the journey! He is too young to make such a journey. And in winter!* They will have to cross the mountains, riding over snow and through storms. Charles Martel has never known cold weather. He cannot possibly survive such a journey!

And then, overriding every other sensation, I am gripped with a terrible fury. My son is the heir to the Kingdom of Naples. They have taken him away from his birthright, from the kingdom that is rightfully his. Taken my son to turn him into a brutal, uneducated Hungarian. More to their point, they have taken him far away so he will not be in King Louis' way when he demands my throne for himself.

I stand up abruptly, barely hearing my chair crash to the ground behind me for the roaring in my ears. I grip the edge of the twenty-foot table, wanting to throw it over onto its side, so full of rage I am certain I could do so. I struggle for control.

"Excuse me," I say in a voice that sounds like no one I know. Louis starts to rise. I stay him with a flick of my hand, never looking at him. Without a glance at anyone I walk rigidly out of the room.

Chapter 14

Judgement

Joanna 1 of Naples
March, 1348

Oh that God would put Louis of Hungary helpless before me and a sword in my hand!

No, too quick. I have seen far worse deaths which I would like to exact upon the monster who has dared to steal my child away and put his life at risk. I have been raised to be womanly but all that has been swept aside in a blind rage to defend my son. He is a baby, not yet three years old! If I had ever thought they would take him away—

I cannot breathe. I was not raised to kill with my own hands, however much they may clench themselves into fists when I think of Charles Martel shivering in the mountain passes and crying for me. I was not raised to fight but I *was* raised to be ruthless when necessary, and ruthless I will be when I return to my kingdom and wrest it back from this vicious usurper who has dared send my heir away from his kingdom.

Anger focuses me. Outrage sharpens my wit, preparing me for the combat through which I will win back my throne: the inquest Louis of Hungary has forced upon me by his slander and spite. I will not allow myself to wallow in grief or fear for my son nor blame myself for leaving him behind. I did what had to be done and now once again I will do what has to be done. And then, when I have regained my righteous name and secured my royal titles and my son's, then I will demand Charles Martel be returned to the kingdom he was born to rule.

I spend hours with Niccolò Acciaiuoli going over the points we will make when I stand before Pope Clement and the cardinals. We discuss the accusations King Louis has made against me and how best to refute them. Indeed I am as well-versed in the law as he, for I am the granddaughter of Robert the Wise who reformed and codified the law in the Kingdom of Naples above any in the world, winning him the respect and admiration of every scholar in Europe. I grew up studying his laws and listening to his lengthy Latin orations on them and other weighty subjects.

Niccolò will accompany me as my lawyer and financier, and Louis, strong and proven in battle, will stand as my champion. They are visible proof of the wisdom, wealth, and force of arms that I have at my command to regain my kingdom and rule it well. But I have also requested, and been granted, the right to speak on my own behalf. I can best represent my own innocence of wrongdoing, for truth is *my* sword, and I would be no fit sovereign if I did not know how to wield the weapon of oratory.

On the appointed day I choose my wardrobe carefully: my primary robe of state, with golden fleur-de-lis on its bright blue background. The French flowers proclaim my royal blood, the blue proclaims my purity. A white headdress, in mourning for my butchered cousin Charles and my captive people, is pinned over my braided hair. Stylish but simple enough to handsomely accommodate my crown, which I place over it.

I ride my white mare to my trial. Louis rides a white stallion on my left, nearest my heart. He wears dark blue velvet the color of the evening sky in summer before night falls, with a jaunty blue feather on his cap, his yellow hair blowing in the light breeze, his head high—still the handsomest man I have ever known. On my right is Niccolò, riding a horse as black as his hair, wearing a green tunic as dark and mysterious as the workings of his clever mind.

Behind us ride a dozen knights carrying pennants decorated with the coat-of-arms of the House of Anjou, the coat-of-arms of the Duchy of Provence, and the coat-of-arms of Avignon. My pennants, for I am Anjou and Provence and Avignon. Their horses are draped in blue cloth with a row of gold fleur-de-lis embroidered on the edges, to match my royal surcote.

At the gate into the Palace of the Pope our escort waits as I, Louis, and Niccolò dismount, before they leave us. Flanked by my two champions I march in behind Cardinal Talleyrand of Perigord, who has come to precede us into the great hall. A good sign, for he is on our side and not afraid to let it be known. I have heard he is so enraged by his nephew's murder he has ordered the Hungarian ambassadors never to appear in the same room as him. I walk in stately measure down the entire length of the great hall toward the dais on which Pope Clement and his cardinals are seated, led by Cardinal Perigord. Among the throng of princes, ambassadors, and nobles on either side of the room, not a single one is wearing the colors and emblem of Hungary. My cousin Charles of Durazzo is serving me better in death than he ever did in life.

This is the Great Audience Hall, in which papal laws and judgements are made; a hall so large it requires pillars to hold aloft the multi-vaulted ceiling above it, a visual reminder that the weight of all Christendom rests upon the decisions made here. Its size intimidates me though I give no sign of that. The ceiling is painted a rich deep blue flung with golden stars, like the vault of heaven. Twenty figures of prophets of the Old Testament stare down on me from the ceiling as I walk, each one bearing a parchment on which is written edicts from their Book. On the north wall is a fresco of the

Last Judgment, peopled with the faces of popes, cardinals, and bishops. Between the two east windows is a painting of the crucifixion of Christ, a judgement on us all. I notice these things without appearing to look, my head held high and straight as I make my stately walk down the length of the great hall. I will not be intimidated, though very fresco I pass is meant to remind those who enter here that they face the judgement of the Pope and the Sacred College of Cardinals.

Cardinal Perigord takes his seat in the semi-circle of velvet-covered chairs to either side of the dais on which the pope sits. There is no second throne beside Clement's today. I am here to be judged, not honored. Yet my royalty cannot be ignored. Three chairs, no less ornate than those of the cardinals, have been placed on the floor facing the Pope and the Sacred College.

I kneel on the white silk pillow and once again kiss the cross on the Holy Father's slipper. He motions me up and addressing me as his daughter in Christ gestures for me to be seated. My husband performs the same obeisance and after him Niccolò Acciaiuoli.

When we are seated, the charges against me are read in Latin, the language of the papal court. I recognize behind the accusations and arguments the voice of King Louis of Hungary and his mother, Elizabeth, the Dowager Queen. I have heard these base allegations before, but I listen closely, trying to hear how they might sound to the ears of those who do not know me, who were not in Naples before and at the time of Andrew's murder. I must not only refute these charges but speak so compellingly that all suspicion is lifted from me, now and throughout my reign.

I am accused of being estranged from my husband, of publicly scorning him and of encouraging my barons and lords to thwart his rule, disregard his commands, and scorn him as I did. Of showing little remorse at his death and no evidence of haste to investigate it or eagerness to bring to justice the perpetrators of the heinous crime.

Finally, I am accused of marrying without dispensation from the Pope a man who rumor claims was already my lover. My marriage is therefore a direct breach of papal law.

I am surprised when the recitation ends. So many vile rumors have been spread about me by my Hungarian relations that I can hardly credit their self-control in stopping here. I have heard it whispered that I lay with all my courtiers, that I operated a brothel, that I am as wanton as the whore of Babylon. I had steeled myself to hear all the disgusting things my Hungarian relatives can conceive of laid at my feet. No doubt their lawyers restrained their imaginations here. Adding in the more lurid speculations would only cast doubt on all. Or perhaps it was Clement, not wanting his scarlet-clad celibates' minds sullied by depraved fantasies. Even so, the case against me is grave, all the more so because there is enough truth behind each of these allegations to give them some credibility.

My husband, Louis of Taranto, rises to speak first. He is of royal blood as am I, both of us direct descendants of Louis VIII of France, and both our mothers sisters of Philip VI, the present King of France. My husband speaks heatedly of my virtue and godliness and cries "For shame!" that I should be called to defend it by villains. He vows there were no unseemly relations between us before our marriage, which was not conducted in secret or dishonor, but was performed and witnessed by the Pope's legate in Naples, Cardinal Bertrand de Deux.

"As concerns the charge that we were married without the proper dispensations, the very man who raises this accusation against us," he glares around the room as though to challenge the Hungarian sympathizers, "is the man who forced that action upon us! King Louis' invasion of my dear Queen's kingdom forced a war upon her, one she neither wanted nor sought, but one she *must* fight, and must do so without a husband and champion. Holy Father, honored Cardinals, *look* at this woman who sits before you. Is she made to lead an army? Can she don mail and spurs and lead men into battle to save her realm?" He pauses to let them look at me, sitting before them pale and slim and feminine, my eyes modestly downcast. "What resort had she but to seek a husband who could raise an army and command it for her, and quickly? Your peer and fellow cardinal, Cardinal Bertrand de Deux, was there at that time, and saw the need and acted on the Holy Father's behalf as his legate should do, to give this beleaguered woman a champion by marriage in her most dire need. Cardinal de Deux would say as much to you today if he were not still trapped in Naples, witnessing the terrible crimes being perpetrated by the same invader who dares charge my virtuous wife and queen with improper behavior!"

He stops, seemingly struggling to control his outrage on my behalf, then concludes, "Furthermore, we have come as soon as we were able, to subject ourselves to Your Holiness and request the necessary papal dispensation for our marriage." He bows reverently to Pope Clement, extends his bow to all the cardinals, and at their leave sits down again.

My heart is full. No man has ever defended me so passionately before. I would throw myself weeping with gratitude into his arms, but I am still on trial for my life and the worst charges have not yet been addressed. I rise, bow low before the Holy Father and his Sacred College, and thank them for allowing me to speak on my own behalf concerning the charges laid against me.

I defend myself as a virtuous and obedient wife in a clear, strong voice, standing with my back straight, holding my crowned head high. I deny publicly scorning Andrew or ever answering his insults in like manner—leaving the image of an obedient wife with a cruel husband. It is a true image and that truth rings out in my voice. I also deny in any manner emboldening my nobles to ignore or thwart his commands no matter how sorely provoked they might be by his behavior, which owing to his youth and frequent merry-making became, on occasion, offensive to proud men. I outright renounce the accusation that we were estranged, offering as irrefutable proof the fact that I was carrying his child at the time of his death.

"We were not estranged but living together as man and wife, and had earlier that month ridden side-by-side to our summer residence in Aversa where we had often played together as children."

I bend my head in sorrow. "My dear prince, wedded to me in childhood, the father of my son and heir. I was and always will be deeply grieved by his foul murder of which I had no part nor any cognizance. To my unending regret Prince Andrew provoked many proud men with threats and insults so that I had to issue a command that none should harm him. All that was in my power to do in order to protect him from those who had grievances against him, I did, as Cardinal Aimeric will attest, having been in Naples at that time." I do not mention that it was Andrew's Hungarian knights and questionable choice of friends who took him outside the castle gates every night of our stay at Aversa to make merry and spend time with the women lingering near the castle grounds while I lay virtuously sleeping. Had he not come back late and drunk and smelling of whores he might not have been so easy a target for his murderers.

Instead, I speak passionately of the shock and grief I felt when wakened with the news that my husband had been most foully murdered, and of my anguish as a loving wife—that part a stretch—and a mother-to-be. That morning is and always will be so vivid in my memory that I am able to portray it in all its horror until, thus reliving it, I am brought to tears and many in the room with me.

Of course I had nothing to do with Andrew's death! From the moment I heard of it I knew with a terrible dread it would eventually bring me to this—my kingdom invaded by Andrew's relatives and I myself pleading for my life before a jury of men who will never be asked to subject themselves to a bestial husband.

But I do not put it to them this way. Instead I present eloquent arguments proving my innocence through sound reasoning.

I marshal the facts of the situation against the rumors: my first act was to have my husband's body interred with all honor in the cathedral of Naples the following day, and to order a Mass be celebrated there daily for him. My second act, within two days of his murder, was to apprehend the villain responsible: his chamberlain Tommaso Mambriccio whose life Andrew had threatened. These actions on my part are a matter of public record. Finally, with utmost delicacy, I remind His Eminence the Pope that his resolve to make the Curia responsible for the investigation of Prince Andrew's murder had in fact caused the delay, for the two cardinals he assigned were both called away elsewhere before they could travel to Naples, and his third appointment fell ill. All this is true and none can deny it. I myself was desperately eager to have the inquest proceed and the culprits responsible for the heinous crime brought to justice not only for my sake and Andrew's but for the sake of my kingdom.

I look at the seated cardinals, their faces impassive as I speak. How many of them have been bought by Louis of Hungary's gold, or swayed by the poisoned tongues of his ambassadors? I can only continue and hope that the truth will leach out his poison.

I impress upon them how much I and my kingdom had to lose by my late husband's murder and nothing to gain by it. What reason, then, could I possibly have to desire so offensive a disaster to fall not only on my poor young husband, but also on myself and my kingdom? Finally I remind them that during the lengthy inquest and trials, not one of the men and women convicted of and executed for my husband's murder ever implicated me in any way in their crime, despite the gruesome tortures they were subjected to, which drew forth the names of their actual accomplices.

In all my impassioned speech I take care to show both my dutiful reverence for the Holy Office—in contrast to King Louis' unruly and unlawful behavior—and my ultimate right and ability to rule the Kingdom of Naples. Pope Clement needs a strong and reliable ally in Naples, especially in these turbulent times.

The room is silent when I finish. I bend my head in reverence to the Holy Father and step back. Beneath my robes I feel my legs tremble as I sink into my chair. I sit erect and queenly, my eyes cast downward modestly. What are they thinking, these men who hold my life in their hands?

And then the room erupts. On all sides men are cheering, calling my name, ignoring the stern looks of the cardinals to voice their approval. I glance up through my eyelashes in time to catch the hint of a smile on Clement's face before he raises his hand to quiet the audience.

Now Niccolò Acciaiuoli, the finance minister of my kingdom, speaks on my behalf of all I have done to maintain the peace, order, and prosperity of my realm, showing me to be a wise, just, and capable monarch.

We wait in silence as Pope Clement retreats with his cardinals to confer. The entire hall is stilled and silent, every breath hushed, waiting for their verdict. I am aware of the eyes of every man in the hall upon me and even more aware of the weight of the crown on my head. *I am* the kingdom of Naples. Only death can remove the sacred right and burden of monarchy from me, and only God's representatives on Earth, the Pope and the Sacred College, can judge my worthiness to bear it.

I sit rigid and regal in my chair barely breathing as I wait upon their judgement. I have been a faithful daughter of the Church all my life but I will never believe I am not the rightful ruler of my kingdom. Better they should remove my head from my shoulders than remove this crown from my head.

Pope Clement and the eighteen cardinals return to their seats. They file in slowly, their faces impassive. I rise to my feet unaware of anyone around me, as though I am alone in this enormous hall facing my judges. There is a ringing in my head so loud I have to strain to hear the voice of the Pope. He announces their verdict in the solemn and timeless language of ancient Rome.

"Innocent of the crimes of which she is accused. Not only innocent but above any suspicion of guilt," he proclaims before the ambassadors of all the Princes of Christendom.

A great cheer goes up from every corner of the hall, shaking the very timbers of the ceiling with their approval.

Chapter 15

A Terrible Sacrifice

Joanna 1 of Naples
April – May, 1348

"No one will support you if you appear destitute." Niccolò's voice is cool, matter-of-fact.

We three, Niccolò, Louis, and I, sit around the table in my council chamber talking morosely of strategy and finances. Since my unequivocal acquittal my fellow refugees from Naples, Enrico Caracciolo, Sybil, Jeanne, Honoré, and my five loyal guards from Castle Nuovo, have been released from their imprisonment at Aix-en-Provence. They traveled at once to join my household here, swelling the number of people I must support. I am delighted to see them well and restored to my service, but I have now expended all the gold and jewels I brought with me.

"Your allies will expect to lend their support to a prince, not a pauper," Louis agrees. He looks me over critically. "You need two new gowns to wear to the banquets we will throw, and I need a new outfit as well. You have been wonderfully exalted, but it does not come without expectations."

I clasp my hands, staring at the two objects in the center of the table which, together, comprise all the wealth I currently have at my command. Is that envy in Louis' voice? No doubt, for I have been honored more than I could have dared hope: I am the only woman ever to receive the papal golden rose.

At first I did not credit the news when I was told I was to receive it. The golden rose is the highest symbol of the pope's favor, awarded in great ceremony on the fourth Sunday of Lent to the most deserving monarch. Everyone believed it would go this year to the King of Majorca, who had come to Avignon with that expectation, and who knows how he must be feeling now. He was at my inquest and cheered at my acquittal, I can only hope his good will has not been stretched too far.

March 30th: I smile thinking back to that day, recalling the pomp and ceremony as Pope Clement entered the great hall followed by his cardinals. They had come directly from their sacred private chapel where they had blessed the golden rose in preparation for awarding it. The rich scent of incense and holy water from the blessing ceremony wafted from their scarlet robes as they walked, surely the very aromas of heaven. The Pope carried the rose before him in his left hand, a single blossom made of purest gold tinted with red, its petals encrusted with rubies, pearls, and garnets, with a large sapphire at the heart of the golden petals. As he passed me at the forefront of the royals and nobles honored to be present this day, the rose emitted the sweet smell of musk and balsam which Clement, while blessing it, had poured into the tiny cup hidden in its center.

Clement held the rose aloft while the cardinals and all the priests in the room sang *Laudemus in Domino*, the powerful chorus filling the hall with its echoing chords of holy reverence. Then he placed the golden rose on a veil of rose-colored silk and sang the Holy Mass himself while everyone in the great hall knelt. After singing the Mass he beckoned me onto the dais and reverentially presented me with the golden rose.

The Pope and all his cardinals progressed with me through the streets of Avignon to my residence, that all citizens might see the honor bestowed on me and gaze in awe at the glittering symbol of his love, which I held in my raised hand. An honor fit to last a lifetime.

I stare at the golden rose on the table before me, still emitting its hallowed scent of musk and balsam. It would be worth a great deal, but would I ever be able to redeem it?

As though he can read my mind, Niccolò gasps. "You cannot sell the golden rose!"

"I will not sell the other."

"You will lose it nevertheless, for if you even attempt to pawn the Holy Father's symbol of honor in his own city—"

"—in *my* city—"

"—the scandal that will ensue will make you unfit to wear the crown of Naples!"

"Then I will sell neither." I reach out a single finger and touch my crown reverently where it lies beside the golden rose. I have risked death twice over to keep it, and sacrificed everything I hold dear, even my beloved son. I will not lose it now.

"You will need allies to defeat an enemy as great as Hungary," Niccolò says, practical as always. "And to find allies you have to maintain the image of Naples' rightful queen with the strength and resources to win back your kingdom. No one will follow you into a lost cause. You must give up your crown to regain your kingdom."

And to regain my son. Only when King Louis of Hungary has been defeated and I am firmly in control of my realm will I be able to sue for my son to be returned to the kingdom he will inherit.

My son and my crown, I swore to myself as I prepared for King Louis' army to strike. I stare at my crown glittering boldly on the table before me. He has taken one from me; how can I willingly give up the other?

"Patience and humility," my proud, impatient husband advises me. "You will regain everything you have lost, but only if you are willing to lose everything in the struggle."

I look at him coolly. He is a passionate man who rejoices in the gamble, be it dice or war or love. On April 22nd Pope Clement issued a bull legitimizing our marriage, proof enough for my audacious husband that his gamble paid off. He smiles at me, eager to take on whatever lies ahead of us, confident that I, too, am ready for the next gamble.

I am. I must be. But I have had many losses. I want a sure thing. I want to keep my crown.

But I must get my kingdom back! Pope Clement has publicly declared the Kingdom of Naples rightfully mine by all civil and religious laws, calling for King Louis to be dispossessed of it. And my son, whose capture and removal from Naples Pope Clement has publicly condemned, declaring it a trespass on Charles Martel's rights, showing an unforgivable lack of respect for him and for me. Further, he calls my brother-in-law Charles of Durazzo's execution unjust and illegal. All this he wrote in a letter to Cardinal Bertrand de Deux, his representative in Naples, instructing him to deny King Louis' demand to be crowned the King of Naples.

But legal and moral right will not secure me my kingdom; they count for little to Louis of Hungary. He does not recognize any authority but his own, and he has always wanted Naples. I will have to fight to win my kingdom back.

And in order to fight, I must have allies.

I give my crown one last stroke before drawing my hand back. What is a crown without a kingdom? Nothing but a hollow mockery.

I glare narrow-eyed at Niccolò. "Take it then. But see that you sell it for what it is worth. And be sure to write into the sale that I will buy my crown back again for the same price when I am able. And they will have my gratitude besides."

In May news comes to us of the troubles in my kingdom, from nobles who manage to slip away and come to Avignon seeking sanctuary with me or one of their relatives here. My Neapolitans, used to a benevolent ruler and a light yoke, are outraged by King Louis' reign of terror as he punishes not only the perpetrators of his brother's murder, but anyone with any leaning toward it. Well, he will have to slaughter my subjects wholesale to achieve that, for Andrew was of his brother's character, cruel and volatile, and had few friends among honest people.

The thought makes me wince. I cannot bear to think how my Neapolitan subjects are suffering under this tyrant, and those who were closest to me are sure to be suffering the most. Although Louis of Hungary is too stupid to recognize friend from foe—I laugh when I hear he has appropriated property of the Pipini brothers and banished the eldest, all unaware that these were Prince Andrew's staunchest supporters. In retaliation the entire family, a tribe of villains and criminals, have gone over against him, where they are still causing their usual trouble—but to my benefit for a change.

Noncompliance is the order of the day, these messengers from Naples inform me. When King Louis summons one of my nobles to his court, all that appears before him is a message of regret; the count or baron has been brought low with a fever and cannot attend. Each time he issues an order everyone is eager to obey, but for this or that reason regrets to inform him they cannot just now. I laugh once again to imagine King Louis' frustrated rage over all these polite excuses. He is unaccustomed to subtlety. He rules with an iron fist which instills terror in his own cowed subjects, but my Neapolitans respond with their own proud fury and a shrewd wit that defies him at every turn while mocking him with the false appearance of obedience. Oh, I do love my people!

May he choke on his rage, I pray as I struggle with my own. The image of my son being carried away over the frozen mountains to Hungary is never far from my thoughts. And all the while I must fawn on ambassadors and princes, courting their support while I bide my time. Change will come. Louis of Hungary will loosen his grip or have it shaken loose or be called home to settle some uprising at his own border which his brother cannot manage. The wheel of fortune will turn and favor me again, and I will be ready. *My son and my crown,* I whisper in my prayers to God, and hiss with impatient fury to Fortune in my dreams.

At the end of April the wheel of fortune turns, but in a manner so contrary I do not know whether it might raise me up or plunge me to my death.

The news which I have been dreading, have been hoping never to hear, arrives: the plague has reached Naples. I know at once that this is my opportunity if I have the courage to take it. This terrible plague which has killed a full third of the people of Avignon and shows no sign of loosening its death grip even now, for all the prayers and wailing of commoner and cardinal alike: This is the chance that Fortune has given me to regain my kingdom. Only it carries a cost I never wanted to pay.

Nevertheless, I am determined to take it. I send for every man who rides in from Naples to come to me at once and tell me what he knows. The news gets steadily worse.

"Your people are dying in the streets like dogs, Your Majesty!" The young baron cries, kneeling before me as though I were his confessor as well as his monarch. "It is rampant throughout the kingdom, but mostly in the cities, because that is where the sin is greatest. Forgive us, Your Majesty."

"What sin?" I ask sharply.

He peers up at me, his head still bowed, as though to see whether I am testing him. "The sins of the Usurper," he says a little tentatively, and waits, darting quick glances up.

"And how shall I forgive you for another man's sins?"

He hangs his head. "We should never have let him in," he mumbles. Gaining strength, as though now he has begun he is determined to continue, he says, "We should have fought for you to a man, knowing you to be our rightful ruler."

"Indeed you should have!" Louis interjects, remembering no doubt that terrible night when two thirds of his army abandoned him.

"How many are dead?" I ask.

"Thousands." He shrugs helplessly. "Tens of thousands." He spreads his hands. "Each day twice as many die as died the day before." Tears spring to his eyes. "It defies belief, Your Majesty. Who would ever have imagined so many corpses?" His voice chokes off. He bows his head, shoulders shaking. "Forgive us, Your Majesty, forgive us!" His voice echoes throughout the hall, a mad cry of despair.

I draw back sharply, compose myself, trying to shake off the horror aroused by his words. I think of my son, so far away. Away from the plague, at least. "Your family escaped with you?"

He flushes scarlet and turns his head, unable to meet my eyes. I open my mouth to express regret at his loss, glancing up at Louis. My husband's face is still, his eyes hard, his mouth a thin, tight line. The horrible truth washes over me.

"You left them." I pause to let him tell me it is not so. "You left them to die," I say again when he is silent. I put my hand over my swelling belly.

"My son took ill!" He sways on his knees, head bowed, protesting to the floor. "His nurse ran off. My wife said it was only a fever and went to him against my command. I would have brought her with me, but he had already looked at her. She let the child look at her! What else could I do?" He stares at the floor miserably. "I could not have come to you if I had let either of them look at me."

"Back up!" Louis commands harshly. The man shuffles backwards on his knees.

I look at him, sickened, not knowing whether he should be punished for his foul desertion or rewarded for his sacrifice in order to bring me the news I need.

"Have you any other information for us?"

"The king has fled, Your Majesty." He delivers this last in a dull tone. Such incredible news, my kingdom freed from a tyrant, reduced to an afterthought by the horrors of the plague.

"Fled?" I look up at Louis standing beside my chair, his expression as shocked as mine.

"None of us would obey him, nor bend our knee when he rode by, and that was before the plague came over the city, proof of his crime for everyone to see. He slipped away by night on a ship with only a small retinue. He was gone a week before anyone knew it, his soldiers all pretending their king had not deserted them. I came here to tell you, Your Majesty."

Just so did I slip away from Naples in the dark of night. And now the mighty Louis of Hungary knows how that feels! But I was faced with a murdering conqueror, my army disbanded by treachery, my death certain. I would never have run for fear of illness or out of frustration caused by my own poor governing!

A smile steals across my face. Louis of Hungary is a strong soldier, but a weak man. I will return in force to show him what strength in a monarch truly looks like.

Chapter 16

A Difficult Choice

Joanna 1 of Naples
June – August, 1348

Over the next week my husband and I immerse ourselves in a storm of activity. There is so much to do, and who knows how long Fortune will wait for us to seize this chance?

Louis writes to the elders of Florence telling them we are preparing to take my kingdom back and asking for their support. I summon my regional government to assemble in Aix-en-Provence in twelve days time to meet with me. Then I turn my hand to writing letters to the nobles still in Naples of whose loyalty I am certain. The Balzo family will support my return; they have strong ties with Pope Clement. Hugo del Balzo, the count of Avellino, has often acted as his nuncio, his official representative abroad, as he did when Andrew was murdered. I have not always approved of his policies or his behavior; I will never forgive him for my Philippa's torture and death. But he and his family are prepared to stand with me now against the Hungarians, since the Pope has ordered it, and I need every ally. I write the letter with distaste, but I write it.

However I cannot mount a campaign on promises alone; I must have money. The sale of my jewels and then of my crown brought me altogether eighteen thousand florins, most of which has already gone to pay for my expenses and maintain my retinue. I have no access to the royal treasury of the Kingdom of Naples—and dread the thought of what wreck Louis of Hungary must be making of it.

I have only one other thing to sell, and a ready buyer, but the thought appalls me. As it should. I cannot eat and dread to close my eyes at night, for when I do I hear my Grandfather, King Robert the Wise, lecturing me from childhood on my glorious ancestry.

Your great-great-grandfather, Charles of Anjou, the youngest brother of Louis VIII of France, was granted the Kingdom of Naples, and thus began the Angevin reign in Italy. His ambition matched his ability; not only did he rule the Kingdom of Naples, but he won Sicily as well, and then married Beatrice of Provence, adding the Duchy of Provence to our realm. Next he turned his eye east, gaining the principality of Aichaia, and buying the right to the title, King of Jerusalem, in the surety of one day making good on that claim, which aspiration he left to his descendants to realize. A giant of a man who laid upon proceeding generations the shadow and example of a true monarch.

The traitorous Sicilians rebelled and asked the King of Aragon to rule them! my grandfather roars again in my memory. *Charles of Anjou died commanding his heirs to retake Sicily and claim Jerusalem as well. It is our duty to finish the work he began and carve out an empire fit to rival France itself in size, wealth, and beauty!*

That is my legacy and my obligation: each successive monarch must hold what is handed down, regain what has been lost, and increase our empire for the next generation.

My grandfather had me memorize this litany before I learned to say my rosary. My own voice rings in my ears at six, at ten, at sixteen sitting by his sickbed, vowing to hold, regain, and increase our kingdom. Over and over I hear myself until I want to scream. For I cannot do it.

The gains of my predecessors since Charles of Anjou mock me—Hungary, Durazzo, Constantinople, I know them all. Nor is it any consolation that my grandfather failed to regain Sicily despite successive attempts, for he increased the Kingdom of Naples in honor and prosperity, such that its laws, its library, and its university are known throughout Christendom and praised by such learned men as Petrarch and Boccaccio. He added luster to our name, making our court one of the most civilized, prosperous and admired courts in all the world.

I have added nothing to our realm, neither by marriage nor by conquest. No, worse than nothing; I am the heir who lost the Kingdom of Naples. I am the queen who sold her crown.

King Louis will take the sophisticated court of Naples and tarnish its name, trample its laws and learning, squander its wealth and prosperity, and destroy the legacy of my grandfather. This is what my grandfather comes in the night to tell me.

I must not shame my ancestors and betray my heirs by losing my kingdom or letting its renown fade. Neither rumors nor false accusations, not treachery nor poverty nor even this monstrous black death creeping over the world can be allowed to deter me.

But I have only one thing to sell which is worth enough to pay for an army large enough to defeat the Hungarians. And that sale is a betrayal in itself.

"You must sell it," my husband once again counsels me. "Accept the lesser loss for the greater gain."

He is a younger son, a man born to inherit nothing, who does not feel the weight of his ancestors except as an unfulfilled entitlement. He knows the glamor of power, the seductive feel of it just beyond his grasp, the bitterness when it goes to someone no more capable or deserving than he. He has looked at me when he thinks I do not notice with the same cold envy I have seen him turn on his older brother, Robert.

He struggles to hide that expression now, to keep the resentment from his voice. A man who has nothing but pride, married to a woman who has more than she could ever need, yet cannot bear to part with a trifle to regain a fortune. So it must seem to him, because he only knows the desire to rule, not the constant, overwhelming responsibility that comes with it. He should know none of it is truly mine.

"You will buy it back when you are once again ruler of your kingdom," Niccolò tells me.

I shake my head. Once he has it, he will never give it up.

Niccolò shrugs, as though I have said the words out loud. "There is nothing else you can do, Your Majesty."

Pope Clement has spent a fortune building, beautifying, and fortifying the papal palace in Avignon as the permanent seat of his court, but he will only be a tenant here as long as I own Avignon.

Avignon, beautiful jewel of Provence. I must sell Avignon to the Pope. Sell one city to regain my kingdom and my crown.

When I ride out in Avignon my people stop on every corner to cheer me, to bless me, deriving courage from my presence among them at this time of their greatest trial. How will they feel when they learn that I have sold them out of a greater love for Naples? I smile and wave back at them as before but my soul is sickened with shame.

I cannot bring myself to meet with Pope Clement to discuss the sale of Avignon. I cannot look upon his eager, avaricious smile, the worldly glint in his eyes, when the Holy Father, my spiritual confessor, negotiates a price for this amputation to my realm.

I am not selling Avignon to a cruel master, nor to an unworthy one. The Holy Father of all Christendom will be their lord. They are blessed in this transaction. So I tell myself, smiling at my subjects as I ride by.

I am not betraying my ancestors, I tell myself as I direct Niccolò Acciaiuoli to have my lawyers draw up the contract. I imagine in the afterlife admitting to my grandfather that I lost the Kingdom of Naples. That I allowed all his light and learning to be snuffed out by barbarians. If I must forfeit something I know he would prefer I lose Avignon, bitter as that may be.

And so I make my peace with what I must do. I accept my failure, and vow that I will make it up in some way.

And therefore I am not pleased when Niccolò Acciaiuoli returns the next day to tell me that there is a problem.

"Avignon does not wish to be sold, Your Majesty."

"I do not wish to sell her," I reply, showing nothing of either the gratification or the guilt his words give me. "But we do not always get what we wish for."

"The citizens of Avignon are devoted to you. You have won their hearts and their allegiance is resolute. Their lawyers argued that you have not reached your age of majority, as stated in your grandfather's will, and thus you cannot sell or otherwise break up any portion of your inheritance."

I stare at him open-mouthed. My grandfather's stipulation on my inheritance was that I would reign under the advice of a ruling council, with my grandmother Queen Sancia at its helm, until I reached my age of majority: twenty-five.

"You know as well as I that that was rescinded when I was nineteen after Pope Clement, at the insistence of the Hungarians, sent a legate to rule Naples in my place." I shake my head, recalling what a disaster that was. "When he recalled his legate, he left me with absolute rule over my kingdom."

"So I told them, and the Pope's lawyers argued it as well, most vehemently. But the citizens of Avignon were insistent that the terms of your inheritance were made for this very situation, so that you would not break up your kingdom thoughtlessly, or be taken advantage of, while you may be still too young to appreciate what you are doing."

"I am twenty-two! If I were a king instead of a queen they would not dare make such an accusation. To imply that I have not carefully considered this—!" I feel my face flush hotly. As though I need to be told my duty like a peasant girl who has been raised without a care for her ancestor's expectations.

"Nevertheless, an heir who has not reached her majority cannot commit an irreversible act, and yours was set clearly in King Robert's will as being twenty-five years of age."

"My Grandfather could not have foreseen this! He would never want me to lose Naples. I must have the money to pay for an army, and I must have it soon, while King Louis is gone and cannot rally or increase the diminished army he left to hold my kingdom."

"All this I told them, and more," Niccolò assures me. "But still they are determined that you cannot make a binding and irrevocable decision to sell any part of your kingdom until you are twenty-five." He arches one eyebrow and gives me a long look from beneath it. "I was unable to dissuade them, Your Majesty, however hard I tried in good faith to do so."

My frown relaxes as understanding dawns. "And so... you were forced to put a condition upon the sale—that I might buy Avignon back before I turn twenty-five at the same cost as I sold it to the Holy Father?"

He looks down at his hands, flicking his fingers lightly as if his accomplishment was of no consequence. "There was no way I could avoid making that a condition of the sale."

"And how did the council of Avignon know to give that instruction to their lawyers?" I ask, giving way to laughter.

Once again he flicks his fingers. "I might have mentioned it in confidence to them a day or two ago…"

"And Pope Clement agreed?"

"But of course!" Niccolò looks shocked. "The Holy Father would not *dream* of taking advantage of a minor."

I receive eighty thousand gold florins in exchange for Avignon. I spend eighteen florins at once to regain my crown and my jewels, and wait anxiously until they are returned to me.

Enrico Caracciolo, my loyal chamberlain, enters my presence room that afternoon, walking solemnly between the four guards who accompanied him on this important errand. He kneels before me and unwraps the velvet in his hands, revealing the symbol of my sovereignty, the crown of Naples. It is all I can do not to weep to see it again.

I take it in my hands and place it upon my head and I am myself again. I feel my back straighten, my chin rise, for the golden, bejeweled circlet raises me up rather than weighing me down. Any trepidation I felt over facing King Louis in battle—for he will surely return with a second army when he hears I am in Naples—fades under the reassuring weight of this crown. My people will flock to support me when they see it, for what is a kingdom without a crown? A body without a head, a lumbering giant acting without reason.

The fear that gripped my heart at the thought of entering a land infested with the uncontainable plague now killing my people with no concern for rank or station, no mercy for the young or the innocent, and no limit to its toll, falls away from me under the golden reminder that I am anointed by God to rule my kingdom and I will do it though Satan himself stand in my way.

Everything falls into place as though God were only waiting for the bracing of my will. My council at Aix-en-Provence promise me two hundred knights; Clement issues a bull granting me one-tenth of the church's income in Provence, normally reserved for crusades, to add to my war effort; and my husband secures us twelve galleys and an armored vessel to carry our army to Naples. By mid-June we receive news that my loyal Neapolitan nobles, to whom I wrote for support, have won two battles already against the Hungarians. A delegation arrives urging me to return to claim my kingdom as soon as possible. My banner has been raised in the city of Naples!

I have stepped upon Fortune's wheel and am dizzy with the swiftness of my rise.

I am also on the verge of childbirth. I cannot risk a sea voyage until our child is born, let alone risk entering plague-ridden Naples in this condition. I promote Niccolò Acciaiuoli to grand seneschal of the Kingdom of Naples and send him ahead to Tuscany to recruit allies and pay for mercenaries.

Having done all that I can, I enter my confinement to await the birth of our child. *I must have another son,* I pray before the temporary altar erected in my chambers. I have postponed retreating from the world as long as possible, there has been so much to prepare. Now I have nothing to do but wait in a fever of impatience for the birth. *And he must come soon!* I add, crossing myself and struggling to my feet.

Sybil and Honoré, my faithful maids who followed me from Naples, rush to help me up. I feel a pang at the absence of my sister. Maria was with me through my last confinement when I gave birth to Charles Martel, a rock I could rest upon in that difficult time. This, too, is a difficult time for both of us. Maria has recently given birth to another daughter, Margherita, named after the faithful cousin of her husband who shared her terrifying journey to Provence. It is bittersweet for a woman to give birth to a child after her husband has died, however frequently it befalls us to do so. Maria herself was born months after our father died of a wound sustained in battle, and I gave birth to my Charles Martel after his father was dead. For all his deceptions and betrayals, I believe Maria loved Charles to the end.

I have sent her a note of congratulations with a little gown for the infant, but have received no reply. There has been a coolness between us ever since I refused her request for money without any explanation. Her anger, no doubt, has increased along with her need since the child is another girl and instead of increasing the family assets, we will be in need of a dowry. But how can I worry about what will become of my sister when my own situation is so tenuous?

She should know that, should guess I could not bring with me much more than she did. I too fled for my life. Yet instead of support I get censure: she does not approve of my selling Avignon, and has sent me a letter of outrage over it, as though it is her kingdom I am diminishing rather than my own. Her censure struck too close to the bone for me to forgive her for it. Perhaps when I have won back my kingdom I can be generous and we can mend our differences.

The child arrives on June 30th, prompt as I requested, but it is a girl. Catherine, we name her, a strong name for a future queen. Her little red face, squalling out her demands as soon as she arrives, makes me laugh. She settles upon the wet nurse's nipple with regal impatience as though she is preparing herself already to fight for what she wants.

We are enclosed together with my ladies and her nurses until my courses stop and I can be churched. Catherine delights me, and I try to enjoy this time with her despite my impatience to reclaim my kingdom. I fear that King Louis will return with a fresh army before my husband and I can arrive and cast out the troops he left to hold my kingdom. I worry about Charles Martel and long for word that he is well after having been torn from all that is familiar to him.

By the end of the month I am able to travel. The citizens of Avignon throng the streets as we ride by on our way to Nice. Not the crowds I once would have drawn, for so many have died and others been frightened by the plague into hiding or leaving the city. But those who come out cheer heartily and wish us good fortune and hail me as their Countess, still refusing to accept Clement as their lord.

On August 1st, Louis and I set sail from Nice to regain my kingdom, once again hailed on our way by my loyal subjects. We travel with the two hundred Provençal knights and bring with us two plague doctors trained by Guy de Chauliac, the pope's plague doctor and most esteemed in Europe. De Chauliac has kept Pope Clement and most of his cardinals alive, even one who broke out in the terrible black boils but under his care recovered—a feat so rare and unlikely as to be declared a miracle. The two plague doctors trained by him cost me nearly as much as a battalion of mercenaries, but if they keep us alive they will have been worth it.

Our precious Catherine and her wet nurse are snug in a cabin beside mine. The sea is calm enough in summer, she will feel she is being rocked to sleep as we sail to the home she has not yet seen. Whatever Fortune may bring, I swear to God I will never again be parted from a child of mine.

Chapter 17

War

Joanna 1 of Naples
August–December 1348

Our ships sail over the turquoise Mediterranean as steadily as the clouds sail across the calm blue sky above. Looking up at those clouds I think we might be the shadows they cast, dark shapes on the sea following behind them, carrying a storm that will break over the land.

The knights of Provence lounge on the deck, playing dice, exchanging stories of past battles, a few practicing their swordsmanship. My husband joins them occasionally but not for long. He prowls the deck as restless as the lion in my grandfather's menagerie, his every muscle ready for action, waiting to be released into battle. He has no time for our daughter Catherine, barely hiding his disappointment at not having a son, and little time for me. He is a man on the verge of winning himself a kingdom.

I do not let myself dwell on the coming battle, but it is never far from my thoughts.

"A beautiful day, Your Majesty."

I look up. Enrico Caracciolo bows low before me. "Indeed it is." I nod, pleased to have him join us.

He gives a courtly little bow to Sybil and Honoré before turning his smile back on me. "The sun shines on the righteous."

"And on the unrighteous."

"So we are taught," he says gravely, taking my rebuke. "We need not hate our enemies to hate their actions and drive them from our lands."

I wish, not for the first time, that my husband understood me as this man does. I glance down the deck to where Louis stands at the bow, his hands gripping the railing as though he would throw himself over and swim if it would get him to the coming battle sooner. My heart stutters as it always does when I look at him, standing half a head taller than the tallest of his knights, the light wind blowing his golden hair back, his blue eyes slightly narrowed and unwavering as though he is reading his future in the waves. His strong young body is taut with muscle, ready for action, his expression proud and fierce and confident.

I swallow a laugh at wishing to be understood. He is what I wish for, what I have wished for ever since he and his brothers rode back into Naples when I was fifteen.

"You chose a fine champion, Your Majesty," Enrico says quietly beside me. "He will win your kingdom back from the Hungarians." There is something reserved in his voice, as though he is thinking more than he is saying, but just then Louis turns and looks at me.

I smile as I always do. He does not smile back but looks thoughtfully from me to Enrico before he turns back again to gaze into the distance.

We cannot land in the harbor. The castles of Naples guard it and they are still occupied by King Louis' soldiers. Our galleys stop up the coast from Naples, dropping their anchors in the sea, and we are rowed ashore, the knights urging their horses into the water and clinging to them as they swim for land. I step from the rowboat, holding my skirts above the warm water, my shoes tied to my girdle like a young girl picnicking at the seashore. I laugh at the feel of the water and the sand squishing between my toes, as though I am coming home, not walking toward my death. I may be doing both.

We make our way to the church of Notre Dame and send messengers to tell our loyal nobles we have landed, and are waiting for them to come to let us into the city.

Louis dons his mail and straps on his sword. The knights remain close to their mounts, vigilant. King Louis' soldiers will know we are here almost as soon as our supporters learn it. I go to the chapel to pray but my thoughts are not on God. My every sense is strained, listening for the thunder of hooves and the war cries of the Hungarians coming to mow us down.

Not that they will have an easy time of it. We are a force of hundreds, enough to hold them off if their numbers have shrunk as much as we have been told. And soon we will be joined by Niccolò Acciaiuoli leading the allies he has won over and the mercenaries he has bought to join forces with the soldiers of Provence here with us.

Through the chapel window I hear the sound of men shouting in the distance, the whinny of horses and sharp clop of their hooves, the tramping of hundreds of feet. I clutch the silver cross at my neck and pray to Mary to intercede and give us victory. But when I rise from my knees and hurry to the window it is not Hungarian soldiers I see but a mass of citizens, dressed in great splendor in silks and velvets of rich colors, carrying my banner before them. Now I hear a medley of instruments playing joyful music, and see that the horses are prancing, having caught the mood of their riders, and those on foot are dancing or singing and shouting my name in celebration.

The church gates are thrown open as I hurry from the chapel to greet my subjects with Louis beside me. Now I see that not only my Neapolitan subjects have come to greet me, but people of every nationality living in Naples, for the court and markets of Naples draw people from all the known world. And all are overjoyed to see us.

"Where are King Louis' forces?" my husband demands.

"Cowering in the castles they have captured," comes the scornful answer from one of my Neapolitan nobles at the head of our welcoming party.

A great feast has been prepared for us at a fortified chateau on the outskirts of Naples. All the company that came to greet us escorts us there and joins the feast celebrating my return. Sitting beside me Louis insists that everyone who bows before me bends to the same degree to him, and scowls at anyone who is not quick to do so. I smile as though I approve. It is hard for a man to be lower in station than his wife, and he has come to liberate the kingdom of Naples for me. I have promised him he will be crowned with me and we will rule as equals when the Hungarians have been driven out, but he is impatient and proud; it galls him to see me honored above him.

When I retire Louis stays to drink with my nobles. I hear their voices grow raucous as night edges toward morning. Louis' boasts of what he will do to the Hungarians become more and more extravagant. Unbidden, the image comes to me of Andrew stumbling back to our rooms at Aversa in this same condition on the nights leading up to his murder. I push the thought from my mind. There is no similarity between the two. Louis is restless, full of pent-up energy and tension over the battle before us and letting some of it out as a young man must. He will sleep better for this night's excess. I close my eyes. I, too, need sleep to face what tomorrow will bring.

"Lorenzo has held Melfi." Niccolò pauses for a delicate moment allowing us all to note the success of his son. Melfi is an important city at the very center of my kingdom. The Hungarian siege to take it was long but Lorenzo is as capable a planner as his father; their supplies held out until the plague disposed of their enemy. I nod acknowledgement but he has continued speaking without noticing me. The three of them, Niccolò, my husband, and his cousin appear to be having a private war council in my privy chambers. I curb my annoyance, deciding to tolerate their unintentional disrespect until they win back my kingdom.

"My spies tell me the Hungarians hold castles in Capua, Aversa, Abruzzi, Campania, Apulia, Foggia, Calabria…" the list includes every major city and province in my kingdom. No, Melfi is ours. Would that Niccolò had more sons at my disposal!

We already know the Hungarians hold Castle Nuovo and Castle dell'Ovo, the two largest and best-fortified castles in Naples. Angevin castles, the seats of my royal court. Every day they are there is an offense and a slur on my reign. And if they are well-stocked they can resist our siege for months; at Castle dell'Ovo perhaps as long as a year. King Louis will be back with more men long before then.

"Their forces will be depleted," Louis says, "by the fighting they have already done, by the resistance of our people—"

"—By the plague," I cut in, a subject they avoid as much as possible. It is everywhere, and with King Louis gone back to Hungary, no one has been in control, no one is dealing with it. Bad as it was in Avignon, it is far worse here. The bodies, invaders and citizens alike, have been left to rot in the streets or in their houses. Wild dogs run snarling through the streets gorging on human flesh and rats likewise, even in the daylight. The putrid stench of disease and decay rises from the city like a poisonous fog from hell.

I have sent soldiers to kill the dogs, given orders for a mass grave to be dug just outside the city, and directed my merchants to supply carts and servants to collect the corpses under the direction of the plague doctors when the site is ready. But it will all take time, and meanwhile more people die every day. How could they have let my beautiful Naples come to this?

"—by being spread so thin across the entire kingdom," Louis continues as if I had not spoken. "Our forces are fresh and eager to fight, and the Church is on our side. The only unknown is time."

Niccolò nods his agreement. "We must strike on multiple fronts, regain as much as we can as quickly as possible before King Louis returns with reinforcements."

"You will have to kill all the foot soldiers," the bishop of Florence advises, "and as many of King Louis' knights and nobles in battle as possible. The mercenaries we can persuade to fight for us. But the Hungarians, all but the highest born…"

I try not to look shocked. It is customary to take prisoners and hold for ransom any who look wealthy, and certainly all those of birth.

"We do not have the time or the men to guard prisoners," Louis agrees sharply, not looking at me but certainly speaking for my ears. I am in their way, his tense body and angry expression says, an obstruction, this is men's work, battle decisions are not meant for women. I shut my mouth firmly over my objections and picture my city as I rode into her last week, my people dead in the streets, my nobles tortured, my cousins murdered or hauled to dungeons in Hungary, my son… I nod. Let them reap what they have sowed.

"We will divide our forces," Niccolò proposes.

"I will take three thousand mercenaries and fifteen hundred horsemen east to Apulia, then south to liberate Calabria," Louis proposes. "We will gain forces as we free each city."

"I will take half the rest of our forces north to Aversa and Capua," Niccolò says.

"And I will command my knights from Aix-en-Provence and the citizens of Naples to continue the siege on my castles here in Naples," I say.

Louis and Niccolò glance at the bishop of Florence, who nods to indicate he will remain here also. As if my Provençal knights, or I, would not know how to lock a castle in siege. As if I have not sat by my Grandfather's side through councils on war as well as on all other aspects of rule, since I was a young girl.

Louis glances at me, his face grim. Is he angry at me, or worried for me? Of course he is worried for me and for our daughter, leaving us here in a city gripped by plague and war. The thought softens me and I let go of my annoyance. But I am no helpless maid trembling in fear. I raise my chin confidently.

"Win back our kingdom while I win back our castles," I tell him. "Louis of Hungary will return to find he is too late, his cowardly flight has cost him a kingdom."

My husband smiles at me across the council table. A tight smile with no warmth in it, as one would give an ally one were saddled with.

No, I will not think so. It is the tension of the conflict before us, affecting us both. It is only the smile of a man planning his battle strategy, his mind on more pressing matters.

I do not wait up for him in my room that night. No man will expend himself on a woman the night before he rides to battle.

The Queen Who Sold Her Crown

Louis and Niccolò leave with their armies at dawn the next morning. I dress to send them off and go down to the courtyard. They are huddled together, the three of them, in a last parley before they separate. As I reach the yard they break off and silently watch me approach. It is an awkward moment, a shocking moment. I am their monarch, they can have no secrets from me.

I hold out my ring, the symbol of my office, for them to kiss as my vassals. Niccolò reaches for it at once and bows low as I bless him in his task to secure my kingdom for me. Louis hesitates when I turn to him. I hold out my hand as though I have not noticed. He takes it and kisses my ring, bowing before me as I bless him. He does not look at me when he raises his head but turns at once to mount his war horse as Niccolò has already done.

The bishop of Florence is left standing beside me. I do not offer my hand—he is not my vassal, but Clement's. Nevertheless, he is below me in position for I am no one's vassal, equal in rank to the pope in all but spiritual matters. I stare at him calmly until he gives me a small, stiff bow before turning to say a blessing on my champions.

They ride off, leaving me filled with an ominous disquiet that has nothing to do with the battles before us, though I try to convince myself that it does. Everything will be put right when I regain control of my kingdom. Louis will love and admire me again, Charles Martel will be returned to me, my kingdom will be a place of peace and prosperity once more. Even the plague will pass, as all afflictions do.

Until then, I have much work to do.

Chapter 18

A Rain of Blows

Joanna 1 of Naples
Spring, 1349

"Close the market? I cannot close the market!" I frown at my two doctors. Did I bring them here from Avignon for foolish counsel like this? "Where will my citizens buy their food? Where will they get the powders and herbs to throw on their fires?" It is known that fires, especially those of richly-scented woods or with powders, herbs and dried flowers thrown onto them, fight the noxious vapors that carry the plague.

"The plague is spread by breath and sight, Your Majesty," the older plague doctor says, as though I do not already know this. "It can travel on a person's speech, as though his very words were infected with the vile contagion. People must not gather. They should stay indoors."

I have already forbidden gatherings as much as I can with the exception of Mass, which people flock to. I cannot deprive my people of prayer, nor would I, for their pleas must reach God's ears. Besides, the plague is already in their homes and in the streets—it is everywhere. Next he will tell me my people should wear masks covering their eyes.

"I have stopped riding through my city although I cannot stop

Louis from doing so." I tell the doctor. Louis will not listen to me and flouts my commands or worse, overturns them when they inconvenience him. We are all disheartened as the war and the plague drag on.

"The markets will stay open." I raise my hand to ward off their objections. "The people must be able to buy and sell goods or they will starve. And Mass. You would not dare suggest I shut down Mass, would you?" I look fiercely into their silent faces. "Good! For I need all my people, religious and commoners and nobility also, praying for an end to this terrible scourge that has come upon us."

I stand up, signaling an end to my daily meeting with the plague doctors. I have done what I can to alleviate the sufferings of my people. I would ease their taxes but Louis will not allow it and we do need the money to pay our soldiers and mercenaries—otherwise they will loot and destroy our cities as King Louis' soldiers did. To raise the morale of my people, or at least not further depress it, I have forbidden public self-flagellation and have ordered the bells not be rung at night. I have also ordered the wild dogs killed. Those poor starving creatures whose masters, dead or unable to feed them, have turned them out are now roaming the streets eating the corpses left for the death-carts to gather. I overturn the law against women practicing medicine in order to allow midwives and those skilled in the use of herbs to care for the sick if they have the courage to do so. Or the desperation. With their husbands dead and incomes lost many women and children are starving to death before the plague can claim them. These are terrible times.

I go to my private chapel to pray as I often do after meeting with my doctors. How jubilant we were at Yuletide! Niccolò's army had won Aversa and Capua, Louis had freed the provinces of Apulia and Calabria. By mid-January the Hungarian soldiers at Castle Nuovo and Castle dell'Ovo had surrendered to my soldiers, worn down by the siege and by their king's desertion. Was it only a few months ago when we were so certain of success?

Then news arrived that King Louis, hearing of our triumphs, was preparing to return with a larger force. His men, spread throughout my kingdom, took heart—or perhaps considered their brutal sovereign's likely reaction if he returned to find they had failed him. They regrouped at Foggia and fought with such ferocity they drove my husband and our army back.

Louis returned to me a changed man. Or perhaps not so changed. Maybe this taciturn, angry man was always there beneath the charming courtier he showed at my court, and bitterness at this second defeat has simply brought it out.

There is much to be bitter about. I, too, could succumb to it if I were not so busy. Or perhaps I keep busy to avoid despair.

The husband I adored has become a cold, scowling presence in Castle Nuovo, locking himself in his chambers with Niccolò and his cousin to discuss battle tactics. They no longer even pretend to include me, and send out ordinances that I have not seen with my royal seal affixed to them, and my personal seal as well, as though the order came from me. Orders to which I object in many instances, making our relations more strained and accomplishing little else. He drinks late into the night until he has to be half-carried to his bedchamber. I see him at dinner, or when we go to church, or on a rare visit to our daughter's nursery if I happen to be there.

On impulse I turn from the direction of my chapel to go to the royal nursery. A while with my daughter will raise my spirits more than prayer. I smile, picturing her as I walk, her yellow curls and rosy cheeks, her sweet, contented nature and avid curiosity. She watches everything with wide eyes and learned to crawl early in her desire to explore every corner of her nursery. She cannot replace Charles Martel, but she is a delight in herself and a consolation while I wait for his return. And she is a bond between Louis and me, one of the few it seems we still have.

The guard opens the nursery door and steps back as I walk through it. Catherine is sitting on the floor looking at her doll and the little wagon with its cunning wooden horse that Charles Martel loved. For the first time since she could crawl she does not come to greet me with her toothless grin, but remains with her toys.

"She has refused her milk, Your Majesty," her nurse informs me.

"Her new toy has distracted her." I smile, pointing to the brightly-painted parrot held tightly in her little fist. A wood carver sent it to me yesterday with his request to have his license renewed as a visiting tradesman, one of the minor matters Louis has left to me. "She will remember to be hungry when its novelty has worn off."

But she is still not eating when I visit her the next day, and now she lies wan and listless in her cot. I send for the palace doctor at once, scolding her nurse for not alerting me sooner.

"It cannot be the plague," he says after questioning her nurse about the symptoms and the time her lethargy began. "I will bleed her."

"No," I tell him, looking at my small, pale daughter. "Let us wait until she is stronger."

That night there is a loud knocking on my bedchamber door. I sit up, startled, thinking it is still part of my dream when Louis runs in ahead of my guard. Behind them I glimpse Catherine's nurse still in her nightdress.

"She is gone!" Louis cries, distraught.

"Gone? Who is gone?" I stammer, staring from him to the nurse.

"Our daughter Catherine! Gone!" he moans.

"Gone where?" I demand sharply of her nurse who stands tearing her hair with a wild look in her eyes.

"Get out!" Louis screams. "Leave the palace at once!" He raises his hand as if to slap her but stops, afraid to touch her. She bobs a curtsy and turns and flees, the sound of her wailing a trail of misery in the night.

One of the plague doctors, whom I had not noticed earlier, steps forward and says quietly, "Your Majesty, the little princess fretted in the night. Her nurse sent for me and I found buboes under her arm and at her groin. I did what I could, but within the hour she was dead." He bows his head in grief.

I stare at him, more disbelieving than grieved. How can my happy, active daughter who was waving her little wooden parrot in the air just yesterday be dead?

Louis looks at my dry, shocked eyes and shouts, for all to hear, "No tears? No tears for my child? You wept enough for Andrew's child who is not dead but only gone to Hungary, but you shed no tears for mine?"

I am too stunned to respond but only stare at him. He leaves the hall in a rage as though our daughter's death is a personal insult I have given him, ordering fires lit in every room of the castle on his way out, and calling for the plague doctors to attend him in his room. Terrified for himself.

And still I cannot cry. I am numb with the horror of it, the suddenness. With death all around me for months I still did not believe it would strike at me or one of mine. I feared it constantly, but still I had not feared it enough.

Fires blaze in every fireplace and the plague doctors bleed Louis and I and any guests who had seen the child. Everything in the nursery is taken outside and burned—her little dresses and toys, her swaddling cloths, her cot, all remembrances of her gone before another night falls. Her nurses are turned out of the castle. I insist they be given some coins to live on despite Louis' objection that it was their carelessness and my unconcern that caused Catherine's death.

When the fires have had time to burn the illness from the air, and Catherine has been hastily laid in her grave, I return alone to the nursery. When we brought Catherine here in January I wept to see it, for every piece of furniture and toy reminded me of Charles Martel and all the times I had visited him here. I thought I would never enter this room without the pain of his absence striking me. But slowly little Catherine filled the room with her presence. The royal cradle became her cradle, the child-sized chair her feeding chair, the toys her toys as she played and chewed and crowed over them.

Now she is gone, and they are gone. Everything that reminds me of love has been buried or burned or taken away from me. I stand alone in an empty, desolate room that once housed my greatest treasures and a pain more intense than any I have ever known sweeps through me. I fall to my knees unable to stand, then all the way to the floor, lying prostrate on the cold tiles with my arms stretched out reaching, reaching into the emptiness, until my fingers curl uselessly against my palms, holding onto nothing.

Niccolò's spies return from Hungary the following month, bringing us word of King Louis' progress in outfitting an army to defeat us. He cannot leave quickly with a small force this time, counting on hiring enough recruits and mercenaries as he travels through the Holy Roman Empire. The Pope has declared his invasion unlawful and the plague has cut the population in half all along his route. Even aside from the fighting men who have died from illness, the numbers of willing mercenaries have been depleted by demand—not only by our conflict but by the larger war being fought between England and France.

King Louis will have to raise his army in Hungary. It will take time for him to muster a large enough force and march them across the mountains and down through Italy. He will have to bring provisions—the peasants raising the crops have been struck down by the plague as well as fighting men; there is famine everywhere.

We have a year, perhaps longer. And all that time we will be consolidating our rule and winning skirmishes against his remaining troops, driving them back.

Still, it is not good news. Good news would be that the plague has hit Hungary and King Louis' nobles are in disarray unable to call up their vassals to fight. The best news would be that King Louis himself had been struck down by the deadly black boils. Instead it is the intelligence we were expecting and we must make the best of it.

Louis and I receive the information calmly, sitting side-by-side in our high chairs at the end of the great hall as though we were already joint rulers. Niccolò and his cousin the bishop of Florence stand one step down on Louis' side. Seated beside the bishop is the court recorder, his writing tablet on his lap, his quill and bottle of ink ready. The bishop has been named the keeper of the royal seal, at Louis' and Niccolò's insistence, and so he is always in attendance when decisions are to be made. He is not one to hold back his advice or wait on consensus. I am more concerned about what he is doing with my personal seal, which I foolishly gave into his protection as well, when I am not seated beside Louis. But even that is not on my mind at the moment.

I lick my lips and swallow to dispel the dryness in my mouth and throat and ask the two men standing before us, just come from Hungary, "What can you tell us of our royal cousins and my son, Charles Martel?"

A terrible silence greets my question. Niccolò's spies hesitate, not quite looking at one another but waiting, as though each is hoping the other will speak first. So it seems to me, but my heart is thudding and my head has begun to pound so that I cannot be sure of what I am seeing. I want to glance at Louis and Niccolò to see if I am imagining the messengers' reaction, but do not want to call their attention to me. A monarch takes bad news in stride and gives no show of weakness to alarm her subjects. My face is calm, without expression as I pray silently, desperately: *Please, merciful Father in Heaven. Please, Holy Mary who knows what it is to lose a son. Please let it be one of my cousins who has died. All of them, if necessary, only spare my son, my sweet, innocent, gentle little boy.*

I am grateful in the end for their brief silence. For those moments to prepare myself. Otherwise how could I have borne what they had to tell me?

"Your cousins are still in prison, Your Majesties." The older messenger, the one who gave us the news of King Louis' preparations, finally speaks, his head bowed. "They are unharmed as far as we know." He stops, letting us surmise the rest. If King Louis wins the war he will not want them disputing his reign and will have them murdered at once. If we win, he will ransom them for as much money as he can get from us to regain the worthless traitors, and we will have to pay or wear the name murderers ourselves as they languish, dying slowly in his prison.

I give it little thought. That was not my question. My question was the one they are not answering. The one that makes Louis shift on his seat and glance at me, that has the bishop bow his head, that stills my heart because their silence is already an answer.

"The little prince died soon after they reached Hungary, Your Majesty. The cold was too much for him."

I stare straight ahead, seeing nothing, hearing nothing. I realize I expected this. The dread of it settled in my breast as soon as I learned he had been taken from Naples. A cold, desolate feeling that never left me, even when I pushed it aside, even at the height of my success in Avignon. I knew this, I knew it as it happened. I torture myself with questions I cannot ask and do not want answered. *Did he call for me? Did he cry for his mother? Did he wonder where I had gone and why I would not come and warm him in my arms? Or was he silent and stalwart, trying hard to be brave, as brave as a king to the end, just as he promised me?*

Distantly I hear my husband asking further questions: How many of his nobles has King Louis called on and how many vassals can each one be expected to muster and arm? I listen to the answers without interest, nod without caring at what is said.

At last the messengers are dismissed. They bow their way out and then I, too, can leave. I rise without a look or a word to anyone and walk out of the hall. Only where can I go? Not to the empty nursery. Not to the gardens where Charles Martel ran shrieking with laughter while I chased him among the trees. Not to my rooms where my ladies-in-waiting sit gossiping and sewing in my presence chamber waiting to attend me.

I go to the plain little chapel where my devout grandmother spent much of her days praying with two little girls beside her, Maria and me, dreaming of what our lives would be when we were queens.

I have no words with which to pray. I bow my head and let the pain sear through me. I do not expect to find consolation as I kneel on the cold stone floor, and I do not seek it. There can be no consolation, no comfort, no healing from this pain.

I am alone to grieve, and that is as close to mercy as I can hope for.

Chapter 19

A Royal Prisoner

Joanna 1 of Naples
April-December, 1349

The silent struggle for power between Louis and I becomes an open battle. I cannot prevent the bishop of Florence from bringing the royal seal to Louis when he calls for it. He is shoring up our army, buying us allies, sending our captains and troops to harass and weaken the forces King Louis left behind with skirmishes and by blocking their supplies.

But he is also undermining my authority, making laws I have not approved, appointments I would not sanction. He revokes the appointments I made in Aix-en-Provence and gives the positions to his favorites, after I so carefully negotiated their allegiance.

"I shall overturn it! Bring me my seal!" I cry, when letters of complaint arrive from the council in Aix-en-Provence alerting me to his foolishness. Some I reverse, but others I cannot for they have been given to generals leading their men against King Louis, and what has been given cannot easily be taken back.

"How else can I ensure their loyalty?" Louis roars at me. "We have no money to pay them! What little there is in the royal treasury I have to conserve for when Louis of Hungary returns with a fresh army. God help us if we cannot pay for soldiers then!"

"That is when we will most need the loyalty of our subjects in Provence!"

"My subjects," he sneers, for in my foolish fondness I bestowed upon him the title Count of Provence while we were in Avignon.

"Not for long if you treat them badly!"

"Then they will learn the consequences of mutiny. They do not have a weak and pliable countess governing them now, but a count who can and will insist upon their obedience!"

I want to shout, *then demand the obedience of our Neapolitan nobles, instead of giving them appointments we cannot afford,* but I bite my tongue. It wounds me, heart and soul, to argue with him and that is all we do these days.

Denied entry to their battle councils, I set myself to governance. I have my own counselors around me, although I invite Louis and Niccolò and his cousin. Niccolò is now seneschal of the Kingdom of Naples, an appointment I made in Provence to reward him for his service before sending him to Tuscany to recruit mercenaries. Louis scorns my discussions of practical matters—the feeding of our people who are starving, actions against the lawless bands of thieves plundering the goods of those who travel our roads and disrupting food supplies, the disposal of the dead. Weary and discouraging work, but necessary to preserve my people and the order of my kingdom. The bishop of Florence comes with the royal seal for any new laws I strike—and, I suspect, to report back to Louis and Niccolò. ... Niccolò. Why does he, whom I have so valued and richly rewarded, not attend? Has he switched loyalties, or is he playing a sly game, biding his time as he watches to see who will win the contest of power between Louis and I? The captain of the city guard, those nobles still loyal to me including the del Balzo family and Enrico Caracciolo, all offer their counsel and support as I try to resurrect order and prosperity out of the chaos my kingdom has become.

In the midst of a discussion on a new burial site for the mounting piles of the dead, we are interrupted by strong voices and the sounds of a scuffle outside my privy council chamber. The door bursts open, revealing four armed soldiers led by Louis.

"Arrest him!" Louis points to Enrico. He does not so much as glance at me, as though I am nothing, beneath his notice or regard.

My council sits frozen in their seats as Louis' guards march down the room toward Enrico, their right hands resting on the hilts of their swords. They reach him in the time it takes me to leap to my feet, the first two already grabbing Enrico's arms and dragging him to his feet.

"Stop!"

The guards dare not ignore me. They stand where they are, keeping hold of Enrico's arms while glancing nervously behind at Louis for direction.

"How dare you!"

"How dare I, Madame?" Louis addresses me without so much as a bending of his head in recognition of my royal rank. He sends a cruel smirk in my direction, daring me to respond before his eyes narrow and his lips thin into a look of outrage. The smirk I believe, but the false outrage freezes my blood.

"How dare you behave as you have with this dog whom you have kept by your side this past year while I have been fighting for your kingdom?"

I stare at him, my mouth falling open. Can he be saying what I think he is?

"How dare you cuckold me as though my noble rank and status as your husband had no meaning? I will not stand for it, *Madame*." He emphasizes once again his reduction of my sovereignty with a sneer. "Take this worm to the dungeon!"

I am shaking with rage and incredulity, unable to think of a retort other than the one he has already mocked, piling lie upon lie atop it.

Louis steps aside as two of his men hustle Enrico out of the room past him. Enrico stumbles once, catches himself. His face is pale but composed. His confidence in the truth, in my ultimate protection, terrifies me. It reminds me of Philippa and Sancia and all those I have not been able to save. I want to scream, and weep, but I compose my face to show nothing but regal disdain as Louis strides into the room to stand in front of his two remaining men. Three more soldiers wearing his colors enter the room. My palace guards stationed at the door are nowhere to be seen. Has he dared to murder them?

Again he smirks at me, an ugly expression I have never seen on his face, cowardly and triumphant at the same time. As though he has me, as though a lie so outrageous is all it will take to destroy me. I recall how his father, Philip of Taranto, dispensed with his first wife of fifteen years, the mother of his six children, with this same accusation in order to marry Louis' mother, my Aunt Catherine, the Empress of Constantinople. Does my husband think to do to a queen what his father did to a minor noble without powerful friends to defend her honor?

"This meeting is over. There will be no more. Your counsel is not needed."

No one moves.

"Get out!" Louis screams. His men's hands move to their swords.

Still my counsellors do not move, looking to me, their eyes nervous but ready. They have not brought swords to this meeting, only the knives they eat with and always carry, and their stout hearts. I nod, freeing them. They leave, but not so quickly as to seem willing.

Louis turns to me, his face stern. As though any amount of play-acting will convince me that he believes a thing he is saying. "You, Madame, will go to your chambers and stay there. You have done me such injury I cannot bear to look on your face. You dare not even deny my accusations."

"Why should I deny what you yourself know is a lie?" I say nothing more for fear my voice will shake with outrage. I turn my back on him and walk with regal dignity to my chamber.

Louis is too clever to act with haste. He is not yet king, although he intends to be. He must either be crowned or have a child with me, a legitimate heir to the throne. And he is well aware of the love my people have for me, of their joy at my return. They will fight for me when Louis of Hungary returns, but would they risk their lives for him, a man with no lawful claim to the throne? He will bide his time, spread his vicious rumors to discredit me, and wait for the final strike when he is secure.

I lie in my bed for days, a cauldron of emotions. Rage at his betrayal after I raised him from the lowly position of a second son, without title or inheritance. Grief at the knowledge that he never returned my affection. Shame at my cupidity. Helpless fury that once again those who are loyal to me must suffer for it. Despair at having my honor besmirched falsely, at being the subject of unspeakable rumors and false accusations for a second time. Where will I find the strength to defend myself again? Who will stand with me, when my previous champions are now my accusers? I have no strength to counter this new attack. And for whom? I have no heir to fight on behalf of, my kingdom is in shambles, my people impoverished, wracked with war, dying of the plague and fallen into lawlessness.

Women are always at the mercy of men, and those who love me, whom I trust because they are so foolish as to put their trust in me, will always be the targets of my enemies.

This is what it is to be a queen in a world where men are the masters.

An odd thought, as though there might be any other world.

An impious and arrogant thought, as though God should have arranged things differently to suit me.

A useless thought for this is the only life I have and the world I live in, a hard, unjust world in which I was born to be a queen.

I wallow in despair until at last it begins to bore me.

To lose your kingdom is to betray the sacred trust of your ancestors, to fail your heirs unborn, and to cast shame upon your name for all posterity. This, above all else, my grandfather King Robert taught me. This is what it is to be a queen.

I rise from my bed as though wakened from a fever and call for Sybil and Honoré to bathe and dress me and comb my hair and plait it up. They smile, overjoyed, when I tell them to do so. I do not share their smile but my face softens briefly at their love and loyalty. A softness I cannot afford, so I say nothing further as they attend me and they respect my silence. But Honoré, her eyes moist, cannot stop smiling and Sybil turns her face away every so often to wipe from her cheeks the tears she tries to hide.

Louis is surprised to hear me announced for dinner. He starts and turns, slack-faced, as I enter in my robe of state with jewels at my throat and wrists and a hard glint in my eye. His face darkens as everyone in the room separates, bowing to the ground as I pass by. These are Louis' friends, his followers. They know the accusations he has made. Yet I am still their monarch.

At the front of the room I stop before Louis and wait. For a moment he does not move. The hall is silent.

Then he bows his head once. With a nod and a rustle of silk brocade I pass him and take the seat beside him, rightfully mine, at the head table.

I avoid looking directly at Louis. He is beneath my contempt. Yet for the sake of everyone watching I smile and chat with those seated near us and listen with feigned interest when Louis speaks. I laugh at the jesters and appear to enjoy the music as I eat. When I have eaten enough to show that Louis' malice has not affected me, I wave over a servant to take my trencher. Since no one may continue eating when I have stopped, the platters of food are quickly removed. I want to laugh at the expressions on some of these fat lords' faces, but give no indication that I have noticed their dismay. Let them return home to eat their own food.

Louis' face is a mottled red as I depart, leaving them all to guzzle their wine on empty stomachs and throw up into their chamber pots.

The next day Louis sends away my ladies-in-waiting and stations two of his guards at the door to my chambers. They will allow no one to pass into my presence except for two maids long entrenched in the Taranto castle, sent to dress and attend me: Louis' childhood nurse and a sour-faced lady who was in his mother's service. Nor am I allowed out. No one who is not loyal first and only to him may see me.

From my window I see counts and dukes, soldiers and messengers, the gambit of royal visitors, come and go in the castle courtyard. By this I know that Louis continues to hear petitions, pass laws, and sign letters of state with my royal seal as though they came from me.

Neither my bitter recriminations nor my tearful pleas prevail upon him. Soon he refuses to come at all when I ask to see him. And so spring turns to summer.

I hear the door to my presence chamber open but I am finishing a complicated stitch and do not look up from my embroidery. It will only be the kitchen servant come to bring a bowl of rosewater to wash the day's heat from me before I go to bed. In the chair beside me Louis' old nurse jumps to her feet, dropping her sewing to curtsy, and then I do look up.

Louis stands just inside the door. He motions his nurse and his mother's old maid, also on her feet now and curtsying, to leave us. I watch with narrowed eyes. He appears to sway a little. Has he come here drunk? I heard earlier the sound of voices, laughter and music as he entertained my nobles with another lavish dinner. Not one of them asked after me, I assume bitterly.

The door closes and we are alone.

"You do not stand to greet your husband?"

"Is that what you are? I thought you were my gaoler."

"I am your Lord husband, your master. Your gaoler, too, if need be."

"You are my subject. You swore fealty to me."

"And you swore obedience to me. It seems, Madame, that we are both liars." He gives a drunken laugh.

"You have had too much wine. Go and sleep it off." I look back down at my sewing, dismissing him.

"Oh, but I am not sleepy yet." He leers at me, swaying a little as he walks forward.

I should use this meeting to learn his plans, to find out what is happening in my kingdom, to plead for my release. Who knows when he will come again? But the sight of him wavering on his feet, the sour fumes of sweat and wine emanating from him, the vulgar sexual innuendo in his sneer and the greedy look in his eyes all disgust me. I stand up, dropping my embroidery into my chair.

"Get out!"

I am a tall woman, and if my formidable grandparents taught me one thing, it was how to command. Louis stops in his tracks.

But he, too, was raised by fearsome parents. We are a pack of wolves, we Angevins, full of a fierce strength and lethal instincts.

Louis' eyes narrow as he takes me in. He licks his bottom lip.

I have taken the wrong tack. The uncertainty of his position as my consort and the tension of waiting for King Louis' army to attack combined with too much strong drink all have him spoiling for a fight. I do not often misjudge an opponent but my emotions for this one have misled me. There can be no backing down now, however. I stiffen my spine and glare back at him, stepping smoothly to the left so the chair is not behind me. I feel my hands curling into fists and hide them behind my skirts. I, too, am tense and angry, spoiling for a fight. But not a physical confrontation. I relax my hands.

"With whom did you dine tonight? Did they promise you their loyalty in exchange for a dinner, or did you give away more of my holdings?"

His lips tighten but he recovers quickly. "Did you expect our nobles to face Louis of Hungary's army in exchange for a smile? We saw how that ended—you fled for your life in the night."

"As did you."

His face blanches. With a snarl he lurches forward and grabs my arms.

"Take your hands off me!" I twist sideways but he has a strong grip despite his state. He pulls me against him. I turn my head aside. "You stink!"

He laughs, a low, ugly sound. "You are my wife and I am in the mood to demand my rights."

I struggle, but Louis is a strong man. He drags me to the door of my bedchamber and kicks the door open.

"How dare you!" I manage to get one arm free and slap him hard.

He slaps me back with such fury my vision blackens and I am deafened by a ringing in my ears. I fear I will faint and try to resist the sickening weakness flooding me.

Louis shakes me. "Oh no. You will feel this, Madame. You will feel every minute."

His shaking clears my head, my vision returns. I see him glance at my bed.

"No," he mutters. "I think I will take you on the floor like the whore you are. Perhaps you will prefer that." He laughs and throws me forward.

Falling forward I stumble, catch myself and rise, running. Before I have taken two steps I feel him grab my skirts and yank me backwards.

"What? Are you not eager to do your duty and give me a son?" This time he kicks my legs out from under me before tossing me to the floor. He falls on top of me as I try to scramble backwards, pinning me beneath him. I bite his hand.

With a curse he slaps me again; not as hard this time, he does not want me unconscious. He grabs my face between his hands forcing me to look at him.

"I could break your neck. It is within my right to punish you for resisting your husband's demands."

I lie still. He would enjoy it. I see the temptation in his eyes, in the flaring of his nostrils, his heavy breathing. I have married a killer, thinking I could control him, that I could divert that ruthlessness against my enemies.

"Good…good…" He struggles to control his breathing, his thumbs stroking my throat longingly. I lie very still, hardly breathing.

"I need an heir and I will have one off you." He lets go of my face, one hand sliding to encircle my neck in case I start fighting again, the other fumbling under his tunic. Freeing himself of his hose he grabs my skirts and yanks them up, raising himself to pull them to my waist. I see with disgust and relief that he has gone flabby. He rubs himself against my mound, playing with himself.

"Think of your lover, Enrico. Think how I will kill him. Slowly. I will make his screams last all day, perhaps two days, as he begs to die." His breathing turns ragged as he hardens against me. My fear changes to disgust. Is it torture, not love, that excites him? He leers down at me. I want to close my eyes but I will not allow myself to.

I stare at him, dry-eyed and coldly furious. He takes me quickly and rolls off, letting go of my neck at last. Freed, I raise my hand to strike him, but he is too fast and catches my hand, holding it as he jumps up. Pulling his hose up, he kicks me in the side, not hard enough to break a rib but enough to warn me to stay where I am.

Scowling down at me, he says, "Go to your chapel and pray that I have got you with child. Otherwise you are no use to me."

He leaves without another word.

The next morning the two old women who are now my maids are back. They tell me Louis has ridden off to check on his troops and the progress they are making against the remaining Hungarian troops. Several smaller cities in my kingdom have been reclaimed from them. I let the maids dress me and do up my hair, then send one to the kitchen to fetch me mulled wine and something to eat. As soon as she has left I order the other to find my musician and bring him to play for us while we sew. Louis' guards are still at my door, preventing me from leaving, but as soon as I am alone I hurriedly get out a piece of vellum and my quill.

Closing myself in my bedchamber I write in secret a note to Pope Clement, who gave me a golden rose and might be convinced to defend my honor once again. I tell him of my captivity and oppression at Louis' hands. I tell him my ladies-in-waiting have been turned away and that I am not allowed to leave even to attend services at the cathedral of San Lorenzo. I write that my husband is listening to his own advisors who have been encouraging him to make laws and administer my kingdom in my name and using my seal, without my knowledge or agreement. Finally I write of the false imprisonment of my chamberlain, Enrico Caracciolo, and the shameful allegations made against my honor concerning him, protesting my innocence. I blush with humiliation as I admit the last, but I have been sick at the thought that these accusations might reach His Holiness before I had the opportunity to persuade him of my innocence.

Hearing the door to my presence chamber open, and the voice of Louis' old nurse and a kitchen wench, I quickly sign my name and wave the vellum gently to dry the ink.

"Your Majesty," the old woman calls at the door to my bedchamber.

I roll up the letter and tuck it under my kirtle before calling, "You may enter."

The musician arrives as I am eating, causing another delay. Having sent for him, I must listen to his playing. I pick up my embroidery and sew with the same impatient lack of interest as I am giving the music, all the while pretending to enjoy both. At last enough time has passed that I may toss down my sewing and say I will go to my chapel and make confession.

This is the moment of decision. Louis has not allowed me to leave my chambers, even to take communion and confess my sins. Now that he has gone his guards will have orders to maintain my seclusion, but will they dare refuse their queen spiritual counsel in the absence of their master?

I do not ask permission but walk at once to the door of my presence chamber, calling the guards to open it. The door swings open. The two guards stand gawking at me as I haughtily order them to send for my confessor to meet me in the chapel at once; I intend to pray for my lord as he rides out to battle, and to receive my palace priest's blessing. "At once!" I snap when they hesitate. "You! Go and give my message to the priest. And you," I gesture at Louis' nurse, the older of the two, who is going blind and deaf and is easy to deceive, "You will accompany me to the chapel. And you," I point to the second guard at the door, "You will follow us and guard the chapel door while I pray!"

Perhaps they are cowed by my air of command, or shamed by how Louis has made them treat me, or reassured that I am not trying to send all Louis' keepers away but will be accompanied by one of his spies and one of them. The guard I ordered to go goes and the one I ordered to follow us snaps to attention and falls in behind me, and the half-sighted old maid scuttles frantically along in our wake.

I request a full service in Latin, with the sort of prayers my Grandmother Sancia could listen to for hours. Each time the priest slows I raise my head and stare at him until he continues. Occasionally I pray aloud myself, always in Latin, my head bent reverently. Until the old nursemaid's eyes close and her head nods. When her breathing is deep and regular I reach into the side of my kirtle and take the letter from under my belt and pass it to the priest, telling him in Latin that he is to see it delivered into Pope Clement's hands himself. He will be rewarded for his service, I promise him, and urge him to leave at once. All this I say quietly in Latin, as though I am praying, confident that the old woman sleeping on her knees will not understand a word even if she hears my voice through her dreams.

Chapter 20

Allies and Adversaries

Joanna 1 of Naples
September - December, 1349

By September Louis is back at Castle Nuovo, having left Niccolò and his son in command of our army. They continue the skirmishes against the Hungarian troops King Louis left behind when he fled.

My husband appears in the night to have his way with me infrequently, always when he has drunk too much. I endure his brutality stoically, showing neither anger nor interest. I refuse to let my mind wander to our sweet and passionate lovemaking when we were newly married and eager to please each other. This is a bleak and bitter transaction on both our parts. Louis needs an heir with a valid claim on the throne to legitimize his position; I, too, need an heir to my throne, and when we have a son Louis will not be able to put me aside without also discrediting his heir.

He has decided it is politic to let me be seen. I am allowed to sit with him at dinner, to listen to petitioners occasionally beside him, although he responds to their requests and dictates when and what I will affix my seal to. These are all minor requests, my presence for show only. When anything important is discussed I am once again locked in my chambers with only the two old ladies attending me.

No one may see me outside of Louis' presence.

I submit to his dictates in public so no one may ever say I was not a dutiful, obedient wife. That would suit his purposes very well. But when we are alone I protest fiercely.

"I am the queen of Naples, not you!" I shout, dodging his slap. "You have not been crowned! You must treat me with respect, as your monarch!"

It is to no avail. I will have to wait until the wheel of fortune lifts me once again above him, and in the meantime pray for a champion; this time, ironically, against the very man I believed would *be* my champion.

In early September the succor I have been praying for arrives. Louis bursts through the doors of my presence chamber with a letter crushed in his hand.

"What do you know of this, Madame?" he shouts, shaking the crumpled letter in my face.

"Nothing, unless you choose to tell me," I reply coolly.

"Ah, you are lying! It is from the Pope."

My heart leaps with excitement. Clement has received my message and replied! But why has he replied to Louis and not to me? What has he told Louis? I tremble even as I maintain a calm expression.

"You wrote to him complaining of me. Spreading vicious lies—"

"Is that what His Holiness says?"

"Of course not. Not directly."

"Then you are imagining things. Out of guilt, perhaps, my Lord Husband?"

"I have done nothing that is not within my rights as the husband of a disdainful, disobedient wife. And yet he says—" Louis looks down, reading from the hastily straightened letter: "*By your union with the Queen who openly honored you above your kindred, you have become possessed of abundance and an exalted position. We* were not unnaturally hopeful that in return you would prove grateful to her, and show her the affection which is not only her due, but would benefit your own honor." Louis shakes the letter fiercely. "He questions my honor? I would call out any other man who did so!"

"And here—" he continues reading, his face twisted with anger, "*You, however, as is a matter of common report (and we are sadly surprised to hear it), not merely do not treat her as behooves a wife and a Queen, but scornfully curtailing the area of her prerogative, you have caused her to be reckoned rather a slave than a spouse. It is further reported that, ruled by the prompting of advisors—*" he crumples the letter once more, his face reddening, "He attacks even my advisors? It is clear you have put him up to this! How else would he know how I treat you?"

I am grimly amused by the unintended admission, but answer him with the simple, shameful truth: "All of Naples knows how you treat me. 'A matter of common report' he writes. Did you think no one would notice? Or that no one would care? I am the Queen of Naples."

A slave, the Holy Father called me. My face burns with humiliation, as though I had not used that comparison myself in my letter to him. How much more demeaning it sounded coming from Pope Clement. Had he truly received similar reports from others?

"It is no one's right to interfere between a man and his wife! And if they noticed, if they care, it is only because you have turned them against me. As you have the Pope." His voice is low, barely audible, his face white and cold, the way he must look in battle as he brings his sword down on the enemy. "Why should I not murder you for your betrayal?" His mouth twists in a smile that stills my heartbeat.

"You will not harm me because I have missed my courses this month," I say in a voice as quiet and cold as his.

His eyes widen. He breathes in deeply.

"Or are you prepared to murder your own heir?"

He stares at me narrow-eyed, his hands clenched at his sides.

I dare not look aside. I dare not breathe.

Until he turns abruptly and leaves.

I do not know what Louis' response to Pope Clement is. I write him myself, thanking him for his support, begging him to continue to prevail upon my husband to return me to his affections and respect, and protesting again my innocence as regards poor Enrico Caracciolo. "*I have never licentiously done anything derogatory to his honor, or forgotten either due respect or submission to him,*" I write, and add, full of despair at the way we women are prey to such rumors: "*I am vexed beyond measure; now this and now that, heaped up or over-colored by repetition, these greater actions are put down to a predilection for disorder, those lesser, to unlawful lapses of the passions.*" I bow my head, briefly overcome. Will I ever escape the false and vile accusations of husbands and kin who want my crown?

It is not as easy to slip this letter to my priest. My attendants have been warned to watch me more closely. But when the good father places his hand on my head in benediction I reach up, overcome, to grasp his hand, and slip the letter from my sleeve into his, murmuring my request that he see it reaches Pope Clement. Fortunately, Louis has not thought of finding a maid for me who speaks Latin.

Louis' public treatment of me improves, at least. He does not want any more rumors reaching Avignon of my ill-treatment. I sit beside him at dinners and may even leave the castle—at his side—to hear Mass sung. He is polite and smiles charmingly as he hands me in and out of our carriage. I am, after all, carrying his heir. And there can be no doubt it is his; Enrico has been in prison five months and no one but Louis has had private access to me.

I play my part, the obedient wife, smiling back at him and accepting his restrictions, making circumspect conversation when spoken to. As a result I am included in more public events, always with Louis at my side to ensure I have no private words with anyone who might take my side against him.

Into this nest of discord my sister Maria plunges. I receive a message that she has returned to Naples and demands an audience. The back of my neck prickles at her words. She wants a public audience? No, she *demands* one? I am about to respond with an invitation to a private dinner when Louis snatches the parchment from my hands and reads her brief message aloud.

"The wife of a traitor is now making demands on us?" he says with an ugly laugh, glancing slyly sideways to see my reaction as he maligns my sister. I bristle. Did not his brother also betray us? But I control my temper.

"Let us hear what she has to say," I answer, endeavoring to sound calm as always despite the jarring warning in my brain. "At lease she had the cleverness not to be taken prisoner, forcing us to pay another ransom."

"I expect she did not want to give you that option."

I am shaken with fury at the implied insult, but also feel a cold trickle of fear and revulsion. Would Louis actually consider refusing to pay the ransom for his own kin?

Maria is ushered into the large chamber where Louis has allowed me this once to sit beside him hearing petitions. Niccolò stands beside Louis' chair where he can lean down and confer with Louis.

I neither glance nor speak to him and he does not try to catch my eye; out of shame, I hope, although I doubt it is an emotion that troubles him. The bishop of Florence, holding the royal seal, sits to the left beside the court recorder at the base of the dais on which we are seated. At the side of the room to our right stand several of our court advisors, nobles of the realm.

Maria marches grandly from the door to our dais, her two eldest daughters walking behind her. My heart lurches at the sight of them. Beneath my wide sleeves I clutch the arms of my chair. Joanna must be nearly six, so self-possessed walking solemnly beside her sister. The last time I saw her she had still been affianced to Charles Martel and played with him in the garden under the fierce watch of his Hungarian nurse. Little Agnes reaches out to hold her older sister's hand, the only sign of her timidity under the gaze of so many powerful men. Maria held my hand that way, her grip tight for such a little hand, when we first came to our grandfather's court. Agnes is four years old now, born a month earlier than Charles Martel. I gaze at her face, unable to look away, for in her blond curls and plump cheeks I see what my son might have looked like now.

"Your Majesty," Maria curtsies low to me and then Louis, forcing my attention back to her.

"Duchess Maria, welcome back to Naples." My voice is warm but formal, the voice of a monarch to her subject, as she chose to present herself to me.

"We are pleased to be safely home and under your just rule once again."

I nod. "Have you come with a petition for me?" I say the words that give her permission to make her request despite my reluctance. I fear I already know what she will ask.

"I and my children have been left destitute, Your Majesty—"

"Your husband's castle has been returned to your family," Louis breaks in, "despite his treachery to us."

"I had no part in his betrayal," she replies with a quiet dignity I cannot help admiring. "But the castle Durazzo is not mine. My husband's title and family holdings are being held in trust for his heir, my daughter Joanna. Until she comes of age I cannot access them. My jewels and personal belongings have all been taken by the Hungarians. I am impoverished, with nowhere to live!" She turns from Louis and looks directly at me. "But I do have an inheritance not yet claimed. Your Majesty, you were with me when our grandfather King Robert dictated his final will."

The memory of that night when we were wakened and escorted into our grandfather's sickroom to hear his final wishes sweeps over me. How young we were, just children, holding hands nervously beside his bed while our destinies were dictated into his will. He could not foresee how far from his wishes our lives would stray, or how quickly it would all happen.

Maria's sharp voice brings me back from my reverie. "You know as well as I, Your Majesty, what King Robert left to me in his will as my dowry. And how little of it I have received." She pulls her daughters in front of her, either as witnesses to my dereliction of duty or as proof of how long she has been waiting.

My lips close in a thin line. I expected her request but not her arrogance in flaunting the children before me when I have so recently lost both of mine. Does she think her cruelty will shame me? She does not think at all. Maria never did. To ask for her dowry—no, all but demand it—when the plague is still raging, my people starving, and we are in the middle of a war with Hungary? Louis and I need every gold florin we can put our hands on—no twice, three times what we have—to hold our kingdom and keep our people alive. I frown at my sister, exasperated.

And notice her pinched face, her shallow cheeks, the look of desperation in her eyes which she tries to hide. Her daughters' clothes look worn and their arms are too thin. But Maria's dress is new. She has a gold necklet at her throat with a fine spray of emeralds. It may be her last piece of jewelry but it will clothe them for a while if necessary. They can stay in Castle dell'Ovo until Louis and I have time to arrange another husband for her. It will have to do. We are no longer those two pampered princesses raised under the stern but protective care of our royal grandparents.

"We will consider your petition," Louis says, dismissing her as if she were a minor noble.

A look of shock and outrage crosses her face, quickly concealed. She stares at me for a long moment, all trace of the love we once shared gone.

Sisters. A relationship born of blood and bound to draw it. A tie that comes with too many expectations and too little gratitude. I expect her to know that our kingdom comes first, she betrays *me* when she forgets that. She expects me to provide her with the luxurious life of a princess as our grandfather did when he was King of Naples, and I betray *her* when I do not. We know each other better than we know ourselves. We are each other's strength, and each other's weakness.

She bends in the shallowest curtsy she can get away with, gathers her children and turns her back on us, hustling them out before her. I observe the looks of mild shock on our courtiers' faces but I let her go, putting my hand on Louis' arm to prevent him saying anything. She has as much right to be angry at me as I have to be angry with her.

The next applicant is announced.

"I expect you are tired." Louis signals one of his guards to escort me back to my locked chamber. The public performance is over.

Chapter 21

Birth and Renewal

Joanna 1 of Naples
March, 1350

Two days after I go into confinement to have our child, Louis has Enrico Caracciolo executed. Another friend murdered for no reason other than his loyal service to me. Louis has claimed this child in my womb, but he cannot allow himself to look a fool for having accused his wife of cuckolding him with no reason. Ah, he had a reason, and still has the same vile reason to maintain his rumor of my adultery: it might be useful at some future time in order to be rid of me. I know how his mind works now.

But he has seen it is not so easy to dispose of a queen, especially one who is loved by her people. I am not powerless for all I am a woman in a man's role. Although I do feel helpless now, fretting in my confinement, wondering what additional problems he is creating in my kingdom. To whom is he endowing titles and appointments now in order to ensure that everyone at court will be beholden to him, loyal to him, dependent upon his good will, not mine?

When I am not worrying, I pray. I must have a healthy son. My kingdom demands it. My people will fight King Louis all the harder if I can provide them with a secure succession to the crown. My marriage depends on my being able to give Louis an heir to our kingdom, and very likely my life depends on it as well. I order the two old ladies Louis has provided to attend me to kneel and pray beside me for hours. Their joints creak when they stand up again and their faces twist with the effort. I think of Philippa, tortured in her old age, along with all her loyal family, and Enrico, and all who have suffered and died for love of me, and I have no pity for these two faithless old crones who have agreed to spy on me for Louis. I lengthen the hours of prayer until even my younger knees protest.

"Holy Mary, Mother of God, bless her Majesty's unborn child. Make him strong and healthy. Give her an easy labor and guide him safely into our hands…" Beside me I hear Louis' old nurse murmuring her prayers under her breath. There is no falseness in her voice, no bitterness over the pain I am inflicting on her with hours of kneeling before the little shrine in my confinement chambers. I hear only the same desperate urgency I feel for a strong and healthy heir. She sways beside me, but does not falter in the quiet crooning of her prayers.

I cross myself, bringing my prayers to an end, and touch her shoulder as I rise, silently offering my assistance to raise her from her knees. She does not move, nor begin the adoration of God that will end her prayer.

On my other side the maid who attended Louis' mother, my intrepid aunt Catherine of Valois, crosses herself and rises. She pays no attention to the audible protests of her body, but cannot avoid a slight wobble as she stands.

"Be seated," I tell her. I bend, my hands clasping the old nursemaid's shoulders. "Rise," I say gently. "We will take some nourishment to strengthen ourselves. There will be time for more prayers later."

Distracted by her pain she leans on me as she rises, but once on her feet she grasps my hand. "Your Majesty, no! You must sit down. Rest yourself. Do not worry about me."

I help her to a chair nevertheless. Did not our Lord wash the feet of beggars, and did I not do so with my Grandmother Sancia before the feast of Maundy Thursday during Holy Week every year of my childhood? Have I forgotten my upbringing in the trials of wearing a crown? I swear to myself to be kinder to these two servants who are naturally loyal to the Taranto family they spent their lives serving.

It turns out we do not have time to pray again. As soon as I finish a small platter of cheese and olives the cramping in my belly begins. I frown, ignoring it. It is too early. It goes away but returns stronger. The third time this happens I have my maid send for the midwives.

I lie helplessly on my bed watching the head midwife's face intently as her experienced fingers stroke and probe my belly. Her face is relaxed, her expression thoughtful. But then, she has trained herself to give nothing away.

"Tell me the truth," I croak, my voice breaking with anxiety.

She probes a few moments longer, her silence bringing me to the edge of despair. I need this little prince so much!

"All appears to be well, Your Majesty," she says at last. "The birth is only a week or so early, nothing to upset yourself over. The infant is a good size, its movements strong. Beyond that, we will have to wait to see."

I take comfort in her words and her calm bearing, though I know she would not show any emotion that might upset me even if she herself was worried. "A calm, happy mother is the best defense against a difficult birth or a fretful newborn," she adds, proving my point.

I breathe deeply, as she has instructed me, and force myself to relax. I have proven I can bear healthy infants. There is no reason to assume otherwise now. Rather than consoling me the thought of my two children, both gone now, brings tears to my eyes. Another contraction begins, forcing out tears and moans as it builds to a crescendo.

Something is wrong. The pain is too intense. I have given birth, and this is different. I writhe on the bed, groaning with agony, my womb bulging and moving like a storm-tossed sea. A cry, jagged with pain and sharp with fear, is ripped from my throat. I clench my mouth tightly, biting my bottom lip. I am not a common woman, to scream when I am hurt. My stomach heaves again, tearing a second scream from me despite my resolve. I am panting by the time it is done, my face damp with sweat. Terrified, I look wildly at the midwife.

"Good," she murmurs, feeling my abdomen which has settled somewhat in the space between contractions. "The child has turned toward the birth canal. It will be easier now, Your Majesty." She smiles, wringing the cloth in the bowl beside my bed and wiping my face. How good it feels, and the smile looks genuine.

"You did not tell me he had not turned."

"There was no reason to think he would not. I have attended your births before, Your Majesty," she reminds me.

I smile at last. Until another contraction comes upon me. This one is normal, rising in a swell, rolling over me and away again, nothing I cannot navigate.

Closer and closer the pains come, each one stronger, until with a great push I finally feel an easing.

"The head has crested." The midwife's voice is pleased. "One more push, Your Majesty."

I feel the tiny body emerge into the midwife's hands. She steps back and sits in her chair, huddled over the infant as the second midwife comes forward and begins packing moss between my legs to staunch the flow of blood. I twist sideways, trying to see the head midwife bending over my son, massaging his chest, inserting her finger into his tiny mouth in the silence that follows.

A silence that steals the breath from everyone in the room. Every eye watches them, my son limp and still, as silent as death in his swaddling cloth.

Breathe, I think, a silent, urgent prayer.

Breathe! I command. *Breathe!*

"Breathe!" I cry.

A thin whimper comes from the midwife's lap, growing in strength into a plaintive cry.

My son is alive! Tears fill my eyes. My kingdom is secure, my marriage validated. "Let me hold him." I stretch out my arms, my voice filled with joy. He must go to his wet nurse soon but first I will hold him.

"Congratulations, Your Majesty." The head midwife folds the blanket around him tightly as she rises from her seat. She smiles, but there is something odd about her smile as she lays the warm, miraculous bundle in my arms. "You have a beautiful, healthy daughter."

Louis is furious with me. He does not speak to me or look at me, let alone bring me a birthing gift as is customary.

His face softens as he leans over his daughter, though, seeing her for the first time two weeks after her birth. He may hate me for giving him a girl, but no one could hate this baby. She is as pretty an infant as ever was born, with her wisps of sunlit-white hair and perfect, delicate features, her large trusting eyes as blue as the sea, her plump, rosy cheeks and rosebud mouth. Her lips curve in a tiny burp as she looks up at him, forming a smile.

"Françoise," he murmurs, the name he sent a messenger to convey to me a week after her birth.

Hearing the tenderness in his voice I release my breath, letting my own face relax into a smile. Surely…

The look he turns on me freezes the unfinished thought. Such a look as Andrew would give me when I mocked him for his stupidity and coarseness. But I have never mocked Louis. I have always loved Louis, admired his strength and confidence, appreciated his quick mind, adored his masculine beauty. I have given him everything. And he loved me, I was sure he loved me. How can he look at me now with such hatred?

Did Andrew love me as well, underneath his vulgar jests, his awkward immaturity, his cruel and sneering intolerance of underlings and superiors both? Was he struck dumb by my beauty as I am by Louis'? And did I return to him a look such as Louis is giving me now? Have I completely failed to understand either of my husbands? Or do I understand them all too well? Their willful masculine pride and ambition unable to accept that God has placed a woman over them.

Louis leaves, having addressed not a single word to me. I refuse to weep and acknowledge neither the scornful look of his mother's maid nor the sympathetic glance of his old nursemaid nor the politely turned-aside head of the wet nurse. There will be only one miracle here today: Louis' hard heart softened by the beauty of his infant daughter. The buoyant hope I felt as I watched him smile down at her is replaced by the more familiar weight of dread settling once again in the pit of my stomach.

I remain confined to my chambers even after I am churched and ready to return to court. Louis locks me in my rooms like a prisoner, worse even than before I went into confinement. Such is my punishment for disappointing him. I submit to it, for I have no choice.

When I insist on seeing him, on knowing what is happening in my kingdom—*my* kingdom, I remind him—he responds with a violent fury that terrifies me. He shakes me, clutches my neck as if to choke me, threatens me with life imprisonment, utters all manner of curses and swears he wishes I had died in childbirth.

"I will kill you!" he whispers more than once, as though a devil has possessed him, throwing me onto the floor and fleeing from the room. Does he fear the temptation to act on his threats might overwhelm him if he stays in my presence a moment longer? Sometimes he stands over me as I cringe on the floor, a terrible, excited look on his face, as though he is daring me to say one more word, to push him beyond his limit. At such times I wait frozen in this tableau, balanced on the edge of chaos. I am not able to breathe, while his breath comes hard and fast as he waits. When I do not respond he turns slowly, as if disappointed, and leaves.

The next time he *will* kill me. I am convinced of it. I live in fear for my life.

Louis' old nurse is afraid for my life, also. I see it in her eyes when she looks at me. Gradually I prevail upon her to arrange a secret meeting, while the other maid is sleeping, between me and a man I can trust to act as my emissary to the Pope. I send him in haste to warn Clement that my life is in danger. When he has gone I pray I might survive long enough to be rescued.

Then the news comes that King Louis and his army have entered the kingdom of Naples and are amassed no more than a day's march away, outside the gates of Aversa, locking it in siege.

Chapter 22

Betrayal

Maria of Durazzo
June, 1350

We are sitting in my presence chamber, Margherita and I, when the letter arrives. Presence chamber. I call it that, though the name makes a mockery of the reality. Perhaps in better days this room was full of ladies-in-waiting and courtiers, sewing, playing cards and flirting with each other, a minstrel entertaining them with music and poetry, a jug of wine beside a platter of figs and nuts on the table.

Now there is only Margherita sitting here sewing with me, and Joanna who is nearly six, old enough to let out the hem of her own kirtle if she must grow so quickly. At least she has one new enough to lengthen. Soon after we moved into Castle dell'Ovo my sister sent her seamstress over to make new kirtles for my daughters, and for Margherita and me a chemise each with a kirtle in the modern style to go over top. The seamstress brought with her an assortment of cloth—not silk brocade, but still good linen with pretty patterns of leaves or flowers woven through it.

A guilt offering, I thought to myself. She would have done better to give me my dowry that I might have the means to support myself and my children, than send us her charity offerings. But I swallowed my pride and accepted the gift. The clothes we had brought with us from Avignon, which my husband's uncle the Cardinal Talleyrand of Perigord had supplied, were already looking worn and my daughters' ankles showed below the hem. Who would have thought I would ever have to worry over how to keep my children dressed? I chose two fabrics for Joanna and told the seamstress to be sure and make the green one larger than needed now and to leave a wide hem in both. The other girls could pass their kirtles down as they grew, but who knew when Joanna would have another new kirtle?

At least the kitchen at Castle dell'Ovo has adequate provisions and two decent cooks, with three servants to bring us our meals and wait on us as we dine, and keep the rooms we live in clean and the fireplaces lit. My faithful guard Lorenzo is still with me, and three others who escaped King Louis' vengeance, as well as a nurse for the girls. It is a more frugal staff than even a wealthy merchant's wife would have, but until my situation changes I must make do.

That is what we are doing this June morning: making do. We sit in the 'presence chamber' with the window shutters wide open to let in sunlight and the summer breeze, with the fresh, salty tang of the sea on its breath, as we let down the hems of all the girls' kirtles. When Joanna grows tired of sewing I have her read to us, her sweet treble voice pausing now and then, stumbling over the difficult Latin words in my Book of Hours, so that it is nearly as painful to listen to her read as it is to watch her sew. She needs a tutor if she is not to grow up ignorant of all she needs to know. If her cousin Françoise dies, she will be third in line to the throne. Not that I wish that, God forbid. There is no money for a tutor anyway.

We have been here nearly four months and I have not been granted another audience with my sister or with her husband. Rumors abound throughout Naples that he has imprisoned her in Castle Nuovo, that he beats her, even that he will murder her.

What should I believe? I have learned not to listen to rumors about me and my sister, but I have never trusted Louis of Taranto. Perhaps she is not imprisoned but ill or weakened with loss of blood from the birth and lying in her bed at death's door? No one has seen or spoken to her since the birth of their daughter. Should I be afraid?

Or glad? She has not been kind to me nor given me what I am due. If she dies, I am the heir to the throne, not Louis. Unless he names their little Françoise queen, and himself as regent.

I shake my head. It is all too improbable. Only weariness and worry could put such thoughts in my head. Louis will not harm Joanna; she is his stepping stone onto the throne of Naples. The people would never rally around him if she died, nor would they want an infant queen. They would want me. And I will never marry a man who has killed my sister.

However often we are at odds she is still my sister.

Oh, but I am so weary of poverty!

"Maman, I will read again." Joanna throws down her sewing. "Unless you think I should go and make sure my sisters are behaving?" She looks at me hopefully. It is the third time she has suggested it in the hour. Not so often as to annoy me; often enough to wear me down.

"Run along," I tell her, wishing there was a pleasanter task I could run off to, also. She jumps up and curtsies, hurrying away without another word for fear I will change my mind.

I sigh. Another endless, boring day. The plague has nearly run its course but one does not walk in the streets; it is still possible, though less and less likely, to come upon a corpse with black boils. No one makes social visits for the same reason. We have grown accustomed to keeping away from each other. I could not afford dinner guests anyway. And Castle dell'Ovo, built on the tiny island of Megaride jutting out into the sea, has no private garden to stroll through.

One of our three servants, the one who styles himself above the others, appears at the door of my chamber. He bows very low—the higher he deems my position, the higher his will be as my steward—and waits for me to bid him rise. "My Lady Duchess," he says when I do, "A letter has arrived for you, from Hungary."

From Hungary? For me? I reach out my hand for the letter. "It is most likely from my brothers-in-law," I say, making my voice sound calm, even a little bored, "wanting me to send them money to bribe their guards for luxuries." It will not be a ransom note, not while the war between Hungary and Naples still rages. But it will not be a request for money, either. My outstretched hand trembles a little as I take the letter, saying, "You may go. If I have an answer I will send for you." He looks disappointed as he bows again and withdraws.

There is some advantage in the lack of servants. I can open my letter in private, save for Margherita whom I trust completely. We have learned to depend on each other after all we have been through together. And who would she have to report to about me, even if she wanted to? It is a form of freedom, not having to worry about spies watching my every move for the first time in my life.

Margherita continues sewing, her head bent over her even stitches, showing no interest although she must be as curious as I am. I put the letter on the table beside me. For some reason I do not want to open it. Whatever Charles' brothers have to say, I doubt I will like it. They know I have no money, that their family assets are on hold until Joanna, the next Duchess of Durazzo, comes of age to claim them. Then some calculating man will force her into marriage for the sake of her title.

No, they are not asking for money, but they will have thought of some way to use my position to benefit themselves. They are Charles' brothers, after all.

Until I open the letter and read it, I am my own woman. Poor, humiliated, perhaps forgotten, but master of my life, such as it is. It will not last long. Perhaps it has already ended with the arrival of this letter. I might soon wish I had complained less as I picked out the hems of my daughters' kirtles, as I ate chicken and onions instead of pheasant or venison.

I glare at the letter. Why is a woman always at the command of men? I will not open it. I will toss it into the fire. I have been the pawn in enough Durazzo plots. I sew furiously.

Beside me, Margherita coughs. Delicately. I look up and wince at the sympathy and understanding in her dark eyes.

Of course I will not throw it into the fire. I will open it and do as I am told, as a woman must. I force a tight smile onto my face. "Perhaps they have died."

Margherita looks shocked. Exaggeratedly so, making us both laugh. What grim humor these terrible times have brought us to, to laugh at the thought of death. It has befriended us, the sickle-bearing shadow, walked so close and so constantly beside us that it has lost its mystery and dread. Life is what frightens us now.

I sigh and pick up the letter. Before I break open the seal I narrow my eyes at Margherita. "If I do not like what it says, I will burn it," I warn her.

"If you do not like what it says, I will burn it," she answers. "By accident, of course. When I was handing it to you to read."

"If you were a man I would marry you."

"If I were a man I would have to think of advancement, of family honor, of commanding those beneath me. You would not want to marry me."

I laugh and break open the seal before I change my mind.

I feel her eyes on me as I read the letter, and then read it again. I look up at her finally, my mouth too dry to speak.

"What is it?" she cries. "Who has died?"

"No one has died." I swallow with difficulty. "It is worse than that."

She jumps up, letting her sewing fall to the floor and comes and kneels beside me, clasping my hands. "Tell me, Cousin."

I look into her face feeling dizzy.

"King Louis of Hungary wants to marry me."

This room has become a presence chamber after all. Lorenzo, Margherita, and Marino Rumba, my chamberlain, have joined me around the table. It is a small and odd assortment of advisors, but with all the members of the Durazzo family in prison or dead I am short on official advisors, and I trust these three people. Marino was assistant to Charles' chamberlain and brought me back my ring soon after I returned to Naples. He had been with his master when he took ill and by some miracle received from him my ring but not the plague. Moreover Lorenzo vouches for Marino, and I owe my life to Lorenzo.

I drop the letter onto the small square table around which we are sitting after I have read it aloud. There is silence as they absorb what they have just heard.

King Louis of Hungary is looking for a wife.

How furious I was eight years ago when I learned that Louis of Hungary had married eight-year old Marguerite of Bohemia instead of me, to whom he had been promised nine years earlier in an agreement between my grandfather and his father. I was a child myself, barely thirteen when he proved false. He was a stranger to me but I did want to be a queen, even if it must be Hungary. I remember hearing of Marguerite's death a year ago and feeling a surly moment of satisfaction before I dismissed it from my mind. She had taken nothing from me that I regretted losing.

And now it is mine again for the taking. The crown of Hungary.

I shake my head, disbelieving.

According to this letter the four of them, my Taranto cousins and my husband's brothers, put forward my name for Louis' consideration from their prison in Visegrad. For the first time, and probably the last, the houses of Taranto and Durazzo are united.

Naturally they expect to be released to attend the wedding. I smother a bitter laugh.

Lorenzo looks at me. "Is this what you want, Duchess Maria?"

Has any man ever asked a woman that question? I hardly know what answer to make. "It would end the war," I offer.

Across the table Margherita gives a little snort. I know what she is thinking: it is not a woman's job to end a war that men began. But if I could, would that not be a good thing for Naples?

I have not thought this way before. My sister should be proud of me, finally putting our kingdom first. I smile grimly at the irony.

Only I know I am not. King Louis' brief reign in Naples was brutal and unjust. He would destroy Naples and all the beautiful memories I have of the elegant, civilized life I spent here.

He will destroy it anyway, far worse if there is a second war. No one can stand against his army, fueled by the inexhaustible wealth of Hungary.

All that wealth…

"It would give our allies pause, if King Louis strengthened his claim on Naples by marriage to a legitimate heir to the throne." Lorenzo's voice is neutral, but I do not fail to catch the words "our" allies. He has already assumed I will do what my brothers-in-law, who speak for the house of Durazzo, have put in motion. Nor do I miss his deflection of my hope to end the war. Of course the war will not end at once. Joanna will never willingly give up Naples. She will have to be beaten.

"I will not marry him if he murders my sister."

There is a long pause around the table. Marino looks at me oddly. I feel my face flush but I return his look levelly. Let him ask my brothers-in-law why *they* are willing to let King Louis profit now from having murdered my husband.

"He will have to execute Louis of Taranto if he is not killed in battle," Lorenzo injects smoothly into the silence. "Louis of Taranto has led troops against King Louis."

I remember Louis' cold disdain as I begged my sister to give me my dowry. At least Joanna appeared regretful. I shrug. I want no say in the retributions men demand of each other. They are all cold-hearted murderers and traitors. "Let him have Louis of Taranto. Or let Louis kill him. That is between the two of them. But I will not marry King Louis if he has my sister killed."

"He will expect to rule Naples if he marries you," Margherita says.

As if I did not know my only value to him. "He will take it one way or another." I sigh. The glorious, enlightened kingdom I remember is already gone, buried under famine and plague and the previous invasion of Hungary. "My sister is the Countess of Provence. Let her keep that title and rule there. They will welcome her back." This last is said with perhaps a little bitterness. Joanna has the knack of being loved by her subjects no matter what she does. Nevertheless, she will be safe in Provence. I would not leave her with nothing when I am Queen of Hungary and Naples.

The prospect brings me little joy. King Louis will be a cruel and demanding husband. But my daughters will not grow up mending patches and letting out the hems of their kirtles, and this marriage will buy my sister's life and the release of our cousins from King Louis' jail.

Joanna will not see it this way. She will hate me for this. It will separate us beyond anything else we have ever done to each other.

I stand and take up the letter and walk to the fire. I look into its flame for a long moment. Am I going to do this?

Do I have any choice? Either Charles' brothers will marry me off for their gain or Joanna and Louis will marry me off for theirs. I am an heir to a kingdom; I must be married. And it is never going to be to someone *I* choose.

I toss the letter into the flames and turn around. "No one must know of this until it is done," I tell my unlikely counselors. "Marino, you will act as my emissary to King Louis. See that my terms are made clear. Do not return until you have his agreement in writing."

Chapter 23

Rescue

Joanna 1 of Naples
July - August, 1350

"Your Majesty! Your Majesty! Look out your window!"
Louis' old nursemaid throws back the curtains around my bed and runs across the room to open the window shutters.

I sit up at once, groggy with being torn from sleep. What can have happened now? In the past two months a volley of letters have arrived from Clement for me, Louis, Niccolò and the bishop of Florence, instructing us all to strive for peaceful relations between Louis and I. Have his directives finally prevailed upon my husband? Will he free me from my chambers at last? Or has the Hungarian army arrived at my gates and King Louis is even now demanding our surrender?

"What is it?" I ask, my voice tremulous with sleep and apprehension.

"Come, look for yourself!" She gestures impatiently to the open window beside her.

Not my husband, then. He would hardly stand outside my window declaring his repentance.

I slip from my bed unwashed, bare-footed and still in my nightdress and go to the window, standing back where I can see but not be seen. There, anchored along the coast between Castle Nuovo and Castle dell'Ovo, bathed in the soft dawn light, is a fleet of six galleys full of armed men. My heart skips a beat. It is King Louis. Did my husband not tell me in a fit of fury that Genoa had promised King Louis ships? So he has finally received them and come for me. I clutch my nightdress to my throat and step back…

Then I notice each ship is flying two banners: mine and the Church of Rome's. *My* banner? I step forward into the window alcove, staring, astounded. The Hungarian banner is not to be seen. Nor is my husband's, I realize.

The church bells ring out the hour of lauds, their loud tolls clanging over the still harbor. When the last peal dies, the men on board the galleys stamp their feet and clap their shields four times in unison. Then, with one voice, they roar, "Long Live the Pope! Long Live the Queen! Down with Louis of Taranto!"

My mouth falls open. Their voices carry the warm Southern accent of Provence. I lean out the window as far as I can, my hair all undone and tangled with sleep, clothed only in a white nightdress, and wave wildly, tears streaming down my face. One man catches sight of me and in a moment the entire troop, all six galleys of men, are cheering and stamping their feet and lifting their swords to me.

I am saved!

I wave until my arm is sore. Then, hearing their voices grow hoarse, I step back from the window. "Dress me! Dress me at once in my royal blue!" I cry to my maids.

They have barely finished pulling the bright blue kirtle over my silk chemise and buttoning it and its sleeves when the door slams open and Louis storms in, his face as pale as death.

"What is the meaning of this?" His voice signals violence. Up to this moment it would have made me cautious and silent.

But now I laugh. "You had best ask the men on those galleys out there. I am curious to know myself. Who commands them?"

Louis glares at me. "The count of Avellino. I have already send messengers to him."

Count Hugo del Balzo? The man sent by Clement to judge and execute everyone loyal to me after the death of my husband Andrew? So now he has come to *rescue* me? I smile to cover my shock. Well, one cannot pick one's savior. I would rather him on my side than against me.

"A competent man," I drawl. "If he sets himself to do a thing, it is done." I almost pity Louis.

Louis' arm twitches. I do not let myself notice it, nor follow the arm to the hand which will be clenched into a tight fist. Let him dare hit me now, with six galleys of armed men chanting my name every church hour!

That afternoon I receive word that the bishop of Saint-Omer, acting as the pope's nuncio, has insisted on speaking with me in private. How Louis must have ground his teeth. He has allowed no one to speak to me privately since long before the birth of our daughter. But he cannot refuse the Holy Father's nuncio.

I curtsy low when he is ushered in. He raises me quickly, his hands gentle and his eyes full of concern. He pretends not to see the dampness on my cheeks as he helps me to a chair. I stare down at my lap while he seats himself, embarrassed at being so easily undone by this first show of kindness and respect after so long.

"Has Louis of Taranto harmed you, Your Majesty?" he asks when we are alone.

I tip my head, demurring, too proud to admit to the bruises hidden under my kirtle. "All will be well, now that you have come. But tell me what is happening in my realm."

He looks taken aback a moment but recovers quickly, making no comment on the state of my ignorance. It confirms all he needs to know.

"When he received your letter, Clement VI wrote to the doge of Genoa, ordering him to protect you. Immediately Genoa rescinded their contract to supply Louis of Hungary with ships and declared themselves for you, a strong message to all Italy. As for your subjects in Provence, they are enraged to hear of your husband usurping your rule. You, and only you, are the rightful heir of King Robert the Wise. The count of Avellino had no difficulty in raising the company of soldiers you see on our ships in the harbor to come to your aid.

"As for your kingdom, the Hungarian siege of Aversa continues. Your people fight for their lives to resist King Louis' rule, having experienced it once. They are united for you, Your Majesty." He hesitates. "It is rumored that King Louis has been injured, that he took an arrow in his leg during the siege. He has not been seen outside his tent in many days."

I do not ask how he heard this. Such information is worth good money to any mercenary wounded or otherwise disinclined to continue a drawn-out siege. If Clement's nuncio says it, it is more than a rumor.

We speak for an hour. Or rather, he talks and I listen as he tells me of Clement's unequivocal support for my cause, of the withdrawal of support for King Louis of Hungary from every city and country loyal to the pope, and of the outrage in Provence over my husband's behavior.

"It is not in my power to order your husband to free you from this room," he says at last, a mixture of regret and disgust in his voice. "My next task is to go to Aversa and speak with King Louis." He touches my cheek as a loving father would to comfort a troubled child. "I will convince him to end this wicked invasion and agree to a peaceful settlement between Hungary and Naples. Meanwhile, I leave the count of Avellino and his six galleys here, to convince Louis of Taranto to see reason."

"God Bless you, Father," I say, kneeling for his blessing and weeping silently as he gives it.

As the door to my chamber closes behind him I feel a strange sensation, one I do not recognize immediately. For the first time in over a year I am feeling hope.

The chanting from the galleys resumes each time the bells of the cathedrals and monasteries toll out the hours: Prime, Terce, Sext, None, Vespers, Compline. Each time I go to my window and wave at my loyal subjects come from Provence to free me. And each time there are more of my Neapolitan subjects come to watch and join in the chant. Was it only four years ago they stood in these streets and yelled accusations, stirred up by my cousins and this same Hugo del Balzo who has now come to rescue me? They cheer me now when I appear at my window, and I wave at them, accepting their tribute without reserve. We have been through a great deal, my people and I, these last four years.

"It is not true!" Louis' old nursemaid limps into my bedchamber as quickly as she is capable of when the bells of Lauds have woken me the next morning. "It cannot be true, Your Majesty," she amends, spilling a little of the rosewater from the washing bowl she is carrying as she curtsies.

"What have you heard?" I ask, sitting up to let her wash the sleep from my face. In the darkness outside the faithful chanting of my saviors on the galleys is winding down. What a blessed sound to wake up to!

"The count of Avellino is saying that my Louis intends to poison you. That his ships have come to besiege the castle and save you." Her face is scrunched up near weeping so torn is she between the queen she now serves and the boy she once nursed.

So Hugo is up to his old tricks, but this time he is turning the populace against Louis instead of against me. Well, I will not intervene on behalf of my gaoler.

"He says he is acting on the Holy Father's behalf," Louis' old nurse continues. Her voice trembles. Her hands as well, washing the sweat of sleep from my face and neck. "But your guard tastes your food and wine before every meal."

I give her a level look. She knows those who guard me now are Louis' men. "You know he has threatened to have me killed," I tell her calmly.

"*I* will taste your food, Your Majesty," she says, her eyes welling.

"No, not you." I take the dripping cloth gently from her trembling hands and return it to the basin. Then I motion to my Aunt Catherine's old maid, standing sullenly just inside the room, waiting to bring me my chemise. "*You* may taste my food from now on," I tell her as I raise my arms for her to remove my night gown, ignoring her gasp of dismay.

"What else does the count say?" I ask as they dress me. My late Lady Aunt's maid still sullenly says nothing, but Louis' old nurse, now equally loyal to me, speaks up.

"He says that if my Louis continues to resist him and if the people of Naples do not act to have you reinstated as their sole sovereign at once, then Pope Clement, or rather he, as the pope's representative, will side with the King of Hungary and use his fleet to take Naples!"

This is alarming. I keep my face expressionless with difficulty. My proud Neapolitans do not respond well to threats. What a gamble Hugo is taking—with *my* throne!

"He says," the old nurse hurries on oblivious to my silence, "that if the people obey the pope and help the count to convince Louis to surrender power to you, then he will force the King of Hungary to retreat and establish peace between our two kingdoms. Can he do that?" She peers up at me, wringing her hands.

I almost smile at the height of Hugo del Balzo's conceit. But it is a good strategy. "Certainly *the pope* can do that and more," I say sternly.

She pulls herself together at my rebuke and reaches to help her silent comrade dress me. I choose my royal blue surcote with gold fleur-de-lis. It is too good for sitting in my bedchamber, but when I go to the window I want my people to see me in my robes of state.

Such small things can turn the wheel of Fortune. A rumor favoring me for a change. A single arrow hitting its mark. The pope finally choosing a side.

In two weeks the people of Naples have so turned against Louis of Taranto that he dares not step outside the gates of Castle Nuovo. One of the castle guards—one of *my* royal guards—comes to my room. Bowing low, he waits for me to bid him rise and speak.

"Your Majesty, I have been sent to escort you to a meeting with Louis of Taranto, Niccolò Acciaiuoli and the count of Avellino. If you care to accept the invitation I will wait outside your doors until you are ready." His eyes shine, inviting me to take all the time I wish to make myself ready.

Louis' old nursemaid grins in delight as she braids up my hair after they have dressed me in my robes of state. I do not hurry them, but I am too eager to hear what Louis has to say to delay overly. My chamberlain arrives, bearing my crown from the royal treasury, as my maids pin my veil in place. I place it on my head and stand still a moment, feeling the weight and authority of it settle over me, bearing me up and renewing me as though I had lost my soul and only now regained it.

When the guards open my door I almost hesitate before stepping through it, so monumental an action it now seems. My royal guard bows low, sweeping me past the moment, and solemnly escorts me to Louis' council chamber, where he has been meeting my advisors and making decisions for my kingdom for so long. My guard snaps his fingers and Louis' men-at-arms push open the door.

Louis sits slouched at the end of the table. His skin is sallow, his eyes dull and underscored with folds that tell of sleepless nights. He raises his head to glare at me as I stand in the doorway, taking in my robes of state and my crown. As though he cannot bear the sight he stares back down at his hands which fidget with a document on the table before him.

Niccolò, Hugo, the bishop of Florence and four other noblemen close to my husband all rise to their feet and bow deeply. Only Louis remains slumped in his seat.

I wait. Without my acknowledgment none of them can rise from their obeisance. We stand in a silent tableaux. Finally Niccolò shifts with what must surely be a nudge of his foot against Louis' under the table. Louis looks up resentfully. No one else moves. Then Hugo, still bent, catches Louis' eye and scowls.

Hugo is not a man to anger. Even Louis knows this. He lurches to his feet and bends into a sullen bow.

I nod at once to all of them and step into the room. Taking my seat at the head of the table I motion for them to be seated.

Without looking up at me again, Louis reads the document before him. It is an official edict acknowledging me as the sole ruler of Provence and the Kingdom of Naples. If I am willing he will be crowned as well, but in name only, as my consort. He will defer to my rule in all matters of state and expect no say in my government.

There is silence when he finishes reading. I wait until he looks up at me, then nod my agreement. There is no need to further humiliate him with a speech of acceptance at this time. He signs the edict and slides it across to me. I sign beside his name. The bishop of Florence affixes the royal seal.

Back in my own rooms I write at once a message of gratitude to Pope Clement, and another to my subjects in Provence thanking them for their support and expressing to them my "best love". My first act, now I am once again the Countess of Provence, is to replace Louis' appointment there with the man I had originally appointed, and to name a new seneschal of Provence, one of their own who has proved his loyalty to me and of whom I know they will approve.

Chapter 24

Marriage

Maria of Durazzo
September, 1350

"King Louis was wounded fighting for Aversa," Margherita tells me, having gone out into the city to learn what news she could. "Both in battle and by siege he tried to capture the town, but it refused to yield."

"What, Aversa? Aversa with no resources and only a single wall for fortification? How could it hold the Hungarian army back?"

"Louis of Taranto sent a battalion to their aid, as he has promised he will do for every city that resists King Louis."

"One battalion against the Hungarian army?"

"He cannot expend his entire force on one battle. He has to keep most of his men here to protect Naples." *Is she defending him? Do the people see Louis as their protector despite what he did to their queen?* Before I can think of a way to ask, she continues. "No one knows how Aversa held out so long. The very impossibility of it has heartened every city in the kingdom. If Aversa could put up such resistance how will King Louis defeat our larger, better fortified cities? They are more determined than ever to resist him because of Aversa's example."

"But he has won her." I signal the kitchen servant who has entered with wine and a selection of cheeses, fruit, and nuts to pour two cups of wine before I dismiss her.

When we are alone Margherita sits in the chair beside mine and drinks from her wine cup. "King Louis has won Aversa. But apparently the effort has given him pause. The bishop of Saint-Omer has convinced him to agree to cease all hostilities for six months, until next April, if Queen Joanna and Louis of Taranto will do the same. King Louis' army will stay in Aversa—" I frown to think they will be so close—"and ours in Naples, but Louis of Hungary, Queen Joanna, and Louis of Taranto must all leave the kingdom."

"Where will they go? And when?" Margherita has contacts throughout the city. People talk freely to her, this relative of the Durazzo's, well enough connected to befriend but low enough in the family for the connection not to harm them. Her news will be reliable.

"King Louis and his barons are preparing to journey to Rome." She takes a sip of wine before continuing. I know her. She is deliberately pausing before a choice bit of news. I wait impatiently.

"Joanna is to be tried again for the murder of Andrew. If she is found innocent, King Louis must give up his claim to Naples and all the lands and castles he has occupied here. If the queen is found guilty, she will lose her crown." Margherita pauses to take a piece of cheese and a fig.

I am dumbfounded. When I regain my voice I can only croak, "And?"

Her eyes twinkle at leaving me again in suspense. She swallows her cheese down with a gulp of wine.

"And you will inherit the kingdom of Naples."

"Me? Do they know of my…arrangement with King Louis?"

"No one has spoken of it. But I am certain it is part of King Louis' reason for agreeing. That and his wound, which has not healed."

"The bishop of Saint-Omer will know of it. That is why Pope

Clement has named me heir instead of Joanna's daughter Françoise. To get King Louis to agree." And if the pope knows, Joanna must know also. I feel sick at the thought. But what was I to do, penniless and obligated to obey my husband's family? Had she given me my dowry I would have refused him!

"Pope Clement has already tried my sister. He has not only declared her innocent, but above suspicion." I gain confidence from my own words. "He would look foolish if he put her on trial again. It is a ruse to get King Louis to stop fighting and leave Naples." I smile at knowing what Louis of Hungary could not deduce for himself. "The pope will not allow King Louis to marry me, either. Not after his brutal behavior the last time he ruled Naples. He will find a way to end the engagement."

So I will not have to marry King Louis after all! I laugh with relief. "We will have a feast, you and I and my daughters. It will only be roast chicken but with orange slices for flavor." I clap my hands and the guard at the door looks in. "Tell the cook we will have a chicken for dinner, with orange sauce. And have him make fruit pastries with sugar. And do not come back to say there is no sugar in the store room; let him find it where he may at any price!"

Margherita smiles at my enthusiasm. "The King of Hungary is still very wealthy," she reminds me.

"After two campaigns against Naples? And the plague? Probably not. If he were still wealthy Pope Clement would not have taken my sister's side. He has a nose for gold."

"You may be right," Margherita says thoughtfully. "The last part of the agreement is that Joanna must pay Louis of Hungary three hundred thousand florins to ransom her cousins."

"Three hundred thousand?" I gasp at the unbelievable sum. "She will never be able to raise so much money."

"She has agreed to it. She and Louis of Taranto are preparing to leave Naples. Will we be going also?"

"I have not been asked to leave." I frown. "No, I will not run from my home again. And if my sister cannot raise the ransom money, what do I care? I will have no brothers-in-law to order me about." I take a drink of wine, pop a fig into my mouth, and chew it with defiance. It is a harsh thing to say but I will not take it back. They thought only of themselves when they arranged this unwanted marriage I could not refuse and that shames me now. Besides, no matter how they deserve it for betraying her, Joanna will never leave them to languish in prison. Somehow she will find the ransom. And I will have to wait even longer for my dowry, no doubt!

I will not let that ruin my happiness now. "The war is over and my sister has regained her kingdom." I shake my head in amazement. "Tonight we will celebrate. I will wear one of my new kirtles for dinner."

What a summer it has been! In the end it was neither Louis of Taranto's prowess nor his skill in warfare that won the war; it was his cruelty to my sister! All the civilized world united to save her, from Pope Clement down to the lowest commoner in Naples demanding her release at the gates of Castle Nuovo. I have never heard of such a thing.

"How everyone loves her!" I mutter. "She is beautiful, brave, intelligent, kind..." I take a sip of wine, glancing sideways at Margherita. Has she nothing to say? About me? "They love her for her passion for justice, her generosity..."

"And she loves them back unreservedly, regardless of station or privilege." Margherita smiles. She loves Joanna also. Does she wish she had stayed in my sister's court and not helped Charles marry me as her family ordered her? And then she *had* to come with me, her second choice. No choice at all, really, once her family had spoken.

"It is in the air, this love of Joanna!" I cry. "I am half in love with her myself! I, who know her flaws as well as I know her virtues. I thought she needed to be rescued, but as usual she has rescued me!"

The Queen Who Sold Her Crown

For all the wealth I would have enjoyed as Queen of Hungary, for all the reasons I told myself I must do it, I knew King Louis would never have trusted or cared for me, the widow of the man he believed killed his brother. My fate would have been no better than Joanna's, locked up and beaten by her husband. Only there would be no rescue coming for me. No, I would have been spurned for what I did, regardless whether it freed my kin and averted a war and saved my sister's life. I would have been reviled and forgotten, not worthy of rescuing.

Well, Joanna has saved me that and averted a war and reclaimed her sovereignty and come out of it all as shiny bright and pure as the morning star. It is annoying beyond words. But even so I am grateful for it.

"As usual?"

I look up from my reverie and realize Margherita has been watching me. No doubt she has guessed at my thoughts. She shakes her head with a bemused smile. "Queen Joanna did not rescue you when the Hungarians came. She did not offer to take you on her boat. You rescued yourself. And your children. You did not leave them behind for King Louis. You are a devoted mother."

"Joanna loves her children as much as I do!" However annoying she is, I will not have my sister unjustly criticized. "It would have been impossible for her to take Charles Martel. She would have been caught at once."

"And it was not difficult for you? Would you not have escaped more easily without two small children and a baby in tow? And a distant cousin-by-marriage whom you also refused to leave behind?" She takes my hand in both of hers. "Duchess Maria, why are you so quick to see your flaws and so reluctant to see your virtues? You are as beautiful and intelligent and certainly as brave as your sister. And you are loyal onto death to those you love."

My eyes well with tears. I look away, blinking. "I have not always been loyal to my sister."

"It is not easy to choose between a sister and a husband. And you have your daughters' futures to consider. Life is not as simple and clear as we thought when we were children. Your sister has not always been loyal to you, either. And she has not always protected those who serve her, as you do."

"She has the kingdom to consider."

"And still you defend her. And still you love her. As do I. But not as much as I love you."

Joanna and Louis leave on September 17th on board Hugo del Balzo's personal ship, accompanied by three of the galleys from Marseille. No stealing away in the night this time—she is given a royal send-off, banners flying, musicians singing her praises, jugglers and jesters entertaining the crowd at the pier. All of Naples, it seems, has come to cheer her off. She has brought them peace—one more reason to love her. My daughters and I watch the spectacle from the south tower of Castle dell'Ovo where we can see the ships in the harbor and the port without danger of infection. The plague is dying down but not yet gone.

Hugo will remain behind with the other two galleys to aid his cousin, Francisco del Balzo, whom Joanna has appointed to govern Naples while she is away. I cannot but wonder how Hugo feels, having rescued her from both Louis' but not being trusted to rule in her absence. She will never forgive him for torturing Philippa and her family—nor will I—but I wonder if I would have had the courage to thwart him in this manner? I study his face as he sits on his horse with a dozen of the royal guard, but I am too far to catch any nuance of emotion beneath his smooth courtier's smile. Well, it is no concern of mine.

We watch until the four ships sail out of sight, taking my sister away. I expect it is not easy for Joanna to leave her kingdom again, even temporarily, but I am glad of the respite. I am more than ready for peace.

When the news arrives that Louis of Hungary and his barons have left Naples the same day, I feel as one does when a storm cloud passes overhead, swollen and dark, and continues on to wreck havoc elsewhere.

A sense of calm settles over Naples. I feel it even here in Castle dell'Ovo, but Margherita is closer to it when she walks through the city on marketing day.

"The war is over. The plague is over," she sighs after one such trip, as she bends to her sewing beside me. "The day of Armageddon did not come, although the world trembled on the edge of it. Even our priests declared the end of the world, you could hear the terror in their voices as they read from the Bible." She looks up, her eyes brimming at the memory. *"There shall be wars and rumors of wars...for nation shall rise against nation and kingdom against kingdom; and there shall be earthquakes in divers places and famines and troubles...for in those days shall be affliction, such as was not from the beginning of creation..."*

She shakes her head as if to clear away the fearful words that describe so well what we have been through.

"And yet we have survived," I remind her, struck by her melancholy. "The war and pestilence and famine—"

"Is it all over? Can it be over?" She blinks and wipes her eyes. "They are saying we who have survived have somehow, miraculously, been absolved of the sin that shook heaven and earth with God's wrath. How can they say that? We know, each one of us, how faithlessly we acted when death walked in our shadow. So why did the sword of God pass over us?"

I frown, uncomfortable with her questions. "There is still hunger," I remind her. Thousands of acres of crops were left to rot when the field hands died.

"But there are fewer mouths to feed. And there is work for everyone, so there is hope. Hope. Who would have believed such a fragile sensation would persist beyond the shadow of death?"

"Yes," I say, for I feel it too, though I have not till this moment put it into words. Today I heard my children laughing in their nursery. I went and sat in a chair by the window and watched them play, letting the sound wash over me, heal me, calm me. Fill me with hope.

"So perhaps we *have* been forgiven. Perhaps we can start to live again." She smiles at me.

I am only one false smile above poverty, I consider reminding her. I am not convinced she is right. But I hope so. I hope the worst is over. I hope we can all, peasants and princes alike, begin to regain the life we have lost.

It is twelve days now since my sister and her husband and Louis of Hungary all left Naples. I am sitting with Margherita and my daughter Joanna, having taken our mid-day dinner in my chambers, when a messenger arrives at the door.

"The count of Avelino is at the gates with his sons, asking to see you before he leaves Naples."

I am aware he has been readying himself and his men to leave, now that the kingdom is at peace. In truth, I am glad of it. I have never trusted him, despite knowing that he has always acted as the Pope's representative. He would gladly have denounced me and my sister as accomplices in Andrew's murder if there had been any evidence upon which to base such a vile accusation. Only our royal blood—and his lack of it—saved us, for he certainly found no proof against Philippa and her family either. I shudder and remind myself that he has given us capable and much-needed assistance this time.

Nevertheless, I will be glad to bid him farewell.

"Open the doors and let him enter," I command my guards. "I will receive him in the great hall. Joanna, you may come with me." Margherita rises also. I am about to wave her back; my daughter must learn how lesser nobles are received by those with royal blood, but there is no need for Margherita to endure Hugo del Balzo's company. She has despised him since he tortured one of her cousins, trying to make the poor man denounce family members as accomplices in Andrew's death. Then I think, the count might have news for me, and I may need Margherita to take Joanna back to the nursery, so I nod for her to come.

I hear the hard stomp of many boots against the tiles before the doors to the great hall swing open. Hugo del Balzo enters, striding like a lord in his own castle, accompanied by both his sons and a dozen of his counselors, all armed. I raise my head, alarmed and angry that they should bear arms in my presence. Margherita steps up beside me, pressing Joanna behind us.

"What do you mean by this, Lord Hugo? Bringing armed men into my hall?" I look around for my guards, but see only men in the livery of the count of Avelina. What has he done with my guards?

"I mean to marry you to my son, Duchess Maria." He smiles, a cruel look of triumph in his eyes, and snaps his fingers. His eldest son steps forward.

I gasp, and only with great effort hold my ground. Marry me? To his son? Robert is a dark, ugly man with small eyes that do not meet mine. His lips are twisted into the same avaricious smirk as his father's. He is perhaps a decade older than I am, tall and stocky, a huge brute. I have feared and loathed him since I first saw him when he came with his father to root out the conspirators in Andrew's murder.

"How dare you?" I cry, still more surprised than outraged, but even I hear the tremor in my voice. There is only one reason he would dare. My own words come back to me: *The pope will not allow King Louis to marry me. He will find a way to end the engagement.*

"I will never marry you. I am of royal blood!" I say to the black-haired beast still leering at me. How could they imagine I would debase myself to marry the son of a count, a man with only common blood in his veins?

Is Joanna aware of this? No, certainly not. She would be furious. Furious! This defiles her as well as me, to force her sister, a royal princess, to marry a commoner. She was furious when Charles took me, and he has the same royal blood as we do!

"There is no use resisting, Duchess. My men are guarding the gates to the castle. No one is coming to rescue you." He glances at his son and they laugh together.

They are enjoying this, I think, sickened.

With a cry of outrage Margherita launches herself at Hugo, her small eating knife gripped in one hand, the fingers of her other hand curled into claws.

Robert's sword is out of its scabbard in a flash and with one lunge he opens Margherita from neck to groin. She falls to the floor, her entrails spilling across the tiles, her eyes wide with surprise.

Joanna screams and screams but I cannot make a sound. I gasp for air, staring at Margherita so suddenly and obscenely butchered before me. *Now we can start to live,* she told me, only three days ago.

Hugo glares at his son. "Clean this up!" he orders two of his men. "We are here for a wedding, not a funeral!"

"My wife should know the consequences of disobedience from the beginning," Robert snarls, wiping his sword on Margherita's dress and sheathing it before the men carry her body away. "Shut that brat up." He points a thick finger at Joanna, still uttering hysterical shrieks.

I turn and hold her, shielding her too late from the brutal sight. "Hush," I tell her. "Hush, my darling. There will be no more violence."

Robert grins as though this justifies his savagery. His father is still frowning but his shoulders relax. I have been brought under submission, however crudely done. He snaps his fingers. A priest steps forward.

"What, *now*?" I gasp stupidly. "Here?" My eyes involuntarily turn to the blood on the tiles between us.

Hugo del Balzo shrugs. "Over there." He points to a window breathing in sunlight, with a tapestry of a garden hanging on the wall beside it.

I look at the window, my arms still around my daughter who is weeping quietly now. I do not think I can move.

"Do you want me to carry you?" Robert grins at me.

I look pleadingly at the priest. His face is impassive. So I am right about Clement, and it will avail me nothing to refuse to say my vows. This will happen with or without my consent. I am being punished for my treachery as surely as the count of Avelino is being rewarded for his loyal service here, and at the same time King Louis' last hope for the crown of Naples is being firmly denied. There will be no second trial of Joanna; Clement will never put Robert on a throne. With one move the Holy Father has taught us all a lesson in obedience.

Joanna's arms are locked around me. Still holding her, I walk the two of us sideways toward the window, my knees threatening to cave beneath me. "Let me send her to the nursery," I beg the priest. "She is only six years old."

"She will be a good witness," Hugo says.

"Stop crying," Robert snarls. "This is a happy day. I am marrying your mother." He reaches to push Joanna's shoulder. I turn so that he shoves my arm instead. He glares at me.

I barely hear the priest as he recites the sacrament of marriage. When it comes time, I say my vows in a calm and steady voice. I am terrified and sickened and above all furious. But Joanna has at last stopped crying and I do not want to frighten her again.

Robert starts when the priest looks up at him and recites his vows slowly, his rough voice slurring the Latin words as though he has memorized them and does not know their meaning. I am marrying an illiterate swine who does not even understand Latin.

And then it is done and he kisses me, a sloppy inelegant kiss which I endure tight-lipped, as though someone were rubbing mud across my face. Or worse.

Only it is not done.

"Down on the floor," Hugo del Balzo says.

I look at him uncomprehending.

"On the floor," he says again roughly. His eyes shift sideways unable to meet mine.

At the corner of my eye I catch Robert's eager leer and freeze. Incredulous, I stare at the count, then turn to the priest. He spreads his hands, a small gesture, as though this is a matter of marital dispute in which he will not interfere, but as he turns his face aside I see a look of revulsion cross his face.

"I will not."

The words have barely left my mouth when Robert grabs me and throws me to the floor, falling on top of me. I slam onto my back hard enough to take my breath and crack my elbow sharply, but in a moment I am fighting, kicking him, twisting and reaching to scratch his face.

He laughs and pins me down, a strong man twice my size. I reach my good hand for my knife, determined to kill him if I can, but he knows my intent and grabs my wrist, twisting it until I fear he will break it. His father obligingly stands one foot on my bruised elbow, hard enough that I gasp with pain and cannot move as Robert pulls my skirts up.

He is brutal and quick and on his feet again tying up his breeches as his brother and their men cheer.

"Married and consummated," Hugo announces, receiving shouts of agreement from his men.

I lie on the floor too humiliated to move, until I see my daughter's face, white with shock, staring down at me from among the aroused male faces.

"Go to the nursery," I croak.

"Take her to the nursery," Hugo instructs one of his men. "Tell the nursemaid to pack them up. They are coming with us, the girl and her sisters and their nurse." He reaches a hand down to me. I have no choice but to let him pull me to my feet. I sway before him, dizzy and nauseous. I swallow hard, refusing to add to my humiliation by vomiting in front of them.

"Tell your ladies to pack your things quickly." He nods to Robert to accompany me to my chambers. "We leave within the hour."

Chapter 25

Captives

Maria of Durazzo
October, 1350

"My children and I must have some fresh air. We are suffocating down here day and night."

For six long days we have been locked below deck in a small, windowless room on Hugo del Balzo's ship. I know neither where we are nor where we are going. Each night Robert descends the narrow steps and enters our cabin and rapes me as he did on our marriage day. I do not struggle. I am careful to make no sound at all, not with my babies and their nurse lying in a huddle on pallets on the floor pretending to be asleep. Even little Margherita, no more than two years old, knows not to make a noise.

The first night she woke and started wailing until Robert rose from our bed and slapped her hard enough to knock her out. I screamed at him and received the same treatment. Now we are all well-trained and silent until he has had his way and lies snoring in the bed. Then I creep out from under him and hold my daughters and whisper reassurances to them that I am unhurt. I would kill him in his sleep if I could think of a way to drag his body upstairs and throw it overboard in secret, so his father would never learn of my revenge and seek his own.

Robert stops pulling on his boots to look at me suspiciously. "How do I know you will not jump overboard?"

I look back at him coldly. "And leave my children to your tender mercy?"

He chuckles. "Ah, yes, I would need to take another bride if I lost you. Your Joanna is of marriageable age, is she not?" He laughs at the expression he sees on my face.

"She is not. Nor would the pope condone such an action."

"Regrettably, we are aboard ship and cannot contact the pope for his direction. Remember that, Lady Wife, when you walk on the deck this morning."

I cannot speak for anger. He is right about one thing: I will not live like this. It is unbearable. I have been married and bedded, it cannot be undone, but eventually he will slip. I will find a way to send my daughters to Joanna and then I will murder him. Or myself. Either way I will be free of this foul marriage. I turn aside, not giving him the words of gratitude he is obviously expecting for granting me a walk on the deck. He shrugs and pulls on his second boot and leaves us.

I think he has forgotten his promise or changed his mind by the time our mid-day meal arrives, but when the boy comes to take away the dishes and uneaten food, he is accompanied by two of the count's men.

The older one looks at the food and frowns. "We have come to escort you around the deck," he says, his voice heavy with disapproval.

I motion my daughters up quickly and help their nurse to tie their cloaks around them before throwing on my own.

The older guard leads us through the low wooden door to the stairs while the younger one waits to follow us. I hear Margherita shriek and turn quickly.

"Na, na," the young guard is saying to her. "You are safe with me, little girl. I canna have you trip on the stairs and fall, can I?" His voice is kind and Margherita, looking up at him wide-eyed, stops struggling and falls silent.

"Are ya comin or not?" the first guard chides. I follow him up the stairs.

A light breeze stirs the tendrils of hair that have escaped my braids as I climb up from below deck. I breathe in eagerly. The air tastes of the sea, salty and fresh and cool, and revives me as nothing else could. I feel like Lazarus emerging from his cave, and cannot get enough of the briny wind caressing my face and arms and neck. I hurry up the stairs into sunlight so bright it blinds me. Shading my eyes I walk to the railing and stare out at the dancing wavelets. I have lived beside the sea all my life and only now realize how much I love her. Hugo's man stands close ready to grab me if I should try to leap overboard. It had not occurred to me before but now, looking out at the clean, free, dancing waves, I think how lovely it would be to escape this filthy ship and be pulled under into a turquoise world. With an effort I turn my back on it.

Joanna has come up beside me, to her nurse's alarm, but the woman is too busy trying to hold Agnes and Clementia back, afraid they might slip under the railing. Little Margherita is struggling in the young guard's arms, demanding to be put down so she can run. The look on his face as he holds her—not a man to hold a woman against her will, even a small one, but too worried for her safety to let her go—makes me laugh for the first time in days. I step toward him holding out my arms and he releases her chubby little body to me with relief.

"You may not run on the deck, it is slippery. Or get in the sailors' way," I tell the four of them. "You must hold nurse's hand or mine, always." When they have all nodded solemnly I let Margherita stand, taking her firmly by the hand, and we walk around the narrow deck.

All too soon the older guard coughs and tells me we must return to our cabin. Before I can protest he grumbles, "I have my orders, Duchess."

"Where is the count? I will demand better treatment!"

"Ah, he is in his own cabin, sick with the gout," the young guard says before the older one can stop him.

"Tell me where we are, then," I challenge them, "if you want me to go back willingly."

The older man rubs his chin and gives a short nod to the younger guard. "Off the coast of Italy," the young man says. "Tomorrow we will dock at Gaeta where Her—" The young man breaks off quickly at a sharp look from his senior. He bends quickly. "I will carry the little one down the stairs."

"No!" Margherita says, her little lips pouting.

"We must go back down, my darling," I say.

Her. It can only be Her Majesty that he started to say. My sister is in Gaeta. I remember now that Hugo said he would rendezvous with her ships before they reached Rome. Does he believe my sister will allow this? I must get word to her that this hideous union has been forced upon me.

Louis and I sit side by side in the hall of the royal residence in Gaeta, hearing petitions from my subjects and receiving gifts or messages from foreign emissaries. We learned this morning that Hugo del Balzo's ships reached dock during the night, and have been expecting him to arrive with a report on our kingdom. But when the doors open next it is not Hugo, or even his sons, who are escorted in, but a miserable sailor unbathed and stinking of sweat.

"What is this?" Louis demands.

"Have you come from the count of Avellino's ship?" I ask.

The man's head bobs eagerly. "Yes, Your Majesty," he says in deplorable French. "With a message you will want to hear."

"On your knees!" Louis orders.

The man falls to the floor, head bowed. When he glances up tentatively I nod for him to give us his message. He bows his head again and mumbles it quickly.

"He has done what?" I grip the arms of my chair to prevent my leaping out of it.

"Married the Duchess of Durazzo to his son Robert, Your Majesty." The man kneeling before us trembles.

"And was the Duchess willing?" my husband asks in a calm voice.

I glare at him. My sister, the granddaughter of kings, willing to marry a count? And such a count as that, stinking of treachery and treason? How can he even ask?

"I believe not, my Lord. They have her and her children locked in a cabin below decks, for fear she will jump overboard and drown herself—"

I leap from my seat with an inarticulate scream. The man huddles on the floor burying his head in his arms. Louis looks amused for one instant before he wipes the expression away, replacing it with a look of outrage. "And what have you done to aid her?" he asks in a haughty voice.

"Me, my Lord?" the man squeaks from inside his arms. "I...I have come to inform you?" His voice rises plaintively.

Louis rises quickly, his hand on the hilt of his sword. I raise my hand to stop him, embarrassed by my own desire to murder this messenger. What could the man do? Mount a ship's mutiny single-handed? "Thank you for your information," I say, though the words come out with difficulty.

"You are on shore leave," Louis observes, looking down at the man crouched on the ground before him as one would look at a spider or cockroach. The movement of the man's arms indicates a nodding head beneath them. "And the rest of the crew are also taking shore leave?"

"Yes, my Lord," the hidden head mumbles.

"And the count of Avellino and his sons? Speak up, man!"

The sailor unwinds his arms and folds them before him as a man in prayer. He keeps his head bowed. "His sons have come ashore but the count is shipboard recovering from a spell of the gout, my Lord."

I watch my husband's face harden. It is an expression I recognize, one that usually precedes violence. He signals two of his men.

"Go with this wretch and find his shipmates. Ply them with drink. See that none of them return to their ship before the bells ring vespers. Especially the count's sons. At vespers you will arrest the older son, Robert, and lock him in our dungeon." He tosses a bag of coins to one of his men.

He stands silent, his anger mounting, while they take their leave. I am not fooled. He is not concerned about my sister, though the outrage done to our royal lineage is just the excuse he has been waiting for. No, he is fueling his hatred of Hugo del Balzo, building it into a blaze. I note the fury growing in his eyes as he prepares himself to enjoy revenge upon the man who humiliated him in Naples. The count who lead the entire city to shout, "Down with Louis of Taranto!" day and night; who demolished his dream of stealing my crown. I shiver, waiting to hear what he will do, but I do not intrude or protest. Hugo has gone too far this time.

When the door closes behind them Louis turns to the man standing rigidly beside him, the arms man he most trusts. "Call up a dozen of my men, those you trust with your life. Tell them to arm themselves and mount up. I will meet you in the courtyard."

It occurs to me as he stalks away that Hugo del Balzo is Clement's man. There may be no written trail from the pope to Maria's abduction, but his hand is behind it. His message has been delivered to all concerned. Good. Let Maria and King Louis consider the fruit of their treachery, let Hugo believe himself safe to enjoy his reward and leave himself unguarded.

There is no trail from me to Louis of Taranto's impending action, either. But let Clement receive this message: I am the sole monarch of my realm and he has overstepped his authority. The royal bloodline of France is not to be trifled with.

Sometime during the night we arrived at Gaeta. I awake in the dark little cabin to the quiet bobbing of a ship at anchor and the clear, mournful cry of seagulls, a sound that should be drowned out by the louder calls of sailors and guardsmen manning the ship. I lie in bed listening. Robert has left some time ago, the sheets beside me are cold. I hear a man's voice. No, two. And a third. Where are the others? There should be dozens.

They have gone ashore! The ship must have only a bare crew manning her. Has Robert gone also? And his father, his brother? I roll off the cot quickly.

"Hsst," I whisper, nudging the nurse with my foot. She shifts with a groan, waking Clementia who opens her mouth—

"Hush!" I put my hand over her mouth quickly. By then the others are waking. I silence them all with a whisper. "The men have gone ashore. This may be our chance. Get dressed, quickly. Quietly."

When I try the door I am not surprised to find it locked. Peering through the crack I can see the bolt was hastily shot and has barely caught. "Find me a knife," I whisper. "Anything sharp and slender! Look around."

Before we can move, however, we hear the heavy tramp of men's boots mounting the gangway. I back away from the door with an unchristian oath. And then I surrender to silent tears. To be so close! Why is God taunting me so?

But the men boarding do not call out to their comrades. Except for their heavy footfalls they make no noise at all. I wipe my cheeks dry and lean against the door listening, hardly breathing.

A man on deck screams. And then another! I hear the scuffle of men fighting, and others running onto the deck. The clash of swords, a sound I will never forget after the night the Hungarians entered Naples. I cry out before I can stop myself and back away from the door. Behind me Clementia screams. I grab her and hold her against me, hushing her.

"Quiet, children, quiet!" Who knows who has come aboard and what their intent? If Hugo del Balzo was acting with the pope's agreement, how much worse might captivity by these men be? Or worse, are they coming to murder us all? "Shush, shush, my darlings." I look around but there is nowhere in this tiny cabin to hide them.

The battle above is short, followed by a violent screaming. I think it is Hugo's voice but cannot be sure. Then comes the terrifying sound of armed men descending the stairs. I back as far from the door as I can, pushing my children behind me and brandishing a plate, the only thing I could find to hit a man with. Their nurse sits in the corner shaking and hiding her face in her hands. I think of Margherita, ever stalwart and brave beside me, and want to weep. But this is no time for tears. "Hush," I whisper to my daughters. "Maman will protect you."

There is a rattle at the door and then it bursts open.

I blink, not daring to trust my eyes. "Louis?"

He laughs, exhilarated. "I have come to rescue you, sister-in-law!"

I peer at the men behind him. Can it be true? "Hugo—?"

"Is dead and on his way to hell. His body is in the sea, not worth a burial." He laughs again, as if it were a joke. I know some men feel truly alive only when they are in battle. I realize Louis is such a man.

Still I dare not believe it. That monster, dead so easily? I feel Joanna's head peek out from behind my skirts and push it back into hiding. "You are certain? You saw him die?"

"I killed him myself. Skewered him a dozen times over with my sword, pitched him into the sea and watched him sink." He sees my children peeking from behind me and his voice softens. "You are safe, Maria. You and your children will come and live with Joanna and me. We will stay in Gaeta for the winter, until we can all go back to Naples."

I lick my lips, beginning to hope I need not die after all. I, too, have been found worthy of rescue.

"And Robert?" My voice trembles.

"He is in chains in my dungeon," Louis replies. "Where he will remain until we return to Naples and he can be tried for daring to violate a royal princess of the house of Anjou." He says this proudly as though he himself is not guilty of the same crime.

I let my children come timidly forth from behind me and thank their cousin for freeing us. I let Louis lead me off the ship, his men surrounding us in a knot of protection. I let him hand me into a carriage, his men lifting my daughters in around me, but then I cannot let go of his hand, so that he has to climb into the carriage and ride with us. I let him escort me into the royal residence in Gaeta, where my sister runs to greet me and embraces me, all sins forgiven. I let her take me to a bedchamber, prettily appointed with tapestries and paintings, with a wide, soft, clean bed where I will sleep alone with my children. "You are safe here," they keep insisting. "We have freed you."

And yet I do not feel safe, or free.

Somewhere below us Robert lurks in their dungeon planning what he will do to me and my children when he is freed and able to take his revenge.

Chapter 26

Return to Naples

Joanna 1 of Naples
February, 1351

I am walking down the familiar streets of Naples, almost blinded by the blaze of sunlight pouring down on me from above.

At first I am overjoyed to be home, but then the sun fades, the warmth begins to cool. As darkness steals over the streets my happiness turns to doubt, then to fear. The streets are empty and silent, every door barred, every window shuttered, every balcony vacant. Where are my people, why have they not come to greet me? I stop walking and turn around slowly, full-circle, searching for the reason behind the sense of dread that fills me.

A solitary figure walks through the shadows down the middle of the street toward me. It is tall, imposing, clothed in white and faceless, like a corpse wound up in its shroud. I draw in a shuddering breath.

The figure walks toward me as though straight from its grave. I dare not move, I dare not run, else it will turn on my people and devour them. I stare at it, willing its attention to me, my back rigid. It is three yards away…two…one. It stops. I feel its breath on my face, stale and choking. Its shrouded arms reach to its head; I notice *only then that it is wearing a crown. Slowly it removes the crown and holds it out to me. The gold, jewel-encrusted circlet shines with a light of its own, like a small sun in the hands of death. I want it. Oh, I want it, but I dare not touch it. The shrouded figure waits.*

"Who am I to rule the dead?" I whisper, staring at the crown lighting the darkness of the shadowed street around it.

The white-clad figure is silent, neither urging me to accept nor acknowledging my fear. It waits patiently, without judgement, as though there is no question of my acceptance. As though I am fated to take this most dangerous gift from its hands.

Now I see that the street is lined with my people, silent witnesses, their faces devoid of expression. How did I fail to see them before? I am certain they were always there, waiting for my decision.

If not me, then who?

With that thought I reach out to take the crown, and the dark bitter death lying within its shining center, and place it upon my head.

Not for my sake, not for love of a binding circle of gold and jewels. But for the invisible people waiting silently in the shadowland of my kingdom for my return.

I awake sweating in the night. Slowly the pounding of my heart eases. Only a foolish nightmare, but the anxiety lingers.

Today of all days! Today we set sail for Naples. I am returning to my kingdom at last.

I close my eyes, trying to picture a pier filled with my people come to greet me when my ship lands at Naples. Three weeks ago, at the beginning of February, Louis and Niccolò led an army from Gaeta down to Naples. Their first battle was to liberate Aversa from the rule of the 5,000 knights King Louis had left behind. A few skirmishes followed, but the Hungarians, realizing their king had given up his attempt to take Naples and abandoned them here, soon left. My husband sent the welcome news for me to come and claim my throne once more. I should be waking with a song of praise in my heart, not a nightmare that feels like an omen. I sit up and call for my maid, determined to shake it away.

The door to my chamber opens admitting my maid with a bowl of rosewater. As soon as she has set it on the table I tell her to open the shutters. No wonder my apprehension lingers, shuttered in this dark room as I am. But the opened windows reveal a dull gray sky casting little daylight into my bedchamber. Too much to light the torches, too little to lighten my mood.

After performing my morning wash the maid retires with instructions to bring mulled wine, cheese and fruit. My three ladies-in-waiting enter as she leaves—young women I have chosen, two from noble houses in Gaeta plus Honoré, who rejoined me as soon as I was released from Louis' enforced imprisonment.

Even thinking his name makes my frown deepen. As if my thoughts have called it up, Honoré tells me, "The Duchess Maria asks to break her fast with you if it pleases you, Your Majesty." I sigh inwardly as Honoré helps me out of my nightdress, but do not consider refusing. No wonder I am having nightmares. Maria's pale face is a blight on my happiness; she has not been the same since Louis rescued her from the del Balzos.

We should never have left her behind when we sailed from Naples, but she was unwilling to leave again and Hugo del Balzo assured me she would be safe. The thought of his assurance makes me grit my teeth. I do not regret that Louis killed him though I wish he had not taken such pleasure in doing so. Hugo was of noble birth and deserved a burial, despite his despicable behavior. Perhaps it is just as well. I can imagine my sister's protests had we given him one befitting his rank if not his character.

I let my ladies dress me and sit still as they braid up my hair. The combing and braiding, as well as their quiet chatter and my occasional murmured response soothes me. I feel my mood brightening. Certainly I have faced down much more than a trivial nightmare to get to this day and I intend to enjoy it. By the time my sister arrives I am smiling, drinking my first mug of mulled wine and have sent my maid for bread and nuts to add to the cheese and fruit I will share with her.

Maria storms into my chamber. "I tell you, I will not stand for it if Louis releases Robert del Balzo!"

I nod to my maid and ladies-in-waiting to leave us. "He will not do so," I say calmly when they have gone.

"'Spare the son from being punished for the sin of the father,'" Maria quotes from the letter Pope Clement sent to my husband, pleading for Robert del Balzo's life.

"Sit down, Maria," I say, too weary of this discussion by now to prolong it by demanding she greet me properly first. "Robert del Balzo married an heir to my throne without my permission, a crime tantamount to treason. He will be punished accordingly." I look at her coolly. She does not meet my eyes, well aware that she conspired to do the same.

I do not press the point. God knows she has been punished enough by the pope's and del Balzo's sly, despicable plot. Still, she is not the only woman whose husband beat her and locked her up. How naïve we both were, raised lovingly in our Grandfather's honorable court, never dreaming we ourselves might one day be subject to the treatment that plagues our sex. Yes, plague, a good word for it. The lot of women is as cruel as a plague and I have determined to look for ways to improve the lives of my female subjects.

"Eat. Drink." I raise my mug to her. "This day we return home to Naples triumphant."

I watch her surreptitiously across the table as she picks at her food, silent and sullen. *Is this what I am returning to?* I wonder. *A country of beaten, broken, hopeless people with nothing left but their anger and pain? Was that the meaning of my dream?*

I take a long drink of my wine and take a fig from the platter. If so, it will be my duty to revive their hopes and heal their wounds. Louis' and mine. However troubled our marriage may be, we are united in our desire to restore the kingdom of Naples to its former glory.

"When Robert is executed I want to watch."

Shaken out of my thoughts, I look up at her in horror. Will she tell me next she wants to wield the sword?

She licks her lips, a quick, nervous movement, and looks away. "I must know it is done. That he is dead," she whispers.

"Maria, he cannot hurt you," I touch her hand, miserable with compassion.

"You do not know his strength, his cruelty…" she stumbles over the words, her voice faint so that I lean forward to hear her words. "My daughters, Joanna and Agnes, even sometimes little Clementia, they wake in the night crying—"

"Maria—"

She looks up. "He said he would take Joanna. He said he would have her if I— And if he cannot get her there is Agnes. Agnes is only six—"

I fold her hands in mine, stopping her rush of words. "They are safe," I tell her. "He will never be released."

"You have a daughter. You should understand." She looks up, her eyes shining with tears.

I lean back. As if realizing she has gone too far she changes tacks. "I am still married to him. Married to a monster! He can do what he likes to any of us!"

"Calm yourself, Maria. Pope Clement will annul the marriage."

"He has not done so. Why is that, Joanna?"

"He will do it," I say grimly.

"But he is taking his time. He is hoping you and Louis will relent. He has asked Louis to spare…" She stops, unable to name the man who has her so frightened. "I am being punished. I know that, Joanna." Her voice is low, angry now. "What I do not know," she looks up at me, sudden and fierce, "is whether you agreed to it."

I take a drink of wine and replace the goblet carefully on the table. "You are distraught, sister." I pause, letting her hear the warning in my voice. "Either you know I would never—*never*—condone your abduction, or you do not."

She bows her head but does not apologize. Nor had I expected it. She has ever been headstrong and impulsive in words and actions. She takes a fig and a piece of cheese from the platter between us. I have lost my appetite but I reach for something, a couple of grapes, so that we can eat together.

"I would never have allowed him to have you murdered."

I realize she is speaking now of King Louis of Hungary. Not quite an apology for her secret betrothal, but close. And ridiculous. After all that has happened, she still thinks she can control the actions of a man? Especially such a man as King Louis? "He would have done so, if you were his wife and the heir."

"I made it part of the contract that he would not."

Neither of us looks at each other and it is a good thing, for I am tempted to laugh out loud. How can she be so naïve? Or is that how she justifies her actions? And does she imagine I will believe it also? Well, *I* will choose her next husband and this time it will be someone who will *not* betray me.

"Where will I live when we get to Naples?" She is still studying the platter as though it holds something of interest. "My husband's—Charles'—castle is abandoned, I am told. It has been stripped of everything, linens, dishes, lamps. The servants and my husband's men have fled or been murdered. We cannot stay there."

I open my mouth to offer Castle dell'Ovo but then remember that Robert del Balzo is locked in its dungeon. "Stay with us at Castle Nuovo. You may have the chambers we shared as children, and your daughters can stay in the nursery with Françoise. She is enjoying having her cousins to play with." I push aside the platter of food we have barely touched. "It is time to prepare for our journey."

"Yes." She does not rise. "Do you remember ordering Charles to have the men who abducted me for him hanged?"

"I remember."

She nods—"Good"—and gives me a level look before she rises from her chair. She bows only as low as she must before she turns and leaves.

Our entrance into Naples is triumphant. Contrary to my dream, large crowds of my people line every street we ride through, cheering as they did the last time I returned.

It was a rough winter sailing and I can still feel the ground heaving beneath me, but I smile and wave at those who have come out to greet us, as do my sister and my husband, riding beside me.

This is where I belong. By all that is holy, I swear I will never be driven out of my kingdom again.

Chapter 27

Unfinished Business

Maria of Durazzo
March, 1351

I am still married to him. The thought fills my every waking moment and insinuates itself into my dreams. I wake in the night and lie listening to the darkness, certain I have heard him enter. Will Pope Clement ever annul the marriage he sanctioned? I no longer believe it. And I am beginning to believe Louis of Taranto will never punish him, not while Clement continues to lobby for a pardon. It suits Louis to have the pope want something of him.

I will never be safe while Robert del Balzo is alive. I am alternately humiliated, revolted, and terrified by the knowledge that he is alive and still my lawful husband. It requires all my strength to attend Joanna's court, to sit at dinner with her other guests and pretend to be interested in their conversation, to laugh at their pleasantries, to remember whatever the current news is in the city or the kingdom. As if any of it matters. I pretend not to see the mockery or pity in their eyes, not to know they will whisper about me as soon as I leave, married by force to the son of a count. I cannot bear it much longer.

I force my mind back to the present. "I beg your pardon, Joanna?"

The Queen Who Sold Her Crown

"I said a holiday would do you good, and be good for your daughters as well."

"I am sorry, sister, but I cannot go to Baia with you and Louis."

"Of course you can, and you must."

"I will not, unless you order me." I say this in such a way that she will know not to. When I first heard her plans to go to their seaside castle at beautiful Baia, all I could think was how wonderful it would be to be left alone. No dinners, no entertainments, no court of ladies-in-waiting and courtiers flirting and laughing in her presence chamber. No pretending.

And then that night I had another thought, a thought borne of darkness and despair. A thought that brought the first honest smile to my face in a year. A thought I dared not speak aloud.

"How can I leave you like this, Maria?"

So today she is my compassionate sister. Other times she is impatient or angry, accusing me of neglecting my children, of casting a shadow over her court, of reminding everyone with one look at my drawn, unsmiling face of all they have been through in the past years of famine, war, and plague. "Do you think they have forgotten?" I asked her once, not sarcastically but wonderingly. Is it possible to forget? Is it something that will ever happen to me?

"Because I wish it," I answer now, a simple answer with no pretense in it. I have buried my thought so deep there is no need for pretense, it will not awaken again until Joanna and Louis and their court have gone to Baia, Then I will be able take it out and examine it alone and see if it might be possible.

Oh, it is possible. I know just how—

I bury it again, quickly. Not until she has gone.

"Why are you frightened, Maman?" my Joanna asks as I bend to kiss her in her little cot.

"I am not frightened, darling," I lie, forcing myself to laugh. "I am happy."

"Maman, I know what people look like when they are happy," she reproves me, her young face as solemn as ever.

I stroke her cheek. When was the last time I heard her laugh, this serious daughter of mine? "Perhaps I am not happy yet, but I will be tomorrow, you will see." I get up to kiss her sisters in their beds, ending the discussion.

"I am not sleepy, Maman," Clementia complains when I get to her cot. "It is still daytime."

"Did you not hear the monastery bells ringing vespers?"

"But they must be mistaken. See, there is still sunlight outside."

I glance at the window, sunlight seeping through the cracks around its shutters. I am glad of the daylight. I want to see what I am about to do. "Summer is coming," I tell Clementia. "The days are longer. But the monks still know when they should pray. And your nurse knows when you should go to bed."

She yawns, slapping her little hand across her mouth to hide it half-way through. "But I am not sleepy," she mutters with a five-year-old's stubbornness as I kiss her.

I open my mouth to suggest she sing to herself. She used to sing herself to sleep, funny little made-up songs that kept us all awake till she dropped off when we were on the road to Avignon. But Clementia has not sung since we were abducted. "Think of something happy," I suggest. "Think of —" But nothing comes to my mind.

"Marchpane," Joanna supplies. "Butterflies. Playing 'find me' in the garden."

"Can we?" Clementia asks eagerly.

"Tomorrow I will play 'find me' in the garden with you," I promise.

Joanna narrows her eyes at me. I have not played with them since

Clementia stopped singing.

"Me too, me too!" three-year-old Margherita shrieks.

"You too. All of us," I agree as I give Margherita her kiss. "Tomorrow after Mass. We will take some cheese and figs and bread and have a picnic there."

Joanna stares at me open-mouthed as I leave their nursery.

A carriage is waiting for me at the gate, and four armed men on horseback. I pull my cape around me against the chill of a wind suddenly come up and let the driver hand me up onto the seat. I tell him where to take me. He bows without comment and springs up to his perch, slapping the reins against the horses' backs.

I am going to do this. Until now it did not seem real, a hazy part of my nightmare. The last tableaux, I tell myself grimly. The way it must end. The only way it can end.

"Hurry," I call to the driver, glancing at the sky. It must be done in the sunlight. I want it to be clear and sharp and very real as I watch.

The carriage drives up to the castle door as I ordered. Let no one say later that I sneaked in like a coward. The wind pulls at my cape as I climb out. I glance anxiously up at a cloud, measuring the angle of the sun, bright behind it. Yes, there will be light when I get there. I walk quickly toward the door, breathless and excited. The guards pull it open for me: I am an Angevin and above question.

My four hired arms men follow me to the entrance to the dungeon. As the door shuts behind us I pause at the top of the stairs to let my eyes adjust to the dim light. The windows on the outer wall are small and high up. Only a small beam of light streams through, but it is enough. I start down.

The unhealthy dampness of the cells below wraps itself around me, the sharp scent of urine and vomit makes me cough. Halfway down the stairs I hear a voice and falter. My breath is coming in gasps.

Is it his voice? I lean against the stone wall, dizzy. He must be talking to a guard. It is too far for me to make out the words but the cold, arrogant timbre of his voice comes up to me. How can I bear to look at him, to see him again? If he speaks to me—

My legs will not hold me; I slide down the wall until I am sitting on the steps. *I cannot do this.* I try to picture what I am about to do. It seemed so easy, so right, back at Castle Nuovo.

This will be with me forever.

"Duchess?" One of the arms men asks. The four of them have gathered around me. "Are you hurt?"

"I am only…" I gasp for breath "…faint," I whisper.

They look at each other over my head. After a moment one of them says, "Would you prefer to wait here with a guard, Duchess? We will return when it is done and help you back upstairs."

"No." My voice quavers.

"No," I say again, more firmly. I reach up and they pull me to my feet. I take a breath and continue down the stairs. The man who offered to leave me there until it was done walks by my side now—to catch me if I fall, no doubt—the others follow close behind. It is dark in the stairwell but there are windows, small and high up. The sun shines fiercely through them.

The gaoler, turning into the stairwell below, looks up at us, startled.

"I am the Duchess of Durazzo," I call down to him. "Take us to the cell of Robert del Balzo." I am proud of my voice, strong and authoritative. I cannot imagine what came over me on the stairs when I heard his voice, but it is gone now.

When the cell door swings open the man inside leaps to his feet. A huge man, Robert, I remember now. His features are caught in the pallid shaft of light descending from the small window high above us, startled and suspicious. Before he can speak, before anything can prevent this, I call out, "Robert del Balzo, you are accused and convicted of conspiring against a royal. Of unlawfully seizing and imprisoning the heir to the throne of Naples against her wishes. For this foul and treasonous crime, you are sentenced to death!" I step back, letting the four men I have hired rush in.

"Quickly," I urge them. "Cut him to pieces!"

He cries out once.

I shudder. Whether from fear of his voice or pleasure at hearing him afraid now, I could not say. And then it is just a matter of watching, of smiling at the ghastly sounds of steel slicing through flesh and striking bone until his body is unrecognizable and the straw is red with his blood. When it is over the last rays of the evening sun stream in through the tiny cell window like a blessing from God.

The men are looking at me, breathing heavily, their swords still unsheathed, awaiting my orders. My breath comes heavily too, I realize, as if I had been wielding a sword of my own. I want to unclasp my hair an do a wild dance of liberation. I close my eyes, and sigh, and open them again, as though waking at last from a long nightmare.

"Dispose of the body," I order the gaoler. "He will not have a Christian burial."

Chapter 28

A Coronation

Joanna 1 of Naples
May, 1352

This is the third time I am being crowned Queen of Naples. The first time was when my grandfather died. The second when I regained my kingdom after the pope's legate took command in the wake of Andrew's death. Now this double coronation after King Louis' invasion. It is my last, for I swear on the graves of my ancestors, I will keep my crown this time until I die.

It is not for me, this coronation. I know who I am and what I was born to be. But my people have suffered greatly. I must give them a vision of stability to end their suffering and despair.

I came back, as my dream foretold, to a desolated kingdom. At the height of the plague, in a mere three months, half the population of the city of Naples died. One third of the towns and villages throughout my kingdom have been abandoned, the people who lived there dead or run off. It is the same everywhere. Niccolò Acciaiuoli, whose family is in Florence, tells me that city has gone from 80,000 souls to 30,000, while Avignon has lost a full half of its population. Everywhere the loss is staggering, barely credible. We have lived through the end of our world as we knew it.

If that were not enough, the war killed thousands who might have survived the plague. Louis of Hungary's army swept across my land burning villages and towns, fields of crops and grazing livestock, destroying everything in their path. And behind them both armies left bands of mercenaries who, having no means of earning a living, have formed themselves into gangs, calling themselves the "free companies". They go about my kingdom pillaging and plundering what little my people have left.

Death and destruction burden my people's souls. I see it in their anguished eyes, their hollow faces, their shambling walk. They have seen so much death they no longer believe in life. Before I can begin to rebuild my kingdom, before my people can heal, I must give them a vision to hold onto, a reminder of the life we knew, the life we can have again.

"This must be the most splendid, most opulent coronation anyone has ever seen," I tell Louis as we break our fast together after morning Mass. He smiles at me, thinking I mean to honor him, a natural expectation in a man and I let him keep it. He has agreed to all the limitations imposed on his crowning: he shall be a king consort only, recognizing my prerogative, and in the event of my death he will lose even that title, though our children will inherit my throne. With that formal agreement between us I have willingly offered to work with Louis to stabilize and rebuild Naples, a goal we share completely.

"We could hold the coronation service inside the Taranto castle," I suggest.

He looks up quickly. "If you wish," he says casually, but I see he is pleased. His pride was deeply wounded when Hugo del Balzo and the six galleys of men from Provence turned our good Neapolitans against him. Holding this most important ceremony in his ancestral palace will declare to everyone that I honor his line and that we are in accord once more.

"There should be entertainments for the entire week leading up to it," he suggests, getting into the spirit. "Tournaments, jousts, pageants and musicians throughout the city, feasts every evening…"

"Yes! And perhaps your brothers might be here by then." Louis' brothers Robert and Philip, along with our Durazzo cousins, are to be released soon to make their way home. In a fit of generosity King Louis forgave their ransom, declaring to Pope Clement that he went to war to avenge his brother Andrew, not to make money. When we received the news from Clement, Louis and I rejoiced together, feeling rich for having evaded a debt we could not pay, and thus we are willing now to incur one we cannot afford.

"They will not arrive in time," he says, unconcerned. There is little love between him and Robert.

We discuss what the occasion will require: silver saddles for our horses, a tunic of pearls and silk for Louis and a silver sword and dagger, rings and gems, twenty-eight girdles adorned with silver for me and my procession of ladies-in-waiting, brooches of gold, rubies, emeralds, sapphires and pearls for our gowns—everything must sparkle and shine and take one's breath away!

"Food and wine and beer for a week of revelry," Louis crows. Giddy with our plans, we draw up a list of who must be invited—nobles and influential churchmen from every part of the kingdom and neighboring regions, Provence, Florence, Siena, Avignon.

We set the date for May 27th, Pentecost. The day the Holy Spirit descended on the apostles: a day of vision and redemption.

The morning dawns as bright as our mood. Sunlight glitters off our jewels and silver as we progress side-by-side on white horses adorned with silver bridles and saddles. A dozen young men in royal livery ride ahead of us, carrying our banners which flutter gaily in the breeze. Our court, richly dressed for the occasion, also precedes us while Louis' men in the Taranto livery adorned with mother-of-pearl buttons encircled with gold and jewels, follow behind us.

The archbishop of Braga, sent by Clement, conducts the service and benediction in front of the massed assembly of our invited guests. He places Louis' crown upon his head, then my crown, which has served me so well in need and in triumph, on mine, while the ceremonial plainsong of a hundred monks fills the air above us with its holy and majestic drone. The archbishop anoints us with holy oil as we make our vows. Its perfume mixes with the heady incense swirling around our heads. I close my eyes and feel for a moment as though I am in heaven.

We rise from our knees and take our thrones at the front of the huge hall where we receive the homage of our barons. Louis smiles, the image of a strong and gracious king at my side, as I had always imagined he would be. I am not fooled by the glitter: Louis is not the husband I hoped for. I keep my personal seal locked in my chambers so he can never again use it against me and I take comfort in the edict he signed stripping him of all power should something happen to me. Our little Françoise will inherit the throne, never Louis. I no longer trust or love him as a husband. But as a king, as the defender of my kingdom, working by my side to restore it, he may do well enough.

A fine feast follows, with jugglers and musicians, five removes of meat and pastries, barrels of beer and tankards of wine. It is late afternoon when we leave the palace for the triumphant procession back to Castle Nuovo, weaving our way through the streets of Naples so all our citizens may enjoy the grand spectacle.

Such joy I see in my people's faces! An almost painful frenzy of hope and delight as memories of the life they thought they would never see again rekindle The narrow streets are crowded, making the horses skittish. I hold tightly to my saddle, smiling and throwing coins to my people as the grooms lead our horses onward. In a balcony above us, a gentlewoman tosses a bouquet of flowers down to Louis, smiling flirtatiously. It slaps against his horse's face. The startled animal shies violently sideways into a stone archway. Louis leaps from its back at the last moment to avoid his leg being crushed.

I watch in horror as the crown flies from his head to land against the cobblestones where it breaks into three pieces. An uneasy silence descends upon the crowd.

"An omen!" a hollow voice cries from somewhere among the press of bodies. The crowd surges back away from us, the ever-present fear returning to their faces.

It is all ruined. My hand rises to my throat; I am as appalled as my people. Surely a shadow follows us, made up of death and broken dreams and things lost that can never be regained.

Louis' expression darkens for an instant. He bends quickly to pick up the pieces of his crown. But when he rises he is smiling. Fitting the three pieces together again he replaces the crown on his head and calls for his horse with a careless laugh.

He knows, I think breathlessly. *He understands what we must do.* Another man would be furious, might order the woman beaten. Louis is angry, I am certain, though he gives no sign of it. I stare at his brilliant smile and I laugh with him. Perhaps I have chosen well after all. This is a man who can rebuild my kingdom with me and return Naples to her former glory. As the groom hefts him up into his silver saddle the people break into cheers.

"Huzzah, King Louis!" "Hail the King of Naples!" they cry, ecstatic in their passionate approval, convinced at last by the strength of his confidence that he will turn evil to good, that together we will lead them back to the splendor that was and will be Naples.

Louis waves to the people, still laughing, then grabs my hand, raising our arms together to the heavens. Vision and redemption. The crowd surges around us, shouting their love as we smile down at them. Anything is possible. Everything is possible. All that I

The Queen Who Sold Her Crown

hoped to achieve when I first took my throne, I will do, and more.

We are unable to move forward for the press of the crowd so I hold Louis' hand high and smile down at our people shouting their devotion around us. There will be trials ahead, the road will not be easy. Louis is still untrustworthy. But despite all that, we will triumph.

By the time we are able to continue and reach Castle Nuovo I am exhausted. The grooms lead our horses through the gates into the courtyard. Louis dismounts in a graceful movement and comes to lift me down from my saddle, grinning at me. He has waited so long for this day. The second son, the one who would not inherit a title, is now a king. I am touched by his gesture, by the gratitude I see in his eyes, and stand in his arms smiling up at him, caught in the last rays of sunlight as it sets on this joyous day.

It is a few moments before I notice the wailing. And a few more before I understand what I am hearing. Louis' face goes from puzzlement to alarm. I turn then and see the palace guards' faces.

"What is it?" I whisper, but Louis is already half-way to the doors. I run after him, filled with a terrible premonition. Inside I race up the stairs, my heart pounding. The nursery! Dear God, not the nursery!

The door to the nursery stands open, the guards' faces pale and anguished as they stare inside, their hands open and helpless at their sides.

Maria kneels on the floor wailing, holding her weeping daughters in her embrace. The nursemaid, moaning and wringing her hands, turns to me, her stricken face all the answer I need. The cradle beside her is still and silent.

"Françoise!" I scream.

"Françoise! Françoise!" Over and over.

As if I could call her back from the dead.

As if I could ever bring any of my children back to me.

Author's Note

Little Françoise' death of a sudden fever while Joanna and Louis were at their joint coronation was abrupt and unexpected. It devastated her parents and ended the brief return of affection between them, although they continued to work together for the good of the kingdom.

The people and events in this story are historically accurate. I have invented conversations and a few minor scenes between characters, but the main events are recorded by chroniclers of the time such as Domenico da Gravina, as well as in letters and in the writings of Plutarch and Boccaccio. When quoting letters between Joanna and Pope Clement VI, I have used the translations in Nancy Goldstone's biography of Joanna, titled The Lady Queen.

Occasionally I have invented a minor character, such as Lorenzo, Joanna's ladies-in-waiting and the various messengers who bring Joanna and Maria reports. Margherita was a real person, Margherita di Ceccano, a relative of the Durazzo's; she did aid Charles in abducting and marrying the willing young Maria as described in Book One, but her role in this book is entirely fictional.

I have tried to portray Provence and Naples in the 14th century as accurately as I can, through extensive research and by travelling to Naples, Avignon, and Marseille, speaking to historians there and visiting the sites mentioned in the book which still exist, such as the cathedrals and castles built in the 14th Century or earlier. However, it is still likely I have made some errors, for which I beg my readers' indulgence.

The painting on the cover of this book is titled *St. Sebastian Interceding for the Plague-Stricken* by Josse Lieferinxe, Provence, France, 1497. Although it was intended to depict a plague in 7th Century Italy, the city in the painting is actually Avignon during a subsequent wave of the Black Plague described in my novel. In the foreground a shroud-wrapped corpse is being lowering into a hastily-dug grave. While a priest is praying over the body, the gravedigger on the left is falling dead of the plague himself. Among the horrors of the Black Plague was the speed with which it killed; a person could go from healthy to dead in a matter of hours. In the background one of the carts sent daily to collect bodies from the street is shown.

The back cover is a view of Avignon from the right bank of the Rhone, showing the Palace of the Popes with the Pont d'Avignon on the left. It was painted by Robert Bonnart in 1700.

Read the fourth and final book in this series for the exciting conclusion of the reign of Joanna 1 of Naples.

The Girl Who Lost a Kingdom (Book 4)

Queen Joanna 1 of Naples struggles to rule a kingdom devastated by war, plague, famine and rebellion. Her niece and namesake, Duchess Joanna of Durazzo, struggles to make sense of a world that has been in turmoil since she was a child. When Queen Joanna swears she will return Naples to its former peace and prosperity, the young Duchess Joanna swears she will always be loyal to her queen. But as their kingdom is increasingly beset with insurrection and war brought on by the terrible "Free Companies"—huge bands of mercenaries and criminals that roam across Europe following the wars and the black plague of the mid-14th C, murdering and plundering everywhere they go—the line between loyalty and survival thins. Will either Joanna be able to keep her oath?

And if you haven't read the two earlier books in this series, they are available in ebook, paperback and hardcover on Amazon:

The Girl Who Would Be Queen (Book 1)

Princesses Joanna and Maria were raised to be queens. When King Robert the Wise, ruler of one of the wealthiest and most sophisticated kingdoms in Europe, died in January 1342, he named his sixteen-year-old granddaughter, Joanna, as his heir or, if she died without issue, her thirteen-year-old sister Maria. Born in a male-dominated world in the passionate south of Italy and surrounded by ambitious male cousins with an equal claim to the crown, will these sisters be able to maintain control over their kingdom? With only their wits, beauty, and the love of their people to aid them, Joanna and Maria, bound together by their strong love and fierce rivalry, are prepared to do anything to hold onto their beloved kingdom.

The Girl Who Tempted Fortune (Book 2)

In the royal courts of medieval Europe, where aristocrats vie for power and royal cousins battle over crowns, is it possible for the lowly daughter of a fisherman to dream of becoming mother to a monarch? Impossible! Yet Philippa of Catania, the daughter of a Sicilian fisherman, risks everything to ride the wheel of fortune to the dizzying heights of power. And in the most enlightened kingdom of all Christendom it might not be so impossible after all. Arriving alone and friendless in the Kingdom of Naples with only her wits, beauty and native intelligence to guide her, she forges allies and finds a love she never expected, as well as enemies who will stop at nothing to destroy her.

About the Author

Jane Ann McLachlan was born in Toronto, Canada, and currently lives with her husband, author Ian Darling, in Waterloo, Ontario. They spend most days sitting in their separate dens typing on their laptops, each working on their next book. When they get out it's usually to do research.

Between books, Jane Ann enjoys gardening, quilting, travel, spending time with family, and getting away from the cold Canadian winters. She is addicted to story, and reads just about any kind of book, but she writes mostly historical fiction set in the Middle Ages and young adult science fiction and fantasy.

You can learn more about her novels and joining her launch team on her author website: www.janeannmclachlan.com

Find resources for creative writing on her website for writers: www.downriverwriting.com

Made in United States
North Haven, CT
26 April 2024